Structure, Process, Principles, and Morality

INTRODUCTION TO CRIMINAL JUSTICE

FIRST EDITION

Edited by **Carolyn Petrosino**
Bridgewater State University

Bassim Hamadeh, CEO and Publisher

Michael Simpson, Vice President of Acquisitions and Sales

Jamie Giganti, Senior Managing Editor

Miguel Macias, Graphic Designer

John Remington, Senior Field Acquisitions Editor

Monika Dziamka, Project Editor

Brian Fahey, Licensing Coordinator

Kat Ragudos, Interior Designer

First published in the United States of America in 2016 by Cognella, Inc.

Printed in the United States of America

ISBN: 978-1-62661-970-8 (pbk) /978-1-62661-971-5 (br)

www.cognella.com   800-200-3908

Contents

Preface

Most introduction to criminal justice textbooks contain appropriate coverage of the full scope of the criminal justice system. Primarily descriptive in nature, these books are designed to provide students foundational knowledge on the history and function of criminal law, law enforcement, the court system, and corrections. But understanding the criminal justice system for new criminal justice majors should require more than just learning the basics. Crime and justice and all of the stages in between can be quite impactful on the lives of many. Each function in the system has real consequences and thus enormous ethical implications.

Issues of morality are inherent in the criminal justice system and therefore should be integrated into the content of such introductory textbooks. In addition, to include a focus on the morality of the system helps instructors bring attention to the interconnectedness of social injustice and criminal justice. This is the central rationale for this book, *Introduction to Criminal Justice: Structure, Process, Principles, and Morality.* The hope is that an earlier introduction to the dimensions of ethics, morality, and social justice as part of the fundamental knowledge of criminal justice will provide students a more realistic view of the system.

Each of the 10 chapters represents an important component of the criminal justice system that is critical to the education of beginning majors. In Chapter 1, I review the scope of the criminal justice system and periodically discuss events that demonstrate the moral challenges besetting the system. In Chapter 2, Wendy L. Wright provides a succinct overview of major criminological theories and reminds us that there are moral consequences to flawed theories, since they produce ineffective crime policies that could be damaging to society. Criminal law and the courts can be challenging areas to new students, but Feyisara Olotu and Mia R. Ortiz in Chapters 3 and 5, respectively, offer their discussions in an accessible style. More importantly, they weave into their chapters questions of ethics that will encourage students to consider the broader issue of justice. John Hobson's approach in Chapter 4, Police: An Experiment in Ordered Liberty, is unique in that he brings the perspective of the rookie officer center stage and his or her exposure to the moral dilemmas that often confront police officers. The next two chapters (Chapter 6 and Chapter 7) deal with community corrections and institutional corrections, respectively. Francis Williams and I approach these areas as comprehensively as possible. Both chapters provide information that is essential about these two areas; and both chapters interject queries and statements that question the moral correctness of some practices and policies routinely employed in corrections. The authors of Chapter 8, Offender Reentry as a Moral Choice, help us understand what makes reentry a moral necessity. Offender reentry is an important process in the criminal justice system, but Trevor Fronius, Anthony Petrosino, and Sarah Guckenburg articulate the many collateral consequences that occur during reentry that interfere with adjustment in the community. The questions provoked in Chapter 8 lead us to Robert Grantham's thoughtful and provocative arguments made in Chapter 9, Are Social Control Efforts Shrinking Crime? Here, Grantham asks students to consider counterproductive policies of governance that may be evocative of criminogenic conditions. He asks whether the government itself is culpable in creating conditions that facilitate deviance, delinquency, and/or crime. If the answer is in the affirmative, the moral implications would be disturbing. Chapter 10, The Future of Criminal Justice, written by myself, reviews a sample of existential and emerging developments that prove challenging to the criminal justice system. These are interesting but cautionary developments that the criminal justice system must prepare for and respond to efficiently and effectively. Changes in the social world will almost always impact the problem of crime and the challenge of justice in society.

In conclusion, each of the contributing authors has expertise in the subjects of which they write. They are all academics and/or researchers, most with strong practitioner experience in the criminal justice system. Their collective backgrounds add integrity and soundness to the entire text as each writes of what they know, experienced and/or studied. Finally, to assist instructors and students who use this text, pedagogical features are included in each chapter. Key terms are identified to underscore important concepts and constructs in the chapter. In addition, the discussion questions that end each chapter will facilitate critical thinking and will provide instructors a platform to begin classroom discussions.

On behalf of all of the contributing authors, we hope that you find this textbook unique and helpful in introducing to new criminal justice students the reality of the inherent moral challenges that exist in the American criminal justice system.

01

What Is Criminal Justice?

Carolyn Petrosino

KEY TERMS

- COMMON LAW
- CONSENSUS AND CONFLICT PERSPECTIVES
- CRIMINAL JUSTICE SYSTEM
- FREE WILL
- PENAL LAWS

A. Introduction

The term *criminal justice* elicits several different impressions, most of which are understandable. One of the most prominent impressions is the irony of the term *criminal justice*. For example, taken separately, the terms *criminal* and *justice* seem antithetical to one another. That which is criminal is far from reflecting justice—and vice versa. The term may also suggest to some that there are different forms of justice, and criminal justice is just one type. There is *economic justice*, *restorative justice*, *environmental justice*, *social justice,* and the familiar term *equal justice*. Whereas *criminal justice* refers to the enactment of **penal laws**, the enforcement of these laws, and the application of penalties that include imprisonment for those who violate these laws, it also reflects most if not all of the other qualities ascribed to the term *justice*.

When you hear the term *criminal justice*, what comes to *your* mind? It is safe to assume that most individuals think of it as representing an official system of governance that dispenses appropriate punishment to those who violate the law. The key word is *appropriate*. Criminal justice, just as all other forms of justice, implies fairness, balance, equal application or nonbias, and effectiveness, all of which are achieved through a civilized and moral process. Now that we've offered a description of what the term *criminal justice* conveys, let us consider the structure of the criminal justice system.

B. The Structure of the American Criminal Justice System

Is the Criminal Justice System a System?

Despite the inclusion of the word *system,* many question whether the **criminal justice system** *is* really a system. Generally speaking, a system is a series of actions or processes that are to some extent related and collectively serve as part of a planned or ordered scheme. This suggests that the various agencies and organizations that engage in the business of criminal justice are aware of one another and subsequently coordinate actions after contemplating effects on other parts of the system. But does that happen? Do legislatures consider whether a law is enforceable by police before passing it? Let's see. According to the Governors' Highway Safety Association, "46 states and the District of Columbia (and other territories) have banned text messaging by drivers."[1] The U.S. Department of Transportation reports that there are more than 250 million registered vehicles in the United States.[2] Let's assume that at least half of the drivers of these vehicles possess cell phones with texting capabilities. How can police effectively enforce this law with such large numbers?

Here is another example. Police using a "broken windows" policing strategy spend precious resources on low-level offenders who tend to be poor, Black, and Brown. How might this strategy impact the communities of these offenders, which have a history of a strained relationship with police? Do law enforcement officials consider that? When sentencing laws changed to became harsher, requiring mandatory prison time for several crimes, were policy makers aware of this impact? Did they anticipate insufficient prison cells? Were they conscious of the fact that the building boom of prisons caused finite tax dollars to be taken away from some prosocial projects to better finance locking up people? The incarceration of more than 2.2 million Americans produced thousands of children who are separated from

---

1 National Conference of State Legislatures. (2015). Cellular phone use and texting while driving laws. Retrieved from http://www.ncsl.org/research/transportation/cellular-phone-use-and-texting-while-driving-laws.aspx

2 US Department of Transportation. (n.d.). Table 1-11: Number of U.S. aircraft, vehicles, vessels, and other conveyances. Retrieved from http://www.rita.dot.gov/bts/sites/rita.dot.gov.bts/files/publications/national_transportation_statistics/html/table_01_11.html

their incarcerated parent. Studies show that this experience produces a greater likelihood that these same children will experience incarceration later in life. Did public officials consider that?

In addition, police agencies, courts, and correctional facilities literally number in the thousands across the country and across states. Their missions and organizational goals are different, and the governments that provide their authority vary as well, (i.e. state, county, local). Neubauer describes these distinctions as fragmentation.[3] It is a separateness that distinguishes agencies in the criminal justice *system*. Each agency seeks to justify its own existence and to demonstrate its efficiency and effectiveness. The presence of fragmentation suggests a *nonsystem* perspective of the criminal justice system. Yet it is also true that interdependence or some level of cooperation exists among criminal justice agencies and components. For example, when police investigate and arrest suspects, it is the courts that must determine the constitutionality of police work. Once courts oversee the conviction of the offender, corrections must take on the responsibility of carrying out the sentence and supervising punishment, whether it is the collection of fines, community service, probation, community corrections, or prison. Therefore, both characterizations are evident; the criminal justice system is both a system and a nonsystem.

Fragmentation is largely caused by the existence of federalism. Federalism is the concept recognized in the Constitution that describes the separation or division of governing powers. Power is not just held by the federal government; power is shared. There is federal authority, state authorities, and county, city, and town authorities. Each has its particular jurisdiction (and limitations), but there are instances in which these authorities may overlap. Since each of these authorities have the responsibility to enforce the laws of that jurisdiction, we recognize that there are sometimes incidents of crime that violate multiple statutes and do so across jurisdictions. In those instances there may be federal law enforcement, state police, and local police involvement—each are justified to participate in the investigation of the crimes committed. An example of this overlap is the recent incident that occurred on June 2, 2015, in Roslindale, a community located in Boston. When two law enforcement officers approached Usaama Rahim, he lunged at them with a large military-style knife. He was then shot to death by the officers, one a Boston police officer and the other an FBI agent. Rahim was under surveillance by federal authorities and specifically the joint antiterrorism task force, which is made up of federal, state, and local officers. He was suspected of planning to carry out ISIS-inspired terrorism. The encounter was caused by recent intelligence indicating that Rahim planned to murder 'the boys in blue' starting that day. There were a number of potential charges that could have been leveled against him; these crossed multiple jurisdictions. To summarize, the structure of the criminal justice system/nonsystem is adaptable to what is needed to respond to the threat and punishment of crime—on any level. So let's now look briefly at the problem of crime in society.

---

3   Neubauer, D. W. (2005). *America's courts and the criminal justice system* (8th ed.). Belmont, CA: Thomson Wadsworth.

C. The Problem of Crime in Society

The U.S. Department of Justice reports that in 2013 a murder occurred every 37 minutes in the United States, a robbery every 1.5 minutes, and a burglary every 16.4 seconds.[4] Crime is not a rare event, but neither does it pervade every aspect of social life in the United States. What is more accurate to state is that reported crime occurs more frequently in some places than in others. Still, it is important to recognize that not every crime that occurs is reported to police. For various reasons, there are crimes that go unreported. Some victims don't think the crime was significant enough to report; others don't want to get involved and invest the time and effort required to report crime and follow up with the demands made by the police and prosecutor to go forward. Still others are fearful of retaliation. There are many versions of the popular crime funnel (see Figure 1.1). It is an effective visual of the screening or "sifting" process that occurs within the criminal justice system in response to crime. It conveys the fact that, *theoretically,* only the most serious reported crimes result in a prison sentence.

Figure 1.1. Crime Funnel Image: The 'Sifting' Process
Source: Macgregor Neighbourhood Watch.

1000 Crimes
500 Reports
100 Arrests

50 Charges
45 Guilty Pleas
3 Guilty at Trial
2 Acquittal

32 Community
Corrections

16
Prison

---

4   US Department of Justice. (2013). Crime in the United States 2013: Crime clock. Retrieved from http://www.fbi.gov/aboutus/cjis/ucr/crime-in-the-u.s/2013/crime-in-the-u.s.-2013/offenses-known-to-law-enforcement/crime-clock

Crime is the violation of social mores, customs, rules, and laws and it is not an artifact of modern society only. Crime occurred in the ancient world as well. In response to 'rule breaking' in society, ancient or otherwise, a set of laws are promulgated to identify what constitutes law violation or wrong-doing. As with any set of laws, the punishments or penalties that may be prescribed are articulated as well. The following section describes some significant historical developments in penal law and the institutionalization of a criminal justice system.

D. The History of Criminal Justice

Code of Hammurabi

Among the earliest written penal laws is the Code of Hammurabi. A king in ancient Mesopotamia, now known as Iran, Hammurabi sought to codify and publicize the laws of his kingdom and make them available to the people he ruled. The code is dated at 1792 to 1750 BCE, and it describes a wide range of wrongful acts as well as the corresponding penalty. Examples include (but are not limited to) laws governing the selling of merchandise, the management of servants and slaves, slander, the marriage contract, assaults, and the theft of property. One of the legal principals most identified with this early set of laws is that of *lex talionis* or an eye for an eye. This is the fundamental concept of retaliatory justice.

Church Law During the Middle Ages

The next significant development in the evolution of criminal justice is the age of church law, par-ticularly during the Middle Ages. Christianity and subsequently the Roman Catholic Church grew as a significant institution throughout Europe. Taking a strong stance against heresy (a violation of theological doctrine), the church structured a process and means modeled after the Roman inquisitorial court system to determine the guilt and the punishment of violators. Better known as the Inquisition era, the church, along with the cooperation and involvement of the state, enforced this system of justice from the 11th through 18th centuries. This period was known for brutal forms of punishment and execution, such as burning the "guilty" alive. But other prescribed punishments that were designed to isolate, stigmatize, or shame were more commonplace.[5] During the Middle Ages and the dominance of the religious perspective in spiritual and secular life, crime was viewed as a result of humankind's sinful nature and/or the result of evil supernatural forces. This period also

---

5   Sparks, C. (2014). Heresy, Inquisition, and life cycle in medieval Languedroc. Suffolk, UK: Boydell & Brewer.

coincided with belief in the divine right of kings. This perspective stated that the king's (or queen's) authority came from the will of God, and thus any disobedience or questioning of his or her rule was a challenge to God's authority and therefore sacrilegious. This view would prevail until it was challenged in the 18th century by those who highlighted the importance of reason, rationality, and the existence of free will.

Principles of Justice—the Age of Enlightenment

The 1700s saw a series of progressive thinkers throughout Europe and England that challenged traditional schools of thought and parochial beliefs regarding major human institutions. Rejecting the notion of the preeminence of supernatural powers in the affairs of humankind, these progressives argued that rationality and the capacity to understand and change the human condition was achievable through the application of reason and analysis. The Age of Enlightenment introduced new perspectives that demystified the role of the state and better qualified its role, as well as the responsibilities of government and those of the individual. Included among these progressives are Jean-Jacques Montesquieu, Charles-Louis Rousseau, Voltaire, and John Locke. However, Cesare Beccaria contributed most to new ideas concerning crime, the criminal, punishment, and the moral duties of the state. His major writing, published in 1764, *Essay on Crimes and Punishments,* largely shaped criminal justice thought for the next 200 years. Beccaria argued that people choose their actions as a result of **free will**. Consequently, they are responsible for the crimes they commit—since they chose to indulge in criminal behavior. He also argued that laws should be fair, published for all citizens' awareness, and that people should receive equal treatment before the law. Other important ideas promoted that would become the framework for the classical school of criminology include:

Beccaria's principles:

1. Laws should be used to maintain the social contract.
2. Only legislators should create laws.
3. Judges should impose punishment only in accordance with the law.
4. Judges should not interpret the laws.
5. Punishment should be based on the pleasure/pain principle.
6. Punishment should be based on the act, not on the actor.
7. The punishment should be determined by the crime.
8. Punishment should be prompt and effective.
9. All people should be treated equally.
10. Capital punishment should be abolished.
11. The use of torture to gain confessions should be abolished.
12. It is better to prevent crimes than to punish them.

Source: Adler, F., Mueller, G. O. W., & Laufer, W. S. (2001). *Criminology.* New York: McGraw-Hill, pp. 63–64.

British Common Law—American Common Law

The Age of Enlightenment also impacted the architects of the new nation, the United States of America. In fact, the influence of Beccaria's writings are still in evidence today. Looking at Beccaria's principles stated above, can you identify contemporary practices in criminal justice that reflect these ideals?

Many of the staples in American jurisprudence (or philosophy of law) are derived from British common law. The term **common law** refers to social traditions, practices, and rules that served as precedents in the doing of justice. A precedent is a legal rule or principle that serves as a guide for subsequent court decisions. Thus, the decisions of judges affirm and formalize these legal principles. Common law, or Anglo American law, is also sometimes referred to as judge-made law or case law. The term was also meant to convey that the law was to be applied throughout a country (Neubauer, 2005). As a body of case law developments, decisions from higher level courts substantiate principles that are observed from lower and higher courts in the same jurisdiction and sometimes elsewhere. This is the principle of *stare decisis,* which originated in medieval England, carried over to young America, and is still evident today.

The result or desired outcome is consistency in judicial decisions. Yet the law itself is not static; it is not set in stone. The law is dynamic; it is alive. Just as the common law reflected the social mores of that period, the law today undergoes change as societal attitudes change. For example, the use and/or possession of marijuana had been criminalized in the United States since 1937. But the movement to decriminalize it and to make it lawful to use medicinally or even recreationally came about, beginning in the mid-1990s, as public attitudes changed and medical studies offered findings that were supportive. The criminal justice system is a powerful governmental institution of social control, but the law itself changes as cultural values, social customs, and attitudes change. The next section briefly describes how an action becomes a crime.

E. Purpose and Goals—the Social Contract and Packer's Models

The purpose and rationale for a justice system in a democratic society derives from the sociopolitical concept of the *social contract.* During the 17th century, philosopher Thomas Hobbes described the following principles of the social contract: In a civil society, (a) individuals should not act in ways that threaten the preservation of life for themselves or for others; and (b) there is an agreement among persons to limit their own liberty in order to gain self-preservation, communal peace, and security. This is the essence of the *contract,* which is the commitment to observe and obey the laws that are enforced by the government. Now that we've described the justification for criminal justice, we will look at the foci of the system through the lens of Herbert Packer's competing models: crime control and due process.

In his book *The Limits of the Criminal Sanction*, legal scholar Herbert Packer describes, as a heuristic tool, two opposing value systems that represent the indigenous conflict within the criminal justice system: the crime control and the due process models. Unpacking these value systems help us to better understand the ongoing tensions that exist within the criminal justice system. The priority of the crime control model is to maintain public safety by swiftly addressing crime. Therefore, the prevention, control, and suppression of crime in order to protect the welfare of the public is primary. In this model, law enforcement is viewed as the most important element of the criminal justice system. Police are prepared to respond to reported crime, investigate, and apprehend suspects—dealing directly with threats against the public. They also engage in patrolling and surveilling—all done with the purpose of preventing and/or quickly responding to crime if and when it occurs. In addition, the crime control model argues that police should be unfettered in their pursuit of fighting crime. Therefore, requiring due process at every juncture (that is, obtaining warrants, administering Miranda warnings, and so on) is viewed as an impediment. Police should be permitted to carry out their work with speed, efficiency, and certainty and without hindrances. In the crime control model, the suspect is presumed to be guilty.

The due process model is concerned with the manner in which crime suspects are dealt with from the time they have contact with police to the time they are convicted and become a probationer or parolee. The entire criminal justice system is the focus—not just police. Therefore, the standard of due process must be met throughout the criminal justice process. Justice and its fundamental quality of fairness is at the heart of the due process model. Whereas the crime control model is operationalized by an unchecked police force, the due process model is demonstrated by adherence to the constitutional protections enshrined in the Bill of Rights.

What is most important in the due process model is not merely arresting criminals, but arresting criminals based on probable cause, using proper warrants, providing the Miranda warning and respecting the right to remain silent, ensuring the right to counsel for eligible defendants, charging offenses according to the appropriate level, ensuring timely court appearances and appropriate bail, and so forth. The abuse of rights or the violation of due process is to be avoided at all costs. Justice cannot be obtained through unjust or illegitimate means; hence, the famous observation of British jurist Sir William Blackstone in 1765, "The law holds that it is better that ten guilty persons escape than that one innocent suffer."[6] Clearly, we see how this model is the antithesis of the crime control model. Where the crime control model tolerates the subordination of the due process protections afforded criminal suspects, the due process model does not. A seminal case that reaffirmed the

---

6   Halvorsen, V. (2015). Is it better that ten guilty persons go free than that one innocent person be convicted? [Article excerpt]. Criminal Justice Ethics. Retrieved from Questia website: https://www.questia.com/library/journal/1G1-135337535/is-it-better-that-ten-guilty-persons-go-free-than

values of the due process model is *Mapp v. Ohio* 367 U.S. 643 (1961). In this case the home of the defendant, Dollree Mapp, was search by Cleveland police; evidence of pornography was found and seized. Mapp was subsequently convicted of possession of porn. But the U.S. Supreme Court decided that the search was unlawful and violated the Fourth Amendment since there was no evidence that a proper warrant was ever obtained in order to conduct a lawful search. Thus, the pornographic material was seized illegally. Her conviction was overturned, and it was established that Fourth Amendment protection against unreasonable searches and seizures also applied to the states. In the due process model, the crime suspect is presumed to be innocent.

F. The Law

How Do Some Acts Become Criminalized?

There are two Latin terms that helps us understand how evil or socially intolerable acts are identified and become criminalized: *mala in se* and *mala prohibita*. *Mala in se* refers to those acts that are inherently evil in and of themselves. Many of them are recognized to be immoral and unacceptable acts, such as murder, torture, sexual exploitation of children, incest, kidnapping, theft, and so on, even across cultures and societies and time periods. These types of offenses have a long history of inclusion in penal codes—even ancient ones. *Mala prohibita* are those acts that became unlawful due to the enactment of criminal statutes.

An act can become a crime due to public response and/or the efforts of advocacy groups to push for legislation. For example, during the 1980s the public saw a number of crimes committed due to the race, ethnicity, religion, or sexual orientation of the targeted victim. Eventually, states and the federal government criminalized *bias-motivated* crimes, now commonly referred to as hate crimes. Another example is illustrated by the tragic victimizations of Jacob Wetterling, Megan Kanka, and Adam Walsh. Each of these children were abducted, sexually assaulted, and/or murdered. The Adam Walsh Child Protection and Safety Act, signed into law in 2006 by President George W. Bush, requires the registration of all sex offenders in the United States. Also known as the Sex Offender Registration and Notification Act, it states that failure of the sex offender to register with local police is a felony. Mothers Against Drunk Driving (MADD) is another organization that advocates more stringent punishment of those who drive drunk. Founded in 1980, MADD was instrumental in seeing more than 100 anti–drunk driving laws passed throughout the country.[7] California's Three-strikes law was largely the result of the persistent advocacy of family members of murder victims whose lives were ended by

---

7   Mothers Against Drunk Driving. (2005). MADD milestones. Retrieved from http://www.madd.org/about-us/history/madd-milestones.pdf

repeat offenders. The 1993 kidnap and murder of Polly Klaas brought national attention to the issue of the violent repeat offender. The Three-strikes initiative was put on the ballot in 1994, and California voters overwhelmingly supported it. The point is that an idea is put forward to introduce a bill to create a crime statute or to modify an existing one, and if it receives enough support (or votes), it becomes law. Criminal laws can be found at the local level (enforceable throughout a county, town, city, municipality, and so on), as state laws (enforceable statewide), and/or as federal laws (enforceable nationwide).

Criminal law can be viewed in two categories: substantive law and procedural law. Substantive law describes those acts that are prohibited by statutes (*mala prohibita*); for example, theft, assault, and distributing drugs. Procedural law describes the administration of justice involved in the arrest, pretrial, trial, and appeal processes and also speaks to the rights of criminal defendants, due process, and equal protection of the law.

Moral Challenges in the Law

As mentioned previously, the justification for the law lies in the idea of the social contract. The theory of the social contract also emerged from the Age of Enlightenment. In summary, it contends that the primary purpose of government is to provide peace and public safety, which is secured by the law. As members of an orderly society, civilians agree to restrict their behavior in order to obey the law, which reflects agreement of the people. Related to the concept of the social contract are the sociological concepts of **consensus and conflict perspectives** of the law. The consensus concept asserts that a stable society reflects agreement among its members on the principles and values reflected in its customs, regulations, and laws. Thus, the law represents the wishes of a society in harmony and in solidarity. Conversely, the conflict perspective states that society is comprised of various social groups, which are in conflict yet hope to have their interests and values incorporated into the law. But only the more powerful and influential social groups are able to achieve this end. Therefore, the resulting law does not reflect the values of all social groups—only the most powerful ones. Subsequently, some social groups *disagree* with the principles, customs, and regulations or laws that structure society.

Ethics challenges us to look at the fairness of the law, particularly when the conflict perspective seems most valid. For example, if the social groups at odds with the law are those that are disadvantaged socially, economically, and/or politically, and if this conflict is persistent and structural, there are moral implications. This would be a powerful limitation placed on those groups that are at the losing end of the conflict. The impact of structural inequality is far reaching and has implications in education, employment, housing, nutrition, health care, and other related areas. How does this relate to crime? There are studies in each of these areas that suggest that deficiencies and disadvantages in these areas increase the likelihood of criminal behavior. What moral implications can you see in the conflict perspective?

Some have argued that the punishment of members of the privileged classes who commit white-collar or corporate crime is minimal relative to the punishment handed down to poor defendants. To illustrate, it became public knowledge in 2001 that Firestone was aware of defective tires that it produced for the Ford Explorer and that Ford participated in a cover up. The flaw increased the likelihood that the tires would blow out from hot temperatures that occur at high speeds. More than 100 fatal accidents and thousands of injuries were linked to these tires.[8] The Ford Motor Company replaced all the defective tires at a cost of $3 billion. No one was criminally charged and held person-ally responsible for these tragedies, although some commentaries indicate prior knowledge and efforts to cover up damning reports. The punishment of these two corporations was monetary. However, poor criminal defendants often have a very different experience.

Twenty-six-year-old welfare recipient and mother of four Elaine Bartlett sold 4 ounces of cocaine in 1983. She didn't sell it to minors, and no one died from her transaction. In fact, the drug sale was prearranged by an undercover narcotics officer. Bartlett had no prior criminal record. But as a result of the Rockefeller Drug Laws, she was sentenced to 20 years to life.[9] Firestone was responsible for multiple deaths and injuries, but not one representative went to prison. Bartlett, a poor African American woman, served 16 years of her 20-year sentence before receiving clemency from Governor George Pataki. If such stark differences are routinely found in the law, what justification might be used to argue that this is morally correct?

G. Law Enforcement

Criminal laws have little effect on society unless they are enforced. Enforcement of the law is a key role of police. In addition to law enforcement, the mission of police also includes keeping the peace, answering calls for service, and fighting crime. Although the popular image of police officers is that of crime fighters, most activities while on duty do not include confronting crime or criminals. Responding to calls from residents for quite ordinary issues tend to dominate police time. Of course, the type of jurisdiction policed shapes the demands placed on officers. It is also realistic that the policy of a given police department determines policing priorities. For instance, in the 1990s, during the Rudolph Giuliani administration in New York City, a new policing strategy was implemented. Often referred to as the 'broken windows' approach, it required police to make arrests for minor crimes as a means to prevent more serious ones. But studies indicate that there were more factors beyond that of broken

8   Pollock, J. M. (2004). *Ethics in crime and justice.* New York: Wadsworth/Thomson Learning.
9   Gonnerman, J. (2004). *Life on the outside: The prison odyssey of Elaine Bartlett.* New York: Farrar, Straus & Giroux.

windows–style policing that impacted the rise or fall of crime rates.[10] A poor economy and joblessness are very powerful contributors to crime rates. Although social scientists may recognize these complexities, how well do police factor in these realities?

Policing With Community

Progressive police officials acknowledge the importance of police–community relations in effective police work. In other words, good policing is done *with* the community and not *to* the community. Much has been learned from the three historical eras of American policing: (a) the political era (1840s–1930); (b) the reform or professional era (1930–1970s); and (c) the community problem-solving era (1970s–2001).[11] What is clear is that police need cooperation from the community in order to be effective. Police cannot be present continuously in any given area; but residents are present by definition. The ordinary citizen recognizes the normal vibes within a neighborhood and notices things that are out of order, strangers, and unfamiliar vehicles—all of which could shed much light on illegal activities that may be occurring. At the same time, police must conduct themselves in a professional manner and in accordance with the law in order to hold the trust and respect from the community.

Policing Minority Communities

Strained relations between police and the African American community are historical and persistent. Beginning with the shooting death of Amadou Diallo in 1999 by New York police officers, it seems that police shootings of unarmed Black men are occurring with greater frequency; some would argue this is the product of entrenched racial profiling and the devaluation of Black lives. The following were all victims of fatal incidents that occurred in 2014: Eric Garner, Dontre Hamilton, John Crawford, Ezell Ford, Dante Parker, Akai Gurley, Tamir Rice (age 12), and Rumain Brisbon. In April 2015 groups of young people in the city of Baltimore erupted into rioting in protest of the killing of Freddie Gray at the hands of Baltimore police (see Chapter 4 for more discussion). Arrested under unclear circumstances, Gray was roughly handled and placed in a police van, where he suffered a catastrophic injury to his spine due to police misconduct. Six Baltimore police officers were indicted for the death of Gray. A week earlier, Walter Scott, an African American man, was shot in the back by a police officer in Charleston, South Carolina. The officer was later indicted by a grand jury for murder. Community

---

10   Corman, H., & Mocan, N. (2002). Carrots, sticks and broken windows (Working Paper 9061, NBER Working Paper Series). Retrieved from http://www.nber.org/papers/w9061.pdf
11   Kelling G. L., & Moore, M. H. (1988). The evolving strategy of policing. *Perspectives on Policing, 4,* 1–15. Retrieved from National Criminal Justice Reference Service website: https://www.ncjrs.gov/pdffiles1/nij/114213.pdf

policing and problem-solving policing are strategies that were designed to improve crime prevention efforts and build healthy working relations between police and community residents. Successful engagement in these areas would help reduce negative stereotypes of both parties, humanize Black men to bigoted police officers, and perhaps decrease the number of fatal encounters between police and African American males.

Moral Challenges in Law Enforcement

Corruption

Policing is a difficult and demanding job. It is also one that requires the utmost in professional training and high ethical standards. Although most law enforcement officers strive to do what is proper and lawful, there have been circumstances in which some officers have committed immoral and at times illegal acts. Probably one of the most popular examples of this failure is in the case of Frank Serpico, a police officer who resisted corruption and paid a high price for being honest. As a New York City police officer during the 1960s, Serpico observed widespread corruption among fellow officers. After supervisors failed to intervene, he eventually testified about the corruption to the Knapp Commission. Serpico was despised by fellow officers for challenging police crime and testifying accordingly. During a drug raid, his fellow officers failed to provide Serpico backup, and he was shot. Soon after this incident, he left the police force. This is likely the first of several major modern day blemishes on police officers in the United States that was well covered by the media. Instances of extortion, bribery, theft, brutality, and the covering up of such illegal acts are part of the ongoing problem areas and challenges in policing.

A more recent version of police corruption occurred in the Los Angeles Police Department (LAPD). During the 1990s, former police officer Rafael Perez agreed to provide information concerning widespread corruption throughout the anti-gang (C.R.A.S.H.) unit in the Rampart Division of the LAPD. It was the arrest and conviction of Perez on multiple state and federal charges such as theft of police evidence, civil rights violations, and possession of an illegal firearm and perjury which revealed the criminal activities of the unit. His testimony revealed pervasive corruption, including some of the most egregious acts that a sworn police officer could ever commit. Approximately 70 officers were implicated in various degrees of misconduct, which included illegal arrests, unprovoked beatings and shootings, planting evidence such as "drop" guns, and stealing and distributing narcotics. At the conclusion of the investigation, more than 20 officers were held responsible, and the lawsuits against the city cost taxpayers millions. Both the New York City and Los Angeles police scandals revealed a criminal netherworld that existed in these departments. This underbelly of flagrant illegality also indicates the absence of a strong moral compass for the police officers involved directly and indirectly in these activities.

But what is moral policing? Perhaps moral policing is policing that comports with the law, police regulations, and state and federal constitutions. It also means that police exercise discretion in ways that reflect sound moral judgement. The following section discusses the next component of the criminal justice system—the courts. In significant ways, the courts act as a check on law enforcement. The veracity of the evidence used in the prosecution of a criminal case is the product of police work. If police conduct a sound investigation in observation of ethical and constitutional concerns, the result will likely be a conviction; an outcome that affirms the work of police. The court system is an essential part of the criminal justice system.

The Court System

Following an arrest and charging, the determination of whether the accused is guilty is the business of the court. According to the Justice Department, 90% to 95% of all criminal cases are disposed of by plea bargaining.[12] But whether a case is handled by plea bargaining or trial, it is in court that criminal cases are managed. Principal parties involved in this critical process include the prosecutor, the defense attorney, and the judicial officer (judge), commonly referred to as the courtroom work group.

H. The General Function of the Courts

The role of the court is to act as a neutral or objective arbiter of justice. This is particularly important considering that the prosecutor and the defense attorneys are zealous advocates for their respective parties. The judicial officer protects all due process matters concerning the case disposition—including that of plea bargaining. Just as the law and law enforcement reflects different levels, so does the structure of the American court system. States mostly have a three-tier court structure: municipal or lower courts, superior courts, and the state supreme court. Likewise, the federal court system includes district courts, appellate courts, and the U.S. Supreme Court (see Chapter 5 for detailed discussions on the court system).

General Court Processes

Many courts, especially lower courts, establish their own routines in managing criminal cases and misdemeanors. However, there are processes and procedures that are common to most courts

---

12 Devers, L. (2011). Plea and charge bargaining [Research summary]. Contract No. GS-10F-0114L. Bureau of Justice Assistance, U.S. Department of Justice. Retrieved from https://www.bja.gov/Publications/PleaBargainingResearchSummary.pdf

and to superior courts in particular. We will briefly describe three of them: arraignments, trials, and sentencing.

Arraignment.

The arraignment is the first formal hearing concerning the defendant's charges. In the arraignment procedure, the defendant, accompanied by a defense attorney, stands before the judge. The judge will inform the defendant of the charges against him or her by reading the criminal complaint. In addition, the judge will advise the defendant of his or her constitutional rights and make sure that the defendant understands this information. The judge will ask the defendant to enter a plea to the charges: not guilty, guilty, or no contest. Finally, if it was not addressed prior to arraignment, the judge will consider bail and conditions of release.

Trial.

If no plea bargain is offered and accepted by either the prosecutor or the defense, a trial is then scheduled. It is the purpose of the trial to determine whether the prosecutor has brought forward sufficient evidence to prove the state's case beyond a reasonable doubt. Whether it is a bench trial or a jury trial, the prosecutor bears the burden to make the case against the defendant. The defendant has no obligation to prove his or her innocence and is not required to testify. In general, the state presents its case, followed by the defense; cross-examinations, rebuttals, and closing arguments are also included. The judge's responsibility is to oversee the entire process, hear motions and attorney objections, determine appropriateness of offered evidence, and make sure the trial is carried out fairly and in accordance with the law.

Sentencing.

Upon a finding of guilt, the judge is charged with sentencing the defendant—now convicted. In keeping with the role of the court—to ensure justice—it is reasonable to expect a fair sentence. But how is fairness determined? Sentencing options are articulated in the penal code of a given jurisdiction. The following are examples of sentencing schemes for second-degree burglary convictions:

- Arizona: Second-degree burglary is defined as unlawfully entering or remaining in or on a residential structure with the intent of committing any theft or felony. This could apply to a home, apartment building, or any place where people reside. It is a Class 3 felony and carries 2½ to 7 years in prison.
- New Jersey: In some cases, burglary of the second degree. This charge carries a potential 5 to 10 year prison sentence. If you commit a burglary, as defined above, and in the

commission of the act you use a weapon, or inflict, attempt to inflict, or threaten to inflict bodily harm on someone, you could face this elevated charge.

- Florida: If you are accused of burglary in an instance where you did *not* have a weapon and where no one was hurt, *and* the property on which it was committed was one of the following, you could be charged with second-degree burglary: (a) a dwelling; (b) an occupied structure or conveyance; (c) an authorized emergency vehicle (police car, ambulance, fire truck, and so on); or (d) a building where the offense to be committed is the theft of a controlled substance. A second-degree felony charge can carry up to 15 years in prison and fines.

Fairness suggests that the same offense categories are punished in a similar manner. Yet this objective is most likely emphasized within a state, rather than across states. Arizona, New Jersey, and Florida burglary statutes have maximum sentences that range from 7 years to 15 years.[13] But the existence of these clear differences does not mean that the sentences are unfair or inappropriate.

The purpose of a sentence is to accomplish one or more of the following correctional aims: retribution, incapacitation, deterrence, and/or rehabilitation. Judges can have multiple purposes reflected in a given sentence. Besides incarceration, defendants can be sentenced to probation, fines, community service, an intermediate sanction, or even diversion.

Moral Challenges in the Courts

The outcome in the courtroom, whether by plea bargain or trial, is the culmination of the efforts of police, prosecutors, and defense attorneys in the seeking of justice. But intentional and unintentional mistakes sabotage the doing of justice. This is the ultimate moral challenge to the court and its primary participants: judges, prosecutors, and defense attorneys. If political ambitions color the discretionary judgement of prosecutors or even judges who are subject to public elections, that would be an instance of *immoral* conduct. All attorneys are officers of the court and as such are held to professional standards of conduct as well as to the common goal of pursuing justice. The American Bar Association publishes the Model Rules of Professional Conduct, which are followed by most state bar associations. But the existence of professional codes of conduct is not sufficient—there must be a commitment to adhere to them.

Luzerne County, Pennsylvania, was the site of one of the most despicable abuses of judicial power in the United States. Juvenile court judges Mark Ciavarella and Michael Conahan took money (kickbacks)

---

13   Burglary Laws. (n.d.). State burglary laws and penalties. Retrieved from http://www.burglarylaws.com

for sentencing juveniles to private juvenile detention facilities by the builders of these facilities. In what became known as the "kids for cash" scandal, Ciavarella and Conahan sentenced children to imprisonment for extremely minor acts such as stealing a jar of nutmeg or ridiculing an assistant principal on the web.[14] They were convicted of racketeering, having received upward of $1 million to keep and maintain a steady flow of juveniles to those facilities. In 2011 Conahan was sentenced to 17½ years, and Ciavarella received a 28-year sentence—both to be served in federal correctional facilities.

I. Corrections

The final component of the criminal justice system is corrections. Corrections involves the administration of the sentence handed down to the offender by the court. The average person may think of prisons first when it comes to carrying out sentences of the convicted. However, the most frequent sentences are not those requiring incarceration, but rather probation. The Bureau of Justice Statistics reports that in 2013 a little less than 4 million persons were under probation supervision. But those incarcerated in jails and prison numbered 2.2 million persons.[15] The network of correctional agencies includes jails, county facilities, state prisons and their federal counterparts, probation offices, community correctional facilities, day reporting centers, drug courts, veterans courts, and community-based counseling and other human services for the offender.

Included in this array are private correctional facilities. These are facilities owned by private companies who bid for contracts to house prisoners—state and/or federal inmates. These companies generally contend that they are able to run a prison in a more economically efficient way than the state can, thereby saving money. The evidence on this is mixed. What is clear is that these companies are for profit and make money in the business of incarceration. There are several ethical questions that arise from this somewhat controversial practice. Which come to your mind? We read in the preceding section on the temptation to 'lobby' for bodies to be sent to such facilities.

A persistent question asks whether the private sector (which is profit motivated) should be involved with a function that is the responsibility of the government—the imprisonment of those who violate public law. Some would argue that it is problematic to permit private companies to carry out punishment. Where does accountability lie? Another formidable question is what resources are skimped on in order to increase profit margins? Some reports indicate that the salary of correctional officers in these sectors are quite low and their training is substandard in comparison to state training programs. If

---

14   Pavlo, W. (2011, August 12). Pennsylvania judge gets "life sentence" for prison kickback scheme. *Forbes.* Retrieved from http://www.forbes.com/sites/walterpavlo/2011/08/12/pennsylvania-judge-gets-life-sentence-for-prison-kickback-scheme

15   Glaze, L. E., & Kaeble, D. (2014). Correctional populations in the United States, 2013 (Bulletin NCJ 248479, Bureau of Justice Statistics). Retrieved from http://www.bjs.gov/content/pub/pdf/cpus13.pdf

these two issues are born out, how would they impact the morale of staff officers? How would it impact the incarceration experience of the inmates?

J. Conclusion

This brief overview of the criminal justice system reflects the complexity of this interconnected system/nonsystem and the implicit ethical issues that are inherent in the system. Each of the subsequent chapters that follow will provide essential information about different aspects of the criminal justice system and also challenge students to consider the various ethical matters that are intertwined with them. The criminal justice system is fraught with ethical issues from start to finish. Some of these issues are blatantly obvious in their lack of moral justification, whereas others are extremely nuanced and colored by context.

DISCUSSION QUESTIONS

1. The history of criminal justice goes back to ancient times. What ideas have remained the same? Where are some of the larger areas of change that have occurred?
2. Are there any common themes when it comes to issues of morality that transcend the law, police, courts, and corrections? Please describe them. What are the differences in ethical concerns?

02

CHAPTER OUTLINE

KEY TERMS

- ANOMIE
- BIOLOGICAL EXPLANATIONS
- CHICAGO SCHOOL
- CLASSICAL SCHOOL
- CRIMINOLOGICAL THEORY
- CRITICAL CRIMINOLOGY
- DIFFERENTIAL ASSOCIATION THEORY
- ECOLOGY
- GENERAL STRAIN THEORY
- ITALIAN SCHOOL
- LEARNING THEORIES
- SOCIAL DISORGANIZATION THEORY
- SOCIAL LEARNING THEORY
- SUPERNATURAL THEORY

Causes of Crime

Wendy L. Wright

A. Introduction

Imagine recess at a local middle school. Children run around the schoolyard, playing soccer or tag. Other children sit in groups talking and comparing the latest toys. Off in the corner, just out of sight of the teacher, is a group of boys circled up. When we zoom in closer, we see that the group is surrounding two boys, and just as we focus in on these two boys, we see one haul back and punch the second with all his might. Freeze!

What might be going on? Perhaps this is a fight that both boys agreed to hold, an illicit way to resolve some common difference. Maybe one boy is bullying the other, driven by poor self-esteem to pick on other children to bolster his own self-image. It's possible that the boy we witnessed punching the other boy was actually standing up for a friend who had previously been threatened or attacked by the child who at first seemed to be the victim. All of these stories—any of which might be true, given our limited information—are theories. A theory is simply an explanation for whatever phenomenon in which we might be interested.

Criminological theory (also referred to as **crime theory**) attempts to identify and articulate the causes of crime. Some criminological theories focus on individual acts and actors, whereas others focus on broader social phenomena. The development and testing of theory is central to the study of criminal justice. People have been developing theories of crime for hundreds of years, each wave of theory reflecting the assumptions, ideologies, and available information of the age. The development of theory is an ongoing process, with new innovations offered every year. Ideas about what human beings are like or what counts as a reasonable argument or sound evidence change over time. Before examining any individual theory, it is important to recognize that theories emerge from a specific historical context and therefore must be considered in light of that context. Further, it is also important to remember that theory never emerges from a vacuum; rather, innovations in theory are *usually* responding both to the immediate context and to other theories. In this way theoretical development might be understood as a long, involved conversation—each new author listening to what others have to say and then adding his or her own perspective. As such, criminological theory has not developed in a linear fashion, with new theories proving to be absolutely "better" than old theories. Instead, more recent theories often have similar assumptions, concepts, and logics as older theories—requiring multiple layers of analysis to truly unpack. Similarly, theories are built on assumptions, biases, and ideas about the world and thus often contain moral judgments or have moral consequences that may not be apparent but are a key part of how a theory works, for better or for worse. In assessing a theory, the morality—not only the logic or common sense—must be analyzed if effective, ethical policies and practices are to follow.

This chapter will introduce the history of Western crime theory, review major contemporary theories, and discuss ways to assess and analyze them. Special attention will be paid to the assumptions and biases that are implicit in each theory. This chapter is largely organized chronologically, but connections across time are also noted and discussed where appropriate.

B. Demons, Devils, and Their Mischief: Supernatural Theories of Crime

In addition to understanding the cause of crime, it is also important to recognize that the explanation of a cause of crime is inextricably connected to two related questions:

1. Whose rights were transgressed when the crime was committed?
2. What sorts of actions count as crimes?

Although it is impossible to reduce the complexity of thousands of years of history into one paragraph, crime was often explained by supernatural influences until the 17th century. That is, it was widely believed that human lives were affected by forces outside of our general understanding or human control, and some of those forces were evil. When evil forces intervened, people might be driven to commit crimes as a result. "The devil made him do it" might be the claim of a person who ascribed to the **supernatural theory** of crime, also called a spiritist or demonological approach to understanding crime. The Salem Witch Trials are a familiar example of the supernatural theory. The men and women accused, tried, and executed were thought to be inhabited by evil spirits, driven to cause mayhem in the Salem community. Their executions were seen not only as a way to combat evil, but even to save the souls of the men and women involved. Here, fighting the crimes of evildoers was considered a moral duty—but with the benefit of hindsight, we can now see the moral perils of judging someone to be a witch.

In the premodern era, crime was often seen as an offense against a deity and/or its representatives on Earth. For example, when Galileo Galilei was prosecuted, his crime was the violation of the Holy Doctrine of the Catholic Church. He believed and wrote that the sun, rather than the Earth, was the center of the solar system. Since this went against the teaching of the time (that Earth was the center of the universe), it was considered a crime. At the time, this sort of blasphemy was a far greater crime than any simple theft or assault. This vision of criminality sees crime as an act of the great battle between the good and evil spirits that work in this world and beyond. Supernatural theory argues that crime cannot be explained through reason but rather is caused, or at least influenced, by forces outside of human control.

In assessing any theory, it is necessary to dig into the assumptions that underpin the theory and see whether those assumptions are defensible when analyzed rigorously. Assumptions of the supernatural theory of crime include that there are one or more evil entities in the universe, that human beings cannot fully understand or control those entities, and that those entities can control or affect how human beings act. Consequently, crime control and punishment are seen as a battle of morality against evil.

Although for the most part, criminologists disregard supernatural theories of crime, these attitudes remain *implicit* in some popular discussions of crime. Consider, for example, the description of some crimes or criminals as "evil." This descriptor is usually applied to particularly heinous crimes and acts of terrorism. But what is this actually saying about the causes of crime? Where is this evil coming from? Sometimes this is a psychological assessment. Other times, however, it contains an implicit judgment of the crime/criminal. For example, when people describe an act of gang violence or terrorism as "just pure evil," they are disregarding other potential causes of crime, such as psychology or environment. Characterizing a person as a "demon" or a "devil," unless one holds the idea that evil spirits can inhabit people's bodies, confuses rather than clarifies a situation. In assessing crime and crime theory, such simplistic approaches may prevent a more morally responsible approach, driven by careful reasoning and ethical judgment.

C. The Road to Modern Theories

Classical School

With the Age of Enlightenment, human thinking on all matters was transformed—from ideas about religion, to politics, to art—including crime, criminals, and punishment. Key to understanding this transformation was the new vision of human beings as fundamentally *rational* or guided by *reason*.

What is known as the **Classical School** of criminology consisted largely of writing what we would now call *normative* texts. That is, members of the Classical School were critiquing society and arguing for progressive changes based on their understanding of the world. Cesare Beccaria is a key figure in the classical school, and his most famous text—*On Crimes and Punishments,* written in 1764—focuses on the proper goals and practices of criminal law and governing. This conception of the world envisions human beings as acting on the basis of rational free will, with the assumption that people act in ways that will make themselves happy and powerful.

Under this view, it is assumed that the reason most people commit crimes is because they think it is a good idea for them to do so. Beccaria (2009) notes that any human being might be tempted to transgress on the rights of others and that a core function of law itself must be to protect each person's liberty from the "usurpation" of that liberty by any other person. Because of this, Beccaria argues that the only legitimate function for criminal punishment is deterrence, or the prevention of future criminal violations. This approach rejects retribution as a source of legal authority, arguing that final judgment about morality is better left to God. Instead, the purpose of criminal law is to ensure that violating the social order is simply not going to turn out well for the violator.

This emphasis on deterrence has some logical consequences for the structure of law and the government. In order for deterrence to work, people have to know what the consequences of committing a crime will be, so tied to classical notions of crime are commitments to a clearly stated legal order and a predictable, fair judicial process. After all, if you committed a crime but did not know the consequences, then you would be acting based on the best information available, and therefore it still might be rational to commit a particular crime. Similarly, if you believed that you would not be subject to punishment—for example, because you could bribe your way out of it—it might be rational to break the law. Beccaria and other classical school theorists can be understood as believing that crime is committed because of bad laws and ineffective punishments.

In many ways, the Classical School subordinates morality to rationality. That is, Beccaria and his cohorts argued that truly rational behavior, made possible by human beings' natural capabilities, was always lawful and moral. The primary moral value that underpins this system is the protection of individual rights and liberties. Unlawful behavior violates the rights of another individual or the community as a whole and thus is also a moral violation. However, the entire purpose of having a government is to protect rights and liberties, so state actions like policing or punishment, if they are not also aimed at the overall protection of rights and liberties, are also immoral. For the Classical School, when laws are rationally developed and the public is effectively educated about those laws, the vast majority of people will follow them, and there will be minimal criminal activity. Beccaria emphasizes that good laws, investment from the community, and a highly educated populace is the best way to ensure public justice.

Despite the emphasis on reason and protection of rights and liberties, the Classical School's reliance on abstract reasoning can run the risk of making assumptions about crime and crime policy that are not based on how human lives actually work, and those incorrect assumptions can result in bad policy. For example, research shows that very long prison sentences, like those passed under three-strikes rules, do not deter people from committing crimes any more than shorter, less costly prison sentences. Therefore, even though it might *seem* reasonable that long sentences deter more, this idea is based on faulty assumptions. Thus, society gets all the negative consequences of long prison sentences—expensive prison costs, hardships for the incarcerated person's family, less likelihood of rehabilitation—without any of the benefit.

Italian School

Another school of thought, the **Italian School** (also known as the Positivist School) emerged at the turn of the 20th century. This movement shifted the focus of criminological inquiry from law back to criminals (and potential criminals). The Italian School was reacting directly to earlier classical notions, arguing that crime was less a matter of rational decision making and something more like a disease—something that had knowable causes that, if effectively diagnosed, might present opportunities to intervene to prevent or minimize the effects of crime (Wigmore & Lombroso, 1911).

The Italian School, led by Cesare Lombroso, argued that there are two distinct reasons that human beings commit crimes: They might be born with characteristics that predispose them to committing crimes, or they might gain those characteristics through the course of their life. As Lombroso's student and daughter, Gina Lombroso-Ferrero described it (2009), the

> *Positive School ... maintains that the anti-social tendencies of criminals are the result of their physical and psychic organization* (sic), *which differs essentially from that of normal individuals; and it aims at studying the morphology and*

various functional phenomena of the criminal with the object of curing, instead
of punishing him. (p. 5)

In his first major text, *Criminal Man*, originally published in Italian in 1876, Lombroso (1876/2006) argued that there existed in society some people who were "born criminals." Born criminals were said to be *atavistic*, or displaying characteristics from an earlier, more primitive era. This theory of criminality builds on a misreading of Darwinian evolution, where some human beings are seen as less developed than others. Lombroso based this theory largely on phrenology, or the study of skulls—which he argued showed that born criminals were likely to have smaller, misshapen skulls (purportedly indicating small, misshapen brains) and that these characteristics were also tied to sensitivities and moral proclivities. For example, those of the "criminal type" were less likely to be graceful or to be able to tell right from wrong. This theory argued that some cultures were more primitive and more criminally oriented than others. When individuals in cultures that considered themselves to be more advanced or superior committed crimes—northern Europeans considered themselves to be more civilized than southern Europeans, most Africans, and most Asians—Lombroso argued that the criminality was a reemergence of a less evolved personality, driven by more "primitive" drives.

Later revisions to the Italian School by Lombroso and his successors, including Enrico Ferri and Rafaele Garofolo, stood by the theory of the born criminal, but also placed greater emphasis on a combination of influences that are always interacting with each other. Or, as Ferri (1910) put it, "in order that crime may develop, it is necessary that anthropological, social and telluric factors should act together" (p. 71–2), meaning that social and environmental effects must also be assessed when attempting to account for the origins of criminality. Language suggesting that social and environmental effects are important might sound familiar to the modern ear, but it cannot be ignored that these explanations for crime are saturated with faulty science, prejudice, and ideologically driven assumptions about different peoples—including, for example, that criminals are more likely to get tattoos because they feel less pain (thus indicating that the tattooed are likely to be criminals!). At its core, the Italian School is invested in distinguishing between higher and lower order peoples; comparing the two, Lombroso (1876/2006) notes, "We [Lombroso and colleagues] have also pointed out that many actions considered criminal in civilised communities, are normal and legitimate practices among primitive races" (p. 135). These assessments are grounded in racism and a belief that northern Europeans and their descendants were more advanced—biologically, morally, and socially—than their counterparts in southern Europe and the rest of the non-Western world. The immorality of such approaches comes not only from the racism and prejudice that motivate these theories, but also from the fact that bad policy and practices are built on such ideas. When governments use immoral theories, they often reenact the immorality inside those theories. So racist theories will be likely to produce racist policies.

At the same time, one must also note the progressive policy reforms that come from this view. In lieu of harming the criminal, or punishing with an ineffective goal of deterrence, Ferri (1910) argued that crime interventions ought to be based on the "fundamental facts of a science of social defense against crime in the human and social life itself" (p. 5). Rather than exclusively relying on penal interventions, Ferri takes a position that the responsible role of the government is one "which does not wait until crime is about to be committed, but locates the causes of crime in poverty, abandoned children, trampdom, etc, and seeks to prevent these conditions" (p. 28). This emphasis on "social defense" sees many types of criminality as preventable, thus making it a social responsibility to intervene to prevent such criminal tendencies from developing.

This double-edged sword of a theory that has problematic and unscientific elements but that may have genuine insights in other respects is a feature of much crime theory. However, it is important to note that parts of theories cannot simply be "cherry picked," mixed and matched depending on what is attractive about them. Indeed, the internal logical consistency of a theory creates a method by which interested students can "check the work" of theorists, ensuring that the conclusions are built on valid and reliable grounds that are ethically and morally defensible.

D. The 20th Century and the Rise of Social Science

The broad schools of thought represented above—that crimes are committed by people with criminalistic tendencies, that crimes are committed because people experience **criminogenic** conditions (conditions that are likely to produce crime), or some combination thereof are the basics of all modern theories of crime. Future theories shift emphasis, attempting not only to identify the sources of crime but also to ensure the validity and reliability of the scientific methodologies that are employed in seeking those sources. These shifts reflect not only transformations in criminological studies, but changes that were taking place across the intellectual landscape as questions of how knowledge itself is produced became open questions for scholars.

The Chicago School

One dominant example of this shift in the process of knowledge production is the rise of the **Chicago School** of sociology, which is broadly associated with an emphasis on empirical analysis. Specific developments included the use of quantitative data, ethnography, and social disorganization theories of crime. This body of thought is known as the Chicago School because the people who were doing the work were based in Chicago (mostly working at the University of Chicago). Starting in the 1920s, under the leadership of W. I. Thomas and Robert Park, they primarily studied social problems, including crime and criminological phenomena, in the Chicago area (Bulmer, 1984). This approach to understanding crime emphasized the particulars of a phenomenon in its context—for example, looking at juvenile delinquency in neighborhoods rather than attempting to make a grand theory emerge out of the ether. As Ernest W. Burgess described it, the Chicago School of sociological inquiry "emphasized science and the importance of understanding social problems in terms of the processes and forces that produce them" (as cited in Bulmer, 1984, p.89).

In 1936 Robert Park published an article, "Human Ecology," in which he argued that human life ought to be understood through the principles of **ecology**, or the study of the relationship between living things and the worlds in which they live. Ecological principles had been developed and applied to the study of plants and animals in the late 19th and early 20th century. An ecological approach argues that nature must be understood as a "web of life," in which all elements—plants, animals, and even the earth itself—"are bound together in a vast system of interlinked and interdependent lives" (Park, 1936, p. 145). For example, as we well know, flowers rely on bees to pollinate them, so if you want to study the reproduction of a flower, you also need to understand what the bees are doing. Park took these principles of interconnection from the study of plants and animals and applied them to the study of human lives.

Like plants and animals, Park argued that human experiences are shaped by symbiotic and competitive relationships—meaning that as we seek to achieve our goals, we are either helped or hindered by others. But in human society, Park argued, we also have the added complexity of culture, history, institutions, customs, and traditions. An effective sociological inquiry thus requires an understanding of the complex balance between all these forces, as well as an understanding of what forces are in play when the balance is upset.

E. Concentric Zones and Social Disorganization Theory

Building on previous Chicago School studies, including Park's model of human ecology and E. W. Burgess's model of urban growth, one of the most important contributions to criminological theory is Clifford Shaw and Henry McKay's *Juvenile Delinquency and Urban Areas* (1942). In this study, Shaw and McKay articulated a **social disorganization theory**, which argued that juvenile delinquency emerges primarily in neighborhoods that are socially disorganized, meaning that people within these neighborhoods are unable to prevent and solve problems as a result of larger structural issues such as poverty, housing instability, and high levels of ethnic difference.

Burgess had argued that cities tend to grow in concentric zones. Imagine the ripples that expand when something is dropped in water—each of these ripples represents a zone that radiates out from the industrial center of the city. The industrial center is zone 1. It is surrounded by zone 2, which is not a terribly pleasant place to live because it is being encroached on by factories and other industrial elements. As a result of this unpleasantness, more affluent families move farther out from the center of the city, meaning that existing real estate in zone 2 is relatively inexpensive. This affordable option leads those without the means to live elsewhere to settle in these areas. These residents are often ethnic minorities and immigrants, seeking to establish some economic stability.

Shaw and McKay, using census and survey data—much of which had been unavailable to previous generations of criminological researchers—noticed that crime was much more common in zone 2, or the transitional zone, than it was in zones farther from the center. Shaw and McKay theorized that the confluence of social problems in this zone led to the breakdown of social ties, thus opening the door to delinquency. The core factors that they theorized contributed to this breakdown include "(1) physical status, (2) economic status, and (3) population composition" (Shaw & McKay, 1942, p. 142. By physical status, Shaw and McKay were referring to the literal state of the roads, buildings, and other physical features of a community. They measured this by looking at rates of building condemnations and buildups of industrial structures like factories and railroad tracks. Economic status looks at rates of wealth and poverty. Population composition refers to ethnicity, race, and national origin. Shaw and McKay found that in these zone 2 neighborhoods, there was significant physical decay, there were many people of low socioeconomic status, and the neighborhoods were often populated by a number of different and rapidly shifting immigrant groups. Shaw and McKay theorized that these factors combined to produce communities that were unable to self-regulate, or provide the kinds of community controls that prevent crime, thus leading to increased crime rates.

There were many critics of social disorganization theory, but by the late 1980s new generations of social scientists were building on the basic premises of the theory. Perhaps most notably, Robert Sampson and W. Byron Groves, in their 1989 article, "Community Structure and Crime: Testing Social Disorganization Theory," developed new methods of empirically analyzing the theoretical claims. They identified measurable markers of social disorganization at the community level and then compared data across hundreds of British neighborhoods. Examples of the kinds of measures Sampson and Groves investigated were answers to survey questions about whether teenagers hung out on local corners and made nuisances of themselves. Using that and other measures, they argued that those people who said they lived in communities with such groups of teenagers were also probably living in communities with high levels of social disorganization—after all, highly supervised teenagers wouldn't be hanging around causing trouble. In the years since, researchers have used social disorganization models to look at all sorts of crime scenarios—from the relationship between the 2007 housing crisis and crime (Wilson & Paulsen, 2008), to terrorism (Koseli, 2007).

Like many well-regarded theories, social disorganization has *intuitive appeal*; that is, there's something about it that just makes sense. When communities don't have strong social ties, young people will fall through the cracks. However, there are a number of less obvious, important things to consider when relying on social disorganization theory to explain the origins of crime. For example, social disorganization theory fails to provide any real ability to explain the causes of the preconditions for social disorganization, or to explore whose responsibility it is or what the best ways are to increase social organization. Imagine that policy makers are looking at social disorganization theory and decide that the best way to reduce crime in their city is to get teens off of street corners; these decisions may have moral consequences. In some political conversations, it is decided that parents aren't stepping up and are failing to provide the structure that their children need. As a result, the policy response might be something like parenting classes or even a crackdown on older child neglect cases. But what if the reason the teenagers are unsupervised is because their parents are working multiple low-wage jobs simply to make ends meet? No amount of parenting education is going to fix that, and it would be immoral to punish parents who are making the best of a difficult situation. Another approach to getting teens off the street might be to increase arrests for loitering. This would have a whole new set of harms as teens are introduced into the criminal justice system, removed from local schools, and made less employable with an arrest on their record. Further, perhaps the reason the teens are hanging out on the corner is not because they are unsupervised, but rather because they live in areas with low employment rates and are unable to find anything more productive to do with their time. Punishing these teens might be immoral, but policy makers might use the strength of a claim backed by a theory to defend their policy as the right thing to do. Assessing the morality of a theory means not only checking to see whether the assumptions within the theoretical framework are ethical, but also ensuring that the *way the theory is applied* is also morally grounded.

Social disorganization theory also fails to make any normative claims about the social inequality that underpins the factors that contribute to social disorganization. For example, it is recognized that poverty contributes to social disorganization, but at its core social disorganization theory has no way to confront fundamental reasons for poverty, which include historical inequities, governmental policies that favor wealth accumulation, and economic and racial segregation. Without accounting for such realities, a theoretically sound explanation might look reasonable at first glance, but because it ignores so much, it ends up being like an empty container that can be filled with whatever political goal—moral or not—that policy makers wish to pursue. Social disorganization offers some crucial insights into the origins of crime, but unless the theory is paired with a perspective that is able to zoom out and take a broader perspective, while also zooming in and taking account of people's lives, one runs the risk of only getting a small part of a larger picture of crime.

F. Differential Association Theory

Differential association theory "postulates that criminal behavior is learned behavior. It is learned through interactions with other persons, usually within intimate personal groups" (Gaylord & Galliher, 1988, p. 4). Originally articulated by Edwin Sutherland, differential association theory follows a development path similar to social disorganization theory. Sutherland originally became interested in criminology while conducting research in the early 1920s at the University of Chicago. He was interested in the fact that crimes happened in different ecological settings, but he sought to explain more specifically how particular social locations or identities lead to crime.

Similar to how social disorganization theory emerged, Sutherland sought to use empirical data as the source for his criminological theory, rather than attempting to develop a theory out of logic alone. Because differential association theory argues that criminal behavior is learned, it is also considered to fall under the broader umbrella of **learning theories**, which argue that behavior is learned as a consequence of life experiences and the influence of other people with whom we come into contact. Sutherland developed nine propositions that theorize how individuals come to adopt criminal behavior:

1. Criminal behavior is learned behavior.
2. Criminal behavior is learned in interaction with others in the process of communication.
3. The principle part of the learning of criminal behavior occurs within intimate personal groups.
4. When criminal behavior is learned, the learning includes (a) techniques of committing the crime which are sometimes very complicated and sometimes very simple, and (b) the specific direction of motives, drives, rationalizations, and attitudes.
5. The specific direction of motives and drives is learned from definitions of the legal codes as favorable or unfavorable.
6. A person becomes delinquent because of an excess of definitions favorable to violation of law over definitions unfavorable to violation of the law.
7. Differential association may vary in frequency, duration, priority, and intensity.
8. The process of learning criminal behavior by association with criminal and anticriminal patterns involves all the mechanisms that are involved in any other learning.
9. Although criminal behavior is an expression of general needs and values, it is not explained by those general needs and values, since noncriminal behavior is an expression of the same needs and values (Sutherland, Cressey, & Luckenbill, 1992).

These propositions together can be summed up to argue that people learn criminal behavior the same way they learn any other behavior—from the people around them and as a result of values and desires. One important feature of Sutherland's work is that it allowed a wide range of different deviant and criminal behaviors to be understood—for example, this framework was seen to be equally useful in explaining the behavior of street criminals and the behavior of white-collar criminals. It is also important to note that Sutherland was primarily interested in the process by which individuals, rather than neighborhoods or larger communities, began to adopt deviant or criminal behavior. The sixth proposition is the core of the "differential association" part of the theory, since it marks the turn of how individuals come to prefer criminal behavior over law-abiding behaviors through the process of associating differentially from those who are learning law-abiding behaviors.

As is common with all important theories over time, subsequent generations of scholars have responded to, revised, and reformulated Sutherland's theory. The most notable revision to Sutherland's theory emerged in Ronald Aker's **social learning theory**, which was "an effort to meld Sutherland's (1947) sociological approach in his differential association theory and principles of behavioral psychology" (Akers & Jennings, 2009, p. 323). Akers argues that social learning theory does not seek to disprove differential association but instead is a "more comprehensive explanation for involvement in crime and deviance" (Akers & Jennings, 2009, p. 323) and seeks to use more sophisticated knowledge of human psychology and cognitive science to investigate how the learning process happens, as well as to focus on developing more robustly *testable* hypotheses based on the theory. More recently, Akers and others using social learning theories have pushed their research into several new directions, including attempts to incorporate the newest science on brains and learning, understanding how social structures affect social learning, and figuring out how to apply the insights from social learning to create meaningful interventions that can be useful for social policy, including reducing future criminality (Akers & Jennings, 2009).

There have also been some major drawbacks to how differential association and social learning theories have developed. Sutherland's work has often been critiqued as being particularly difficult to test empirically. Akers made it testable but in ways that are somewhat limited. For example, the vast majority of testing that Akers and his colleagues carried out was through surveys of college students. The results of these surveys were strong, but it is unclear whether these results are reliable—that is, whether they are generalizable to other forms of criminal association. Further, this model of crime is only capable of measuring crime done by individuals or in small groups. It is incapable of making any claims on definitions of deviance, instead simply reaffirming conceptions of deviance and crime that already exist in society. For instance, social learning theory might provide good insight as to why groups of young people choose to smoke marijuana. Young people see their friends and other peers smoking marijuana and conclude that it is not a big deal—thus, they choose to also smoke marijuana. They have learned this criminal (depending on where you are) behavior through social learning. However, learning theories cannot tell us much about other kinds of crimes, such as why a government leader might carry out acts of violence against his or her own people. A president does not look around and see "everyone else doing it." Instead, the reasons are probably far more complex. These failings do not make social learning theory useless, but they should give students pause, since the assumptions that underpin the theory tend to define crime in a relatively narrow way—a way that may demonize some actions while affirming that other actions should not be thought of as crimes at all. These definitions of crime may prevent the public from defining crimes in such a way that improves people's lives and contributes morally to the community.

G. Anomie, Strain, and General Strain Theory

As mentioned earlier, theories do not necessarily develop in a linear way. Robert Merton's strain theory reintroduced the earlier concept of anomie in a way that looked backward and forward at the same time. That is, rather than being a steady progression of theoretical development, Merton built on contemporary developments in theory, but then turned back in time and brought anomie into the conversation. Strain theories argue, in general, that overarching structures in society—economics, institutional power, historic oppression—will both determine definitions of crime and induce some members of a given society to engage in criminal behaviors.

Anomie is the experience of isolation, feeling disconnected from society in a way that affects one's behavior and produces deviant outcomes. Anomie, which Merton later took up in his theory of strain, was a concept articulated by French sociologist Émile Durkheim in the late 19th century. Durkheim studied a range of social problems, from crime to suicide to war. Anomie played a significant role in much of his work. Durkheim theorized that anomie was an unavoidable side effect of modern society, since rapid changes in human life transform expectations and opportunities (think of changes in the kinds of jobs, technologies, and recreations that have occurred even just in your lifetime). Anomie is not as simple as saying that people act in deviant ways because life is difficult. Instead, it is the result of a mismatch between reasonable human expectations and experienced outcomes, and of what happens when this mismatch is too large for general social norms to govern behavior. In other words, deviance is a result of a "lack of regulation of the individual by society" (Durkheim, 1966, p. 15).

When Merton revisited the concept of anomie in articulating his strain theory in the 1930s, he sought to understand not why crime existed at all (which was part of Durkheim's project), but instead why crime rates were higher in some societies versus others. In looking at American society during the Great Depression, Merton explored why crime was more prevalent in communities with low socioeconomic status. He theorized that because in the United States the goals of economic affluence and social ascent were considered desirable to all citizens, despite one's original socioeconomic position, those who had little chance to achieve those goals through traditional means—such as going to college, getting a well-paying job, and owning a house with a white picket fence—were likely to try to achieve those goals through nontraditional means, such as criminal activity. One thing that is particularly innovative about Merton's (1938) theory is that he recognized that the goals of criminals might not actually be any different from what anyone else wanted, meaning that criminals might be less deviant than others have supposed. Strain theory remained an important criminological theory through the 1960s but lost influence in the 1970s and 1980s.

In 1992 Robert Agnew published a landmark article, "Foundation for a General Strain Theory of Crime and Delinquency," in which he argued for a new interpretation of strain, building on modern understandings of emotions, stress, and individual psychological drives. In addition to strain caused by a break between an individual's circumstances and society's norms, Agnew argued it was also important to understand the strain people experienced as a result of a mismatch between expectations and achievements, as well as disappointment and other kinds of stressful events. Further, in thinking about how to assess general strain theory empirically, Agnew emphasized that it was important to seek to understand the "cumulative effect on delinquency after a certain threshold level is reached … [as well as] the magnitude, recency, duration, and clustering of strainful events" (Agnew, 1992, p. 74). Agnew's version of **general strain theory** work remains an important theory for empirical testing.

Questions of morality that emerge from strain theories emerge from the emphasis on the individual. Even though larger social pressures are recognized, often strain frames the individual as the one who adjusts poorly to those conditions. This theory, in centering the emotional–psychological status of the individual, often puts the focus of crime policy on individuals, rather than creating opportunities to question the norms and structures of society that produce experiences of strain.

H. Theories Against Crime

Running almost parallel to the entire modern history of mainstream criminology have been theories that have pushed against the grain of traditional theories of crime. Instead of asking why criminals commit crimes, these theories turn these questions on their heads by asking questions like: Why do we call act X a crime? Why do we say that a behavior when done by this person is a crime, even when done by someone else, it is not? Why do we fear some actions as crimes but write others off as accidents or simply to costs of doing business?

In some ways these questions are counterintuitive; we all know what are crimes, right? Killing someone seems like it should be a crime—but if we dig a little deeper, we see that circumstances, social expectations, and political contexts all matter in how we determine whether or not something is a crime. Killing someone may seem like a crime, but there are many situations where it is not: the death penalty, war, self-defense. There are also cases where something might be a crime in one place but acceptable in another, such as an honor killing or a killing based on the castle doctrine. When even something that seems so black and white as killing can be so gray, it calls for a much more careful examination of what is happening when some things are called crimes and others are not.

What much of this comes down to is power—who has the power to decide what counts as a crime and what does not. When a mugger takes your wallet, it is considered a violent crime, but when a bank uses misleading paperwork to extract additional fees, it is rarely considered anything more than bad business practice. These determinations are made by governments through the creation, interpretation, and execution of laws, led by people who hold positions of power within governing institutions.

The branch of crime theory that attempts to account for crime by engaging these systems of power has come to be known as **critical criminology**. Though there are many different paths under the broad umbrella of critical criminology, a reasonable definition is that critical criminology is "a perspective that views the major sources of crime as the unequal class, race/ethnic, and gender relations that control our society" (DeKeseredy, 2010, p. 7). Critical criminology has its roots in 19th-century political thought, most notably in the theories of Karl Marx and Friedrich Engels. Marx and Engels theorized that in a capitalist economy (as had developed in western Europe and was developing in the United States), those who controlled the means of production would organize society—including criminal laws and social institutions—in a way that ensured their continued control over the workers of society, known as the proletariat.

In regard to crime, this would have two main consequences: (a) criminalization of the behaviors of poor and working class people and (b) the production of a disaffected class of society dubbed "the lumpen proletariat," who, because of the structure of the economy, are excluded from the normal labor force and are thereby inevitably going to be engaged in antisocial behaviors (stealing, prostitution, extortion).

Although much has changed in the past 150 years, many theorize that power relations are still central to understanding how crime functions in society. This has been picked up in contemporary discussions in criticisms of the control that the wealthiest "1%" exert over politics. Critical scholars like Jeffrey Reiman posit that through this control, the harms of the rich and powerful are ignored, whereas the harms of the poor, who have less sociopolitical power, are criminalized and emphasized. Reiman points to the contradiction between medical malpractice, wherein doctors often do not even lose their medical licenses, and street crime, which is zealously prosecuted even though most people are more likely to be victims of a serious error in medical care than they are to be victims of a violent crime. Reiman (1990) argues that "the label 'crime' is not used in American to name all or the worst actions that cause misery and suffering to Americans. It is reserved primarily for the dangerous actions of the poor" (p. 58). Because of this, critical criminologists push back against traditional approaches to crime theory, attempting to define the boundaries of violence in ways that identify and analyze all kinds of harm and violence, rather than the narrow slice that currently gets called "crime."

Since the 1980s researchers have also developed a number of critical theories and methodologies that focus on *identity*, or a person's social category—such as race, gender, sexual orientation, or a combination of them—as an important means of theorizing crime. These theories often take the position that ignoring identity often has the consequence of making the same mistakes over again—often with people from disadvantaged backgrounds bearing the brunt of those mistakes. Although there are a number of scholars who have approached crime theory in this way—from feminist, queer, and anticolonial perspectives, among many others—crime theory that centralizes issues of race have had a larger influence on both critical and mainstream criminology.

I. Race and Criminology

A key study in the role of race in crime theory is Shaun L. Gabbidon's work in *Criminological Perspectives on Race and Crime* (2010), in which he reviews the sometimes underappreciated role that race places across criminological theory, from traditional to critical perspectives, and explores how that lack of attention can produce devastating errors in criminological research, policy, and practice. In an early chapter, Gabbidon reviews **biological explanations** for crime as biological theories that are in many ways very much like the 19th-century theories of the positivist school, which reemerged in the 1980s and 1990s. The new biological school focused largely on intelligence, as measured by IQ, and argued, for example, that studies showed that people with lower IQs were more likely to commit crime and that African American communities score lower overall on IQ tests, indicating that it is because of native intelligence that African Americans have higher rates of certain crimes. Gabbidon points out, though, that the empirical studies relied exclusively on White communities—not differences across racial groups. Further, these studies ignore other research that shows that IQ tests are not accurate representations of intelligence but instead tend to produce results that are favorable toward the dominant (White) culture. A critical approach would suggest that it is because of preconceived stereotypes about racial difference that these errors in logic and analysis seem like legitimate arguments. Reviewing a wide range of crime theory, Gabbidon points out the importance of engaging social structures and identity when conducting criminological research, identifying sites again and again where the failure to account for the complex social realities of identity undermines scientific validity.

Identities and critical perspectives offer much both as countertheories and as elements to be integrated into traditional theorizing, because when researchers fail to acknowledge identity, they have the tendency to create theories about imaginary people. These imaginary people resemble populations under study, but they tend to be flattened, stereotypical versions of human beings, rather than the complex individuals with histories and cultures that we all are. When this flattening occurs, the immoral biases that researchers bring to the table threaten to dominate the findings of research.

J. A Whole World of Theories: Conclusion

There are far more theories than the ones thus far discussed, including social control theory, developmental and life course theories, and labeling theory, all of which build on, revise, and respond to the theories already discussed in this chapter. Each of these theories has its own strengths and weaknesses and its own assumptions and biases. Further examination of these theories and others enables a more sophisticated understanding of crime, criminals, and the world around us. Remember, we are all using theories all the time. We are developing stories about why things happen, how they happen, and why they happen to particular people, in certain places, and at a specific time. When we formalize a theory, we are making a claim to understand how the world (maybe a big part, maybe just a tiny bit) works. We are responsible for the assumptions, biases, and stereotypes that can become embedded in our theorizing if we are not attentive and careful. If we fail to take this responsibility, we become morally complicit in reproducing false information and understanding—which, particularly in criminal justice research, can have real effects on people's lives.

DISCUSSION QUESTIONS

1. What are the ethical issues involved in choosing a particular theory to use to explain a particular crime phenomenon?
2. Choose one of the following theories: social disorganization, general strain theory, or social learning theory. Identify how race might need to be accounted for in applying the theory to a case.

REFERENCES

Agnew, Robert. "Foundation for a generalism strain theory of crime and delinquency." *Criminology* 30 (1992): 47.

Akers, R., & Jennings, W. (2009). Social learning theory. In J. Miller (Ed.), *21st Century criminology: A reference handbook* (pp. 323–332). Thousand Oaks: Sage.

Beccaria, C. (2009). *On crimes and punishments and other writings.* Toronto: University of Toronto Press.

Bulmer, M. (1984). *The Chicago school of sociology.* Chicago: University of Chicago Press.

DeKeseredy, W. S. (2010). *Contemporary critical criminology.* Abingdon, UK: Routledge.

Durkheim, E. (1966). *Suicide; a Study in Sociology* (p. 15). New York, NY: The Free Press.

Ferri, E. (1910). *The positive school of criminology: Three lectures given at the University of Naples, Italy on April 22, 23 and 24, 1901* (E. Untermann, Trans.). Chicago, IL: Kerr.

Gabbidon, S. L. (2010). *Criminological perspectives on race and crime* (2nd ed.). New York: Routledge.

Gaylord, M. S., & Galliher, J. F. (1988). *The criminology of Edwin Sutherland*. New Brunswick, NJ: Transaction Books.

Koseli, M. (2007). The poverty, inequality and terrorism relationship: An empirical analysis of. *Understanding terrorism: Analysis of sociological and psychological aspects, 22*, 109.

Lombroso, C. (2006). *Criminal man*. Durham, NC: Duke University Press. (Original work published 1876)

Lombroso-Ferrero, Gina. *Criminal Man: According To The Classification Of Cesare Lombroso*. 1st ed. Ann Arbor: The Project Gutenberg, 2009. Web. 4 Nov. 2015.

Merton, R. K. (1938). Social structure and anomie. *American sociological review, 3*(5), 672–682.

Park, R. E. (1936). Human ecology. *American Journal of Sociology, 42*, 1–15.

Reiman, J. (1990). *The rich get richer and the poor get prison*. Boston: Allyn and Bacon.

Sampson, R. J., & Groves, W. B. (1989). Community structure and crime: Testing social disorganization theory. *American Journal of Sociology, 94*, 774–802.

Shaw, C. R., & McKay, H. D. (1942). *Juvenile delinquency and urban areas*. Chicago, IL: University of Chicago Press. .

Sutherland, E. H., Cressey, D. R., & Luckenbill, D. F. (1992). *Principles of criminology*. Lanham, MD: Rowman & Littlefield.

Wigmore, J., & Lombroso, C. (1911). General introduction. In C. Lombroso (Ed.), *Crime: Its causes and remedies* (H. P. Horton, Trans.) (pp. v–ix). Boston: Little, Brown.

Wilson, R. E., & Paulsen, D. J. (2008). Foreclosures and crime: A geographical perspective. *Geography & Public Safety, 1*(3), 1–2.

03

CHAPTER OUTLINE

KEY TERMS

- *ACTUS REUS*
- BURDEN OF PROOF
- COMMON LAW
- CRIMINAL LAW
- JUSTICE
- MENS REA
- PROCEDURAL CRIMINAL LAWS
- SUBSTANTIVE CRIMINAL LAWS

Criminal Law

Feyisara Olotu

A. Introduction

This chapter will take you through the journey of exploring criminal law in the American jurisprudence system. By the end of this chapter, students should have a thorough understanding of criminal law; we will discuss the history of criminal law, the social contract theory, how laws are created, the different categories of crime, various sources of law, how we classify crimes, elements of crime, legal defenses to crime, and white-collar crime versus street crime. When you are dealing with criminal law, you must also deal with the moral and ethical issues that come with it. Morality and ethics play an important role in the study of criminal law. Ethics help develop the moral reasoning used when defining the following fundamental questions:

1. What is criminal?
2. Are street crimes more criminal than white-collar crimes?

3. Does one criminal act deserve harsher punishment than another?
4. What about drug abusers—should they be sentenced to prison? What about people who commit tax fraud?
5. Can a killing ever be justified?
6. These are questions that will be discussed in this chapter with moral lenses. Morality, norms, rules, and consequences for breaking the rules have always been on the forefront of establishing a society in which people can coexist, live in one accord, feel safe, and flourish. This becomes clear by examining the history of criminal law.

B. The History of Criminal Law

Criminal law is a living document that is constantly evolving to keep pace with society and its needs. Because the law defines crime, punishment, and procedure, which are the basic concerns of the criminal justice system, it is essential for students to know something of the nature, purpose, and content of criminal law.

The roots of the criminal codes used in the United States can be traced back to early legal charters such as the Babylonian Code of Hammurabi (1750 BCE) and the Mosaic Code of Israelites (1200 BCE). Another early code is the Roman Twelve Tables (451 BCE), which was the first written code in response to complaints of the lower class of the arbitrariness of the existing unwritten legal codes. Although the original legal formal codes were lost during the Dark Ages, German and Anglo–Saxon societies developed legal systems featuring monetary compensations (wergild) for criminal violations. Guilt was determined by two methods:

1. Compurgation: This involved having the accused person swear an oath of innocence while being backed up by a group of 12 to 25 oath helpers, who would attest to his or her character.
2. Claims of innocence and ordeal: This was based on principle that divine forces would not allow an innocent person to be harmed. This method involved measures such as having the accused place his or her hand in boiling water or holding a hot iron. If the wound healed, the person was found innocent. If not, the accused was deemed guilty. Another method employed by this method was trial by combat. This allowed the accused to challenge his accuser to a duel, with the outcome determining the legitimacy of the accusation. Punishments included beheading, public flogging, burning, and branding.

Common Law

U.S. state and federal civil and criminal law is derived from English **common law**. This term refers to those customs, traditions, judicial decisions, and other materials that guide courts in decision making. These laws are not embodied in the Constitution or enacted by legislatures. English common law developed after the Norman Conquest in 1066. Prior to that, there were no distinctions among laws, customs, and religious practices and morality, and judicial decisions, which differed from community to community. With the goal of providing unity, the king employed representatives (judges) to travel to different jurisdictions with news of what was happening in each one. Over time legal principles began to be common among the lands; thus the phrase *common* law. Afterward, English common law was brought by the colonists to America and became the basis of many early laws in this country. Common law offenses have been kept alive and interpreted by judicial decisions, which are an important part of American law today. How did humankind live prior to the implementation of formal governments? Philosophers theorize communities formed social contracts to protect themselves and their property.

C. Social Contract Theory

The concept of social contract theory is that in the beginning, humankind lived in a state of nature. There was no government, and there was no law to regulate them. Seventeenth-century philosopher Thomas Hobbes believed that as a result of this deplorable state of nature, there was hardship and oppression in parts of society. Life consisted of fear and selfishness. Consequently, the desire for security and order compelled society to voluntarily enter into a contract surrendering all their rights and freedom to an absolute ruler in order to secure self-preservation and protection. Hobbes's theory explains and supports monarchy governments.

In contrast to Hobbes's theory on the social contract, 17th-century philosopher John Locke believed that the state of nature was good and enjoyable. However, men's property was not secure in the state of nature. Locke theorized that the need to protect their property is the only reason men voluntarily entered into the social contract. According to Locke, men did not surrender all of their rights to a single individual but only surrendered their right to individually enforce law, maintain order, and preserve the law of nature. The individual retained all other rights—the rights to life, liberty, and property. The purpose of the government and law is to uphold and protect the natural rights of men. So as long as the government fulfils this purpose, the laws given by it are valid and binding, but when it ceases to fulfill this purpose, the laws have no validity and the government can be thrown out of power. In Locke's view, unlimited sovereignty is contrary to natural law.

Finally, we have a French philosopher from the 18th century, Jean-Jacques Rousseau. Similar to Locke, Rousseau believed that life in the state of nature—life before the formation of societies—was happy, and there was equality among men. But as the population grew, private property was invented, as were greed, inequality, competition, and so on. For this reason, individuals in society surrendered themselves to the community or the "general will.' In return, the general will is to provide civil liberties such as freedom of speech, the right to assembly, equality, and so on. According to Rousseau's theory, the majority ruled society and the minority view was ignored. Unlike Locke, Rousseau's theory did not just focus on the protection of private property; it also included the importance of an individual's civil liberties.

Though the theories of Hobbes, Locke, and Rousseau seem different from one another, they all share a common set of principles. They all believe that:

1. law is an agreement from members of society on what constitutes wrongdoing;
2. cooperative behavior is rational and reasonable;
3. those living under a government are parties to a social contract in which each person agrees to follow the laws of the state on the condition that everyone else does the same; this way we are all relatively safe from each other and we all benefit; and
4. everyone will end up worse if they individually pursue their own interest.

These principles and beliefs make up the consensus views, and all three philosophers subscribe to this way of thinking.

Though some see the social contract as the development of rules and laws that resulted from the cooperative behavior of the majority of a community or society, some dispute this claim. Nineteenth-century philosopher Karl Marx is one of those people. According to Marx's theory, the social contract reflects the wishes of the powerful and controls the poor. Marx's conflict theory states that the social contract is just a tool developed by the wealthy in society to maintain the position of the wealthy, and it deems anyone who does not show respect for authority as deviant and criminal. People who are unemployed are seen as deviant and criminal. A high school dropout is seen as deviant and criminal. Most importantly, the weak of society, such as drug abusers and prostitutes, are seen as more criminal than the wealthy who harm society for the sake of profit.

THINKING POINT

Which social contract theory do you agree with more? Is today's society molded toward any one of these views?

Moral Implication

Today members of society can reasonably be expected to follow the rules. If everyone in society were to ignore or break the law, not only will it undermine the law, it will also endanger the well-being of society. It is rational to obey the law only on the condition that others are doing the same; this is known as reciprocity. However, when someone violates the condition of reciprocity, he releases us, only to a certain extent, from our obligation toward him. That is why society has developed self-defense, castle doctrine, and stand your ground laws. In other words, if you break the contract, then others aren't bound by it.

Example: If you point a gun at me, I have the right to defend myself and shoot back without breaking the law. If you break into my home, I have the right to defend my home and myself against you without breaking the law.

D. How Laws Are Born

Laws begin as ideas. An idea for a law can come from a variety of places ranging from your next-door neighbor to the president of the United States. Once the idea for a law comes into fruition, it must be sponsored by a member of the U.S. House of Representative. Megan's Law is an example of nationwide wide law that stemmed from an idea.

Megan's Law[1]

In 1994, 7-year-old Megan Kanka was raped and murdered by her neighbor Jesse Timmendequas, a convicted sex offender who had been released after serving a maximum sentence. The neighbor who invited Megan to see his puppy was a twice-convicted pedophile. Megan's grieving parents said they never would have let their daughter travel their neighborhood freely if they had been alerted to the presence of a convicted sexual offender living across the street from their residence. In response to this event and other sex crimes, community members successfully lobbied for the enactment of a law requiring sex offender registration and public notification that a sex offender is living and working in the community.

Currently, all 50 states and the District of Columbia have passed similar legislation, collectively referred to as Megan's Law. Underlying these laws is the belief that notifying the public of the presence

---

1   National Institute of Justice, 2009.

of sex offenders in the community allows citizens to take protective measures against potentially dangerous sex offenders who live nearby.

With Megan's Law, we see how a law is created. But what is the actual definition of *law*?

What Is Law?

The precise definition of *law* varies. However, all definitions of *law* will always have the following four characteristics:

1. What is made into law is dependent on the political climate at the time.
2. A law must be specific. A law must describe the offense and the punishment if this offense takes place.
3. A law is uniformly applied. A law must be applied equally to every individual and should not be discriminatory.
4. The law contains penal sanctions that are enforced by the state.

Moral Implications of the Law

Criminal law is generally understood to codify society's reaction to acts that are morally blameworthy, as we saw with Megan's Law. Laws intend to promote order and safety to the public. Law is supposed to encourage fairness in society so that everyone can be confident that their rights will be protected as citizens of a society. This doctrine is derived from the consensus theory previously discussed. This equality of rights, protection, safety, and fairness is one of the primary reasons the law is made to be *uniformly* applied. In order to sustain its moral authority, criminal law should strive as much as possible to remain in step with the basic moral intuitions of the surrounding community.

After an idea is created into the legal definition of a law, it is then categorized into a specific type of law.

E. Types of Law

The U.S. legal system has several types of laws, but for the purposes of this text, we will be focusing on only three types of laws: criminal law, civil law, and administrative or public law. We will touch briefly on common law and constitutional law as well.

Criminal Law

Criminal law is a body of rules that define crimes, set out their punishments, and mandate procedures for carrying out the criminal justice process. Criminal law is divided into:

> Substantive criminal law. *This category of law is probably the most easily recognized by the public. It comprises a body of specific rules that declare what conduct is criminal and prescribe the punishment to be imposed for such conduct.*
>
> Example: *Murder is the unlawful killing of another human being without justification or excuse.*
>
> Procedural criminal law. *This category of law is concerned with the methods that must be followed in obtaining warrants, investigating offenses, effecting lawful arrest, conducting trials, introducing evidence, sentencing convicted offenders, and reviewing cases by appellate courts.* **Procedural laws** *set out the basic rules of practice in the criminal justice system and are mainly contained in the U.S. Constitution and state constitutions.*
>
> Civil law. *This category of law includes all law that is not criminal, including tort, contract, personal property, maritime, and commercial law. Civil law is the set of rules governing relations between private parties, including both individuals and organizations (such as business enterprises and corporations). Civil law is used to resolve, control, and shape personal interactions such as contracts, wills, trusts, property ownership, and commerce. The most relevant to criminal law is tort, the law of personal injury.*
>
> Public law. *Also known as administrative law, this is the branch of law that deals with the government and its relationships with individuals or other governments. It governs the administration and regulation of city, county, state, and federal government agencies.*

Criminal and civil law can be interrelated and can be brought to bear on the same criminal act. A crime victim can sue the accused for monetary damages in civil court. It is possible to seek civil damages from the accused even if he or she is found not guilty in criminal court. The surviving family members of

Nicole Brown Simpson and Ronald Goldman filed and won a wrongful death suit against O. J. Simpson in civil court. The *evidentiary standard* in a civil trial is less than that of a criminal trial. In a civil trial the *plaintiff* must show that the defendant is responsible by a *preponderance of the evidence*, whereas in a criminal trial the *prosecution* must show that the defendant is *guilty beyond a reasonable doubt.*

A law is derived from various sources as can be seen in the next section.

F. Sources of Law

Law is derived from four sources: statutes, constitutions, judicial decisions (case law), and regulations.

- Statutory law. Most states have codified their previously unwritten customs and laws. Each state's criminal statute defines the crimes and penalties applicable to the state.
- Constitutions. To a limited extent, criminal laws are contained in constitutions. Each state's constitution may contain definitions of crime applicable only to that state. The U.S. Constitution deals primarily with procedural criminal law—methods by which law can be enforced. It describes the minimal protections of rights and guarantees of individuals. States can enhance these protections, as long as they meet the minimum requirements provided in the U.S. Constitution.
- Judicial decisions (case law). Law also comes from decisions of judges, as well as customs. The doctrine of *stare decisis* (let the decision stand) is derived from case law and judicial decisions made by that court.
- Administrative law. A less emphasized but still important source of law, administrative law is a body of regulations and rules that come from administrative agencies empowered by Congress (state or federal) to make and enforce rules and regulations. Most administrative laws are civil laws, yet if violated they can be enforced through criminal court. Some examples of administrative agencies include but are not limited to the Internal Revenue Service (IRS) and the U.S. Food and Drug Administration (FDA).

G. Classification of Crime

The decision of how a crime should be classified varies from state to state. Decisions on crime classifications are usually determined by the seriousness of the crime and its impact on victims and society. Most modern criminal codes divide crimes into violations/infractions, misdemeanors, and felonies.

Infractions/Violations

This category of offenses is the least serious which often involve criminal traffic violations.

Misdemeanors

A category of criminal offenses punishable by up to 1 year in jail. Punishment can also include probation, fine, community service, and restitution. Defendants charged with a misdemeanor are entitled to a jury trial and an attorney if they are indigent.

Example: Lucy is convicted of furnishing alcohol to a minor. The state defines the offense as a Class C misdemeanor. If state law provides that Class C misdemeanors are punishable by a fine of up to $100, that is the maximum sentence the judge can impose on Lucy. If the state law provides that Class C misdemeanors are punishable by up to 1 year in prison, Lucy is entitled to a court-appointed attorney if she cannot afford one.

Felonies

This is the most serious of criminal offenses. A felony usually involves serious physical harm (or threat of harm) to victims. Felonies also include white-collar crime and fraud schemes. Offenses otherwise categorized as misdemeanors can be raised to felony status if the defendant is a repeat offender. The punishment for a felony ranges from 1 year in prison to life without parole, and sometimes even the death penalty if the crime was a murder that took place in a jurisdiction that utilizes the death penalty.

Example: Bill is charged with assault with a deadly weapon, even though the bottle that he threw at another patron in a nightclub missed its intended target. Bill will probably be convicted of a felony because even though he failed to injure the intended victim, his behavior was intended to (and did) create a risk of serious physical injury.

Example: Louis was convicted of shoplifting, which is categorized as a misdemeanor in his state. However, 15 months later he is charged with another shoplifting offense. State law may allow (but not require) the prosecutor to charge Louis with felony shoplifting.

A person convicted of a felony may be barred from certain fields of employment, like law, medicine, and public office. He or she may lose the right to vote, and a felony conviction can also affect the status of an immigrant of the United States.

Moral Implications: Felony Disenfranchisement Laws

Disenfranchisement involves taking away voting rights. Most states in the United States have disenfranchised convicted felons and ex-felons. Are felon disenfranchisement laws a form of racial discrimination? The reality is that throughout the United States, 2.2 million Black citizens—1 in 13—are banned from voting because of these laws. One in 5 Blacks are banned from voting in Florida, Virginia, and Kentucky. The impact of felony disenfranchisement laws on communities of color remains disproportionate. *"In many states, felony disenfranchisement laws are still on the books. And the current scope of these policies is not only too significant to ignore—it is also too unjust to tolerate"* (Holder, 2014, para. 19).

The war on drugs has left a staggering number of nonviolent individuals released from prison who are not on probation or parole and have committed no further crimes forever prohibited from voting. And a majority of these individuals are people of color. *"The racial disparity in arrest rates has been absolutely devastating to the black community"* (Rand, 2013, para. 6).

In New Jersey 60% of the individuals subject to the state's disenfranchisement law are African American or Latino. As a result, the political power of the African American and Latino communities in New Jersey is diluted because they are disproportionately excluded from voting.

Some argue that felon disenfranchisement law can be separated from race. State laws are literally race neutral, in that all who are convicted of felonies are subject to the same sanctions. Modern defenders of the practice draw on nonracial reasons for their positions, such as, *"Blacks are disproportionately affected by felon disenfranchisement because a disproportionate number of Blacks are felons."* However, this simplistic rationale ignores compelling evidence of discriminatory racial dynamics in the criminal justice system, such as racial profiling by law enforcement, racially disparate prosecution of the war on drugs, and inequities in adequacy of counsel as a function of both race and class.[2]

H. Elements of a Crime: The Legal Definitions of a Crime

In general, to fulfill the legal definition of a crime, the U.S. criminal justice system requires that four elements be proved:

1. *actus reus*—a criminal act
2. *mens rea*—a criminal state of mind; intent
3. concurrence of a criminal act and a criminal state of mind
4. causation—actual harm was caused

---

2 Mauer, 2004.

The prosecution has the burden of proving all of these elements *beyond a reasonable doubt.*

Actus reus—a criminal act or an act of omission (failure to act) that causes social harm. This is the physical component of the crime. It eliminates the possibility of criminal punishment for one's thoughts. To fulfill the *actus reus* element of a crime, the illegal act must be voluntary; this excludes any act that was made without the person's determination or effort.

Example: A man has an epileptic seizure while driving on a public highway, loses control of his vehicle, and kills four people. This man knew he was subject to epileptic seizures at any time, yet he got behind the wheel alone. Do you think he is criminally liable for the four deaths?[3]

Omission or Failure to Perform a Legally Required Duty

Relationship status creates a duty to act. Parents have a duty to provide adequate care for their child. A spouse has a legal duty to come to the aid of his or her spouse. Doctor have a legal duty to aid their patients. Legal duty might also exist when a person takes affirmative action that creates a situation of danger to a person to whom no duty previously existed.

Example: While driving, Sophia hit a homeless man, and the impact propelled the victim onto her windshield. Sophia drove the car home and parked it in her garage with the victim impaled on the shards of glass. He bled to death. A medical expert testified that the victim would have lived had he received immediate medical attention. Sophia will be convicted of murder for failing to make sure the man received immediate medical assistance.[4]

One important thing to note is that the duty to act is a *legal* duty, not a *moral* duty. There is no affirmative duty to act to prevent a crime.

Example: In New Bedford, Massachusetts, people watched and cheered as a gang rape occurred. Morally, this act was reprehensible; but legally, it is allowed.[5]

THINKING POINT

Imagine you walk into a casino restroom and witness a 7-year-old girl being raped. She is later killed. You walk out and do not even report what you saw to authorities. Are you criminally responsible for her death? Did you commit any crime at all?

---

3   People v. Decina, 1956.
4   CNN, 2003.
5   Vespa, 1984. .

It is important to remember that even though you have no legal duty to act when it comes to a stranger, once you start helping, you must finish. In other words, if you have no legal duty to act, but you start to act and then quit, you will have a legal duty if by starting then quitting you put the person in a worse position than if you had done nothing at all.[6]

THINKING POINT:

Should the law require bystanders to go to the aid of others? Should the law require bystanders to call the police if they witness a crime?

Mens rea—a criminal state of mind. Under common law, for an act to constitute a crime, the actor must have criminal intent. In order to intend to commit a crime, the person must have clear knowledge of the consequences of his or her actions *and* must desire those consequences to occur. *Mens rea* is one of the most debated and frequently litigated terms in criminal law.

Some crimes require specific intent, or willful and intentional mental purpose. With theft/larceny, for instance, it must be proved that the person took the property of another and intended to deprive the owner of the property permanently or for an unreasonable length of time. Simply taking away someone's property, without the intent to permanently deprive him or her of it, is not enough to prove a crime of theft/larceny.

Moral Implication

The *mens rea* requirement is a hurdle intended to ensure that criminal law punishes only the blameworthy or culpable—those individuals who consciously choose to do wrong. From a moral standpoint, why do you think your intention to commit a crime needs to be proved before you can be convicted of a crime?

---

6   *People v. Beardsly*, 1907.

THINKING POINT:

Your classmate, who sits right next to you, takes one of your expensive textbooks without your permission or knowledge. He leaves the class with it. You search for the book for months, make announcements, and even fill out a police report. Two months later you discover the textbook in your classmate's bag. Is he criminally liable for the theft of your textbook? What if 2 months later, he returns the book to you and says, "Here you go, I was just borrowing your book for an important project I had to do. I hope you don't mind." Now is he criminally liable for the theft of your book? Why or why not?

When no specific intent is stated in the definition of a crime, you must refer to the Model Penal Code's (MPC) general requirements of criminal culpability. The MPC recognizes different levels of *mens rea*:

1. Purposely—conscious objective to do the conduct or cause the result.
2. Knowingly—aware that the result is certain to follow.
3. Recklessly—consciously disregard a substantial and unjustifiable risk.
4. Negligently (gross)—conduct that is more culpable than ordinary negligence.
5. Transferred intent—when a person intends to cause harm to another person but instead erroneously inflicts harm on an unintended target, the law can transfer that general intent to the party actually harmed.

    (a) *Example: Marsha is angry at Eric. In a moment of rage, she throws a glass bottle in the general direction of Eric. The glass bottles hits and seriously injures an innocent bystander. Is Marsha criminally liable for the unanticipated harm? Yes, under the doctrine of transferred intent, Marsha can be legally viewed as having general intent to harm the bystander, even though she held no willful or purposeful intent toward the bystander. Further, Marsha acted recklessly and consciously disregarded a substantial and unjustifiable risk by throwing that bottle at someone. Now, what if Eric, seeing the bottle coming, pulled the bystander in front of him to use her as a shield? Does this change anything for Marsha? No.*

Concurrence of the *Actus Reus* and *Mens Rea.*

The third element needed to prove a crime was committed is the concurrence of the act with the criminal intent or result. In order for a defendant to be convicted of a crime, he or she must have the requisite intent when he committed the unlawful act. Further, the law requires that the defendant's unlawful act be the proximate cause of any injury resulting from the criminal act.

Example: A person with the mens rea *for murder fires a gun at another person, misses the heart, and hits the arm. The targeted victim dies 2 weeks later from cancer. What can the defendant be charged with?* **Attempted murder only, because the victim died from cancer, not from the gunshot.** *Now, what if this victim is taken to the hospital after being shot, and he has a heart attack during surgery and dies. Can the defendant be charged with murder?*

In order to obtain a conviction of a crime, the prosecution has the burden to prove all of these elements beyond a reasonable doubt. In summation, *when a criminal act or omission combines with a criminal state of mind to cause harm, criminal liability results.*

In the criminal justice system, there is a category of crimes defined as white-collar crimes. These types of crimes differ from well-known street crimes.

White-Collar Crime/Suite Crime

White-collar crime was initially defined as *"a crime committed by a person of respectability and high social status in the course of his occupation"* (Sutherland, 1974, p. 35). Now it can be more broadly defined as *"violation of the law committed by a person or a group of persons in the course of an otherwise respected and legitimate occupation or financial activity"* (Sutherland, 1974, p. 36). Crimes by those in positions of high status and power still constitute the core of the problem of white-collar crime. The lawlessness of the privileged and powerful cause subtle damage to the social fabric that is impossible to measure in precise quantitative terms. Most people are more concerned about street crime than about white-collar crime. The media focuses so much on street crime that the public does not realize how much more costly white-collar crime is. Many argue that though the cost of white-collar crime may be high, it involves nonviolent crimes that pose no threat to the public. However, the reality is that the National Safety Council has estimated that thousands of people are killed each year in industrial accidents. It is hard to ascertain exactly how many of these deaths and injuries are a result of violation of laws or are fraudulently represented by manufacturers, but one can be sure that illegalities are involved in most of these cases.

Moral Implication: More Money, Less Punishment?

Most white-collar criminals serve their prison sentences in federal prison camps (FPCs). FPCs are thought of as the country clubs of prison. They typically have amenities like yoga, e-mail, a TV room, and even a hospital as opposed to an infirmary. Some people even call them "camp cupcake." FPCs are exclusive to white-collar criminals, celebrities, the wealthy, and nonviolent criminals. Victor Conte, former president and founder of BALCO, a sports nutrition center in California, served time in prison in 2005 after pleading guilty to conspiracy to distribute steroids and money laundering. Conte, a white-collar criminal, described his time at the Taft Correctional Institution, a privately run minimum security federal prison with 1,700 inmates, and his account of the goings on there is astounding. Conte reports the following:

Sports complex *"The first morning, when I woke up it was a kind of university-campus like setting. I walked out and in the middle of the courtyard was a huge sign that said 'Sports Complex.' Basketball, football, baseball. ..."*

Rec center *"I looked over I saw the rec center. And I walked over to that and looked in and there were ... pool tables ... foosball tables ... ping-pong tables."*

Music department *"Then I went through this door and there was this huge music department. Three different musical groups were practicing. ..."*

Drugs *"... anything that you wanted—alcohol—any and every type was $25 for 8 ounces. They had meth, steroids, and cocaine."*

No fences *"There's no fences around the place, about every 200 feet they have a sign on a stake that says 'Out of Bounds.' I got there on December 1 of 2005. That Christmas, about 25 guys just walked out on the freeway and they had their families pick them up and they left. So it's kind of an honor system."*

Some prisoners don't want to leave.[7]

The picture of crime that dominates the popular imagination is one of unambiguous wrongdoing—manifestly harmful acts that are clearly worthy of condemnation, such as street-level crimes with a recognizable victim. White-collar crime, by contrast, is pervaded by moral and imaginative ambiguity. Such crimes are committed by society's success stories, by the rich and the powerful, and frequently have no visible victim at their root. Is embezzlement less criminal than robbery? *Some famous white-collar criminals include: Bernie Madoff, Ponzi schemer, incarcerated at Butner Federal Correctional Institution in North Carolina; and Martha Stewart, incarcerated at FPC Alderson in West Virginia.*

---

7 Frauenfelder, 2012.

I. Legal Defenses to Crime/Criminal Defenses

The moral or blameworthy element of punishment through criminal law (criminal culpability) is critical to the topic of defenses. Most crimes require intent as an element of the offense; therefore, disputing the existence of *mens rea* is pivotal to establishing a defense.

Affirmative Defenses: Justification and Excuse Defenses

Justification defense: *a defense for a criminal act claiming that the criminal act was reasonable or necessary under the circumstances.* For example, the accused admits to committing the act but offers evidence that he or she had a right or duty to do so. With a justification defense, the *mens rea* is not in question; the criminal act is based on individual rights and duties. For example, a police officer has a duty to protect the public and can raise an affirmative defense to homicide if he or she killed an *armed* suspect. Or an individual has a right to defend him- or herself against an armed attacker. Some justification defenses discussed in this chapter are self-defense, consent, necessity, and duress.

Self-defense, the right to defend oneself, is a long-standing tradition under English common law. Generally, self-defense justifies physical injury to an aggressor. Statutes differ from state to state on the specific elements of self-defense, but generally a citizen can legally use force when:

(a) the citizen reasonably believes that she is under some unlawful threat of serious bodily injury or death,
(b) force must be necessary to avoid harm, and
(c) the force used was reasonable and proportionate to the anticipated harm.

A person verbally threatened by another is not justified in striking the other party with his or her fist. In general, state laws regulating self-defense are equally applicable to the defense of others. Laws regarding the defense of property are slightly different and normally do not permit the use of deadly force to protect possessions. The use of deadly force is generally limited to situations in which the actors have reasonable belief that such force is necessary to protect them from harm that might cause serious bodily injury or death, kidnapping, or rape. Some jurisdictions require a person to retreat if and only if it can be accomplished safely before resorting to force—especially deadly force.

The **castle doctrine** provides that individuals have no duty to retreat in certain circumstances. The majority of American jurisdictions recognize this doctrine pursuant to which a person attacked in his or her dwelling is not required to retreat before using fatal force to repel.

The Shooting of Renisha McBride

On November 2, 2013, homeowner Theodore Wafer of Dearborn Heights, Michigan, shot and killed 19-year-old Renisha McBride through his front door. Wafer believed McBride was an intruder. McBride was unharmed.

The issue in this case was whether the legal boundaries when it comes to using deadly force for home protection were met. Michigan law states that a homeowner can use deadly force if he or she has an honest and reasonable belief that imminent death or bodily harm will occur. This is known as the castle doctrine. Wafer was charged with second-degree murder, manslaughter, and felony use of a firearm. He invoked the castle doctrine as the basis of his defense. The prosecutors in the case stated that Michigan law permitting deadly force does not apply to Wafer because he shot through a screen door that was locked even when police arrived; nor was there evidence that McBride entered his home, which therefore negated Wafer's claim of facing an imminent threat inside his home. Does Wafer have a defense? Why or why not?

Wafer was convicted and sentenced to 17 to 32 years in prison.

Stand Your Ground Laws

In recent years some jurisdictions have given more leeway to persons who use force to protect themselves and others. These states have enacted legislation with fewer restrictions on the use of force for self-defense, including the duty to retreat. This is a change that some refer to as stand your ground laws.

An example is the Florida statute made famous in the Trayvon Martin killing in February 2012. The statute states:

A person is justified in using force, except deadly force, against another when and to the extent that the person reasonably believes that such conduct is necessary to defend himself or herself or another against the other's imminent use of unlawful force. However, a person is justified in use of deadly force and does not have a duty to retreat if:

"He or she reasonably believes that such force is necessary to prevent imminent death or great bodily harm to himself or herself or another or to prevent the imminent commission of a forcible felony." Justifiable Use of Force, Fla. Stat §776.031.

The statute also grants civil and criminal immunity to anyone found to have had such reasonable belief. Florida's stand your ground law became the focus of national protest in 2012 after George Zimmerman shot and killed 17-year-old Trayvon Martin, a young, unarmed African American, inside a gated community in Sanford, Florida. After much public outrage, Zimmerman was arrested and charged with second-degree murder. Zimmerman invoked the stand your ground law as his defense. He was acquitted of all charges in July 2013.

In November 2007 a 61-year-old computer technician named Joe Horn shot and killed two men who were burglarizing his neighbor's home in Texas. Horn went outside his home, despite the instructions from the police dispatchers telling him not to kill anyone over property and to stay inside his own home. The 911 dispatcher warned Horn to stay inside at least a dozen separate times, telling him, "*An officer is coming out there. I don't want you to go outside that house.*" Horn says he came out his front door, down the steps of his porch, and confronted the two burglars. Horn fatally shot the burglars in the back, two illegal immigrants from Colombia named Diego Ortiz and Miguel de Jesus. In 2008 the grand jury refused to return a criminal indictment against Horn. Texas law permits the use of deadly force against another in defense of person to prevent the other's imminent commission of aggravated kidnapping, murder, sexual assault, aggravated sexual assault, robbery, or aggravated robbery. Horn's life and property was not threatened by the intruder, and according to the Texas statute, his actions were not permitted by law.[8]

THINKING POINT:

Did the grand jury's failure to indict him essentially allow him to get away with murder? Explain.

Consent

This is a defense that negates culpability. Consent is a viable defense when it is an element of a crime against a person, such as rape or theft. The victim must have capability and authority to give consent. For example, having sexual relations with a person underage is considered statutory rape, regardless of whether that person was willing. The consent must have been voluntarily granted. Force, fraud, and other means of unreasonable or unlawful coercion are unacceptable means of obtaining consent.

EXAMPLE: If Lily consents to sex with Bob under the threat of death, the consent was obtained illegally and is not a defense for rape.

---

8   Bury, 2008.

EXAMPLE: Bob tells Lily that he will break up with her if she refuses to have sex with him. She agrees to have sex, then later claims rape. Consent is a defense because no true threat ever evolved.

Consent also is applicable in defense of injuries caused through sanctioned sports.

EXAMPLE: A football player breaks another player's leg while tackling him. This is covered under consent.

Duress

The defendant claims he was forced to commit a crime as the only means of preventing death or serious harm to himself or others. Duress is only applicable if no other alternative is available. This defense is not a viable defense for murder, but evidence of duress can be a mitigating factor of *mens rea*.

Necessity

The defense of necessity is used when a crime is committed under extreme circumstances and could not be avoided. Unlike duress, this involves threats made by another person, people act out of necessity according to their own judgments.

EXAMPLE: A mother and child are traveling on a deserted road in the middle of winter when their vehicle breaks down, and she has no cell phone reception in this area. There are no other vehicles traveling on the road. They see a gas station that is closed with no pay phone in sight. They are cold, hungry, and dehydrated. The mother decides to break in to the gas station to retrieve water, food, and clothing to survive the night. Does the mother have a defense to the charge of burglary? **Yes, considering there were no legal alternatives to breaking the law. They could have either starved and frozen to death or broken in to and stolen from the gas station. It was the lesser of two evils**.

Excuse Defenses

Insanity

This is a defense to criminal prosecution in which the defendant's state of mind negates his or her criminal responsibility. It is a controversial defense that is not frequently used, and when used it is rarely successful. A successful insanity defense renders a verdict of not guilty; however, the defendant is not released into society but confined to a mental health facility for an indefinite amount of time. Over the years several tests have been developed to define and measure insanity.

The M'naghten Rule

Formulated in England in 1843, this also known as the right versus wrong test. If this rule is invoked, the defendant must show that he or she did not know the nature and quality of the act committed or that he or she did not know the act was wrong. Twenty-five states use this rule.

The Irresistible Impulse Rule

This rule was formulated in Ohio in 1834 and is often used in conjunction with the M'Naghten rule. This rule defines a person as insane if he or she did know that his or her actions were illegal and because of a mental impairment could not control his or behavior.

The Durham Rule

This rule was developed in Washington, D.C., in 1954 and states that an accused is not criminally responsible if his or her unlawful act was the product of mental disease or defect. The Durham rule drew clear distinctions between mental defect (a permanent, unchanging condition) and mental disease (a condition that can improve or worsen over time). Only the state of New Hampshire uses it today.

The Substantial Capacity Test

This test argues that insanity should be defined as a lack of substantial capacity to control one's behavior. It combines elements of the M'Naghten rule with the concept of irresistible impulse.

Intoxication

This refers to the diminished mental capacity caused by alcohol or drug use. Voluntary intoxication is intoxication brought on by free will and is not a defense. At most it could be used as a mitigating factor regarding intent for specific-intent crime but never general-intent crime. So it could possibly be used in a murder case to reduce the charge from first-degree murder to second-degree murder. Involuntary intoxication is intoxication without choice or will, such as that which occurs when someone slips drugs into the food or drink of an unsuspecting person. When involuntary intoxication occurs, a person may have a legal defense. This defense also includes unforeseeable reactions or interactions of substances, like an allergic reaction to a substance or a side effect of a prescription drug.

Mistake of Fact

This can be used as a defense when the offense resulted from an honest mistake.

EXAMPLE: A cab driver charged with aiding and abetting an escaped inmate could argue mistake of fact.

EXAMPLE: A man steals a car and later realizes a child was in the backseat. The mistake of fact defense is not applicable to his crime of kidnapping, because his initial intent was to commit a crime; thus, the thief is responsible for consequences subsequent to that action.

Mistake of Law

This is an honest and genuine belief of the accused that he or she acted in accordance to the law. As a general rule, ignorance of the law is no excuse. However, this defense can generally be used to negate specific elements of a crime.

EXAMPLE: An immigrant enters into a contract with a 14-year-old girl to bear him a son. The girl has a baby, and the immigrant is charged with statutory rape. He invokes the mistake of law defense, saying that in his native country it is not illegal to have sex with a juvenile and that he did not know it was against the law in the United States. Does his ignorance of the U.S. law shield him from being convicted of statutory rape? **No, ignorance of the law is not an excuse, especially when the law has been made public.**

Infancy

Under common law, children below age 7 could not be convicted of a crime because of a conclusive presumption that they were not capable of forming the requisite criminal intent. Children between ages 7 and 14 years were refutably presumed to lack the mental capacity to form criminal intent. So the use by a child under age 14 of the infancy defense could be subjected to being refuted by evidence proving they did have the *mens rea*. Children 14 and older were presumed to possess the mental capacity to distinguish right from wrong and therefore were capable of forming criminal intent. Today the concept of infancy is not used in the U.S. legal system. Instead, the United States has developed a juvenile justice system, which eliminates the need for an infancy defense. The man-date of the juvenile justice system is to provide for the care and protection of children under a given age that varies from state to state. In certain situations, when a juvenile is a repeat offender or thought to be beyond rehabilitation and has committed a serious crime, he or she may be transferred to the adult criminal court. Juvenile offenders may not be subject to the death penalty or life without parole without violating their Eighth Amendment constitutional right against cruel and unusual punishment.[9]

J. Justice for All?

As you have learned in this chapter, laws were created in order to develop some order in society, preserve individual rights, and protect property. However, sometimes we fail to see whether the law provides **justice** for all. In fact, historically the law has been both unjust and just. An example of an unjust law is the constitutional law that declared slavery to be legal, which went even further by classifying Blacks as less than human by making them only three fifths a human. This legal injustice went on for almost a century before it was formally outlawed. However, the abolition of slavery did not stop legal injustice. Racism, racial discrimination, and total injustice for Black Americans were promoted by the passage of Jim Crow laws. Jim Crow excluded Blacks from public transport and facilities, juries, jobs, and neighborhoods.

Jim Crow states passed statutes that severely regulated social interactions between the races. Jim Crow signs were placed above water fountains, above door entrances and exits, and in front of public facilities. There were separate hospitals for Blacks and Whites, separate prisons, separate public and private schools, separate churches, separate cemeteries, separate public restrooms, and separate public accommodations. In most instances the Black facilities were grossly inferior, older, and less well kept. In other cases there were no Black facilities: no public restroom, no public beach, no place to sit or eat.

Historically, other legal injustices against Blacks included the denial of the right to vote by grandfather clauses (laws that restricted the right to vote to people whose ancestors had voted before the Civil War); poll taxes (fees charged to poor Blacks); White primaries (only Democrats could vote, and only Whites could be Democrats); and literacy tests (name all the vice presidents and Supreme Court justices throughout U.S. history).

The type of legal injustice we see today is less blatant and direct and more subtle and institutionalized. It is actually very difficult to recognize it. We see injustice in the legal system when it comes to crime and punishment. Street-level crimes—crimes that are proved to be committed more by poor, inner city people of color—are punished more harshly and more severely than white-collar crimes, which are proved to be committed more by upper class Whites and the social elite. Further, after the punishment stage we still see legal injustice with laws such as felon disenfranchisement law. Many

---

9   Ropers v. Simmon, 2005; Ghram v. Florida, 2010

communities of color have lost their voice in elections, and their right to vote has been diminished due to the felon disenfranchisement laws mentioned earlier in the chapter. In today's society, laws are not blatantly discriminatory on their face, but many laws consistently prove to have discriminatory impact, affecting the lives of inner city communities and communities of color differently than their White and upper class counterparts.

THINKING POINT:

Is it morally wrong to obey unjust laws?

K. Conclusion

This chapter focused on the nature and purpose of U.S. criminal laws by discussing the history of the law and exploring the social contract theories of philosophers John Locke, Thomas Hobbes, Jean-Jacques Rousseau, and Karl Marx. The chapter also explained how the law was born, including a brief discussion on the definition of law, the types of law, and the sources of law. The chapter went on to explain how crime is classified. There is a distinction between infractions/violation, misdemeanors, and felonies. An important discussion in this chapter focused on the moral implications associated with criminal law, such as the *mens rea* element of crime, the different treatment of white-collar criminals, and felony disenfranchisement laws. Finally, the chapter concluded by touching on the injustice in our justice system and how historically, not all of the laws in place are fair, equal, or just.

DISCUSSION QUESTIONS

1. What do you think about felon disenfranchisement laws? How would you feel if the right to vote was automatically restored to convicted felons after they served their sentence? Do you see this as fair? Would you consider felon disenfranchisement a lifetime sentence for felons? Do you see it as a form of racial discrimination? Why? Why not?

2. Is it ethical to allow citizens to take the law into their own hands, no matter what the provocation? Think about self-defense laws, including the castle doctrine and stand your ground laws in your response.

REFERENCES

Bury, C. (2008). Man cleared for killing neighbor's burglars. ABC News. Retrieved from http://abcnews.go.com/TheLaw/story?id=5278638

CNN. (2003). Motorist given 50 year-sentence in windshield murder trial. Retrieved from http://www.cnn.com/2003/LAW/06/27/windshield.death

Frauenfelder, M. (2012). Former inmate's description of minimum security federal prison: Sex, drugs, and rock 'n roll. *Boing Boing*. Retrieved from http://boingboing.net/2012/10/23/former-inmates-description-o.html

Ghram v. Florida, 130 S. Ct. 2011 (2010)

Holder, E. (2014). Attorney General Eric Holder delivers remarks on criminal justice reform at Georgetown University Law Center. Retrieved from US Department of Justice website: http://www.justice.gov/opa/speech/attorney-general-eric-holder-delivers-remarkson-criminal-justice-reform-georgetown

Mauer, M. (2004, Winter). Felon disenfranchisement: A policy whose time has passed? *Human Rights Magazine*.

National Institute of Justice. (2009). About Megan's Law. Retrieved from http://www.nij.gov/topics/corrections/community/sex-offenders/pages/about-megans-law.aspx

People v. Beardsly, 113 N.W. 1128 (Mich. 1907)

People v. Decina, 138 N.E.2d 799 (N.Y. 1956)

Rand, P. (2013, September 20). The devastating collateral damage of an insidious drug-war weapon. *Washington Times*. Retrieved from http://www.washingtontimes.com/news/2013/sep/20/paul-the-devastating-effect-of-a-drug-war-weapon/?page=all

Roper v Simmons, 543 U.S. 551 (2005)

Sutherland, E.H., & Cressey, D.R. (1974). *Criminology* Philadelphia: Lippincott.

Vespa, M. (1984). No town without pity: A divided New Bedford seeks justice in brutal gang rape case. *People, 21*(10). Retrieved from http://www.people.com/people/archive/article/0,,20087332,00.html

04

Police: An Experiment in Ordered Liberty

John Hobson

CHAPTER OUTLINE

KEY WORDS

- AURAL GRAFFITI
- CORRUPTION
- FIELD TRAINING OFFICERS
- POLICE CULTURE
- RACIAL PROFILING
- ROOKIE SOCIALIZATION
- SPATIAL POLICING
- SYMBOLIC ASSAILANT
- "MASK OF A THOUSAND FACES"

James Madison, the fourth president of the United States (1809–1817), was regarded as a founding father of the U.S. Constitution. In addition, he was hailed as the architect of the 10th Amendment, the provisions of which helped ensure that states would retain their sovereignty to prevent the government from denying the people their individual freedoms. The 10th Amendment allowed states to draft, ratify, and enact laws; to increase the power of police to enforce those laws; and to ensure the sovereignty of the local government. In this context, states were empowered to govern themselves.—United States v. Sprague, 282 U.S. 716, 733 (1931).

Madison said that the mission of the police in the United States, as in other democracies, was to play a rightful part in the nation's experiment in ordered liberty. He added that since the rule of law requires the keeping of the peace, the U.S. government was also an experiment in law enforcement and peacekeeping.

A. History Simplified: Roots of American Policing

The narrative of the first structured American police department is open to debate. However, early police departments most likely found their roots throughout the New World colonies. Neighbors watched out for neighbors. This was known as the mutual pledge system in England, the vow to be on the lookout for trouble; it was generational and intrinsic. In larger towns fire brigades watched the property for incendiary trouble to protect life and livestock, community structures, and churches. Fire brigades acted as night patrols and wandered the streets keeping the peace. In colonial America, the purists, or Puritans, were very much a part of law and order, since church elders watched the behavior of their congregations and acted as moral police officers. The elders considered themselves empowered to protect all that was good and righteous.

Throughout the early history of the United States, stories of vigilante groups and posse's told of well-paid mercenaries deputized to capture, dead or alive, those considered criminal, immoral, or anarchic. Punishments, reparations, and reimbursements were levied by the town and church elders or by those appointed to protect church and community interests. As the northern New England towns matured into larger cities, and as industrialization grew populations with the promise of employment, mercantile interests and investments became lucrative. As a result, the job of private security watchman become commonplace. The watch system was composed of community volunteers whose primary duty was to warn of impending danger. Boston created a night watch in 1636, New York in 1658, and Philadelphia in 1700. As wealth, organizations, and power increased, so did the need for organizations to protect these assets. Organized policing was born.

The genesis of policing in the American South found its impetus in America's original sin: slavery. In 1704 the first formal slave patrol was created in the Carolina Colonies. These patrols were designed to protect the interests of property owners, and because slaves were considered property, their safe return was paramount. In addition, because of their semi-militaristic organizational structure and their mission to capture the runaway slave (synonymous with "escaped criminal"), these patrols constituted the first policing organizations in the pre–Civil War South.

Tragically absent from slave patrols, vigilante groups, and the capture posse was the idea of due process. That is, the official and proper way of doing things in a legal case; the rule that a legal case proceed in a way that protects the rights of all the people involved. Out of tragedy came the principles of due process and our democratic system of fair play and justice. Fatefully, it took years of legislation and the lobbying of politicians and policy makers to sustain the premise of the Constitution; that is, that all men are created equal. The struggle to free slaves was long and hard fought, and in theory, ended with President Abraham Lincoln's Emancipation Proclamation.

B. Modern Police Jurisdictions: Sovereign States

On the local and state level, most police officers are generalists, jacks-of-all-trades, skilled in enforcing basic criminal law and investigating both civil and criminal transgressions. Civil infractions (which are primarily minor offenses such as traffic violations) are usually settled by a monetary fine or minor penalty. Criminal deeds are decided by a court of law, with incarceration as the decisive consequence. Federal law enforcement agencies enforce federal laws, protect areas of national interest, and ensure internal and external protections. State law enforcement agencies enforce state laws enacted by state legislatures. Local law enforcement handles cities and towns small and large, municipalities that govern themselves and enact by-laws specific to that locale, such as parking restrictions, curfews, and access to public areas. Both state and local police agencies enforce federal laws in conjunction with, and often parallel to, federal law.

The mission of modern American policing is multifaceted. Many believe that the primary work of the police is crime prevention. Others emphasize peacekeeping and the maintenance of order. Still others stress that law enforcement, practiced by those of good character who grasp what is morally necessary, possess the integrity to attend to a myriad of circumstances that describe the human condition.

This chapter explores policing, law enforcement, police cultures and subcultures, and the idea of a police "working personality." It will also look at the predicament of the disenfranchised, the minority symbolic assailant, and by extension, the ideas of symbolic racism. Paramount within this chapter is the ethical training of the new generation of police officers. In this respect, this chapter addresses the rookie as an agent of change.

C. The Rookie Experience: Police Culture and Training

Before entering the world of **police culture** that awaits the rookie officer, there is one caveat: a belief that exists within the minds of all police and in their sacred brotherhood. Sparrow (Sparrow & Moore, 1990) embodied this idea when he said:

> No one else understands the real nature of police work. That is, no one outside the police service—academics, politicians, and lawyers, in particular—can comprehend what we have to do. The public is naive about police work. People are unsupportive and unreasonably demanding. They all seem to think they know our job better than we do. They only want us when they need something done. (p. 51)

Early Studies

Westley (1970) conducted one of the first studies on the socialization of the rookie into police culture. He described four mechanisms in the rookie's full acceptance of the culture:

1. Expediency
2. Categorical reaction
3. Application of sanctions
4. Maintenance of personal integrity

It is because of these four variables that rookies come to accept the socialization process and police culture. Expediency describes the need for the way a police officer behaves; this leads to the internalization of behaviors available to the rookie. It is because of expediency that rookies begin to model **field training officers** (FTOs) and other peers with high levels of experience. In this mind-set, solidarity and loyalty become part of the rookie's working personality. Moreover, for the first time, the rookie begins to perceive the idea and strength of the "brotherhood," the essence of police culture. During the implementation stage, away from supervisors and other administrative forces, the rookie may undergo peer correction, situational isolation, and chastising by veteran officers. The idea is that the rank-in-file, in other words, the boots on-the-ground protect, condemn, and censure their own by reeling in and correcting unacceptable behavior. Finally, the rookie seeks to maintain self-esteem and integrity through his or her identification with the group. This is accomplished as the rookie begins to understand the new values of the organization.

In 1975 Van Maanen followed Westley's study. Van Maanen's study took a more dynamic look into the rookie experience. He offered four phases of socialization: entry, introduction, encounter, and metamorphosis. The ideas contained within the research of Westley and Van Maanen added to those of Crank and Caldero. The police cultural onion, Caldero and Crank's (2010) notion of the cultural resonance of police culture, aligns with Van Maanen's four stages of police socialization. These four steps are part of the wider view of police culture. To explain, Caldero used a multilayered onion analogy. The analogy describes four cultural layers:

1. The heart
2. The "street" environment
3. Solidarity
4. Supervisors

As we descend through the multiple levels of the cultural onion, we find the heart, protected and insulated by another stratum. The heart is protected and shielded from danger and all threats from the outside world by many layers.

The first layer of the heart represents the individual values that give meaning to police work. The heart is the place where ideas, values, and ethical and moral behavior intersect with situational and fair policing. The heart is where all of the world's problems become police problems.

The second layer, the protective shield around the heart, represents the uncertainty of the street environment. Police work in a fishbowl environment where their reputations and self-esteem rise and fall in tides of emotion: Fear, stress, and anxiety are linked to how well they protect their territories.

The third layer of the police cultural onion is solidarity. Solidarity is called the "**mask of a thousand faces**." The mask reference indicates the sheer numbers of police officers, bonded together, protecting each other, offering support and solace. Solidarity is a product of conflict. It finds its genesis in public perceptions of police work. If ordinary citizens back an officer, in a literal or philosophical sense, then conflict declines. An example would be the D.A.R.E. (Drug Abuse Resistance Education) officer. D.A.R.E. officers teach children how to resist unhealthy decisions and behavior. These officers also receive specialize training that is designed to help empower parents to recognize many of the prominent risk factors that develop throughout adolescence. In this context, the D.A.R.E. officer is welcomed as a role model, and his or her position is supported by the public. However, building proactive bridges with community groups creates feelings of mistrust from other members of the department, officers who do not trust the public view. For example, the proactive officers assigned to community policing activities are often accused of conniving with the enemy: the public.

The fourth cultural level, and one that patrol officers and rookies cannot escape, is the pressure exerted by those of higher rank: the supervisors. Reuss-Ianni (1983) expanded on this idea of tension between the ranks, stating that two cultures of policing exist: the troops or "boots on the ground" and management. He thought that this divide was between the outside and the inside—street cops and their supervisors. Officers must protect each other from supervisors, who are often viewed as being out to make officers' jobs difficult.

D. The Rookie Experience: Four Stages of Socialization

The journey of an ordinary citizen from recruit to rookie officer to peer acceptance is a rigid, relentless, four-stage socialization process. As argued by Westley, Van Maanen, and Crank, socialization is a fluid process, developing and maturing throughout an officer's career trajectory. Career trajectory is the very essence of a rookie's immersion into police acculturalization. Van Maanen's ideas of rookie development, juxtaposed with the preceding studies, will be viewed through the eyes of this writer, a 33-year police veteran. This four stage preoccupation is as follows:

1. Entry
2. Academy training and cultural exposure
3. Encounter: Field training, environmental criminology
4. Metamorphosis: Acceptance and the cultural shield

Phase One: Entry—Interviews and Tests

Entry into the police application and the employment process constitutes phase one. During this stage, a perspective recruit is tested on multiple levels. There are written IQ and problem-solving evaluations. Simple interest is furthered by taking a series of exams and sitting through interviews that address complex scenarios. These interviews explore a recruit's morality, integrity, and ability to follow orders. Equally important is the recruit's capacity to understand discipline and ability to take responsibility for his or her actions. Many of these tests or inquires represent a character inventory. In other words, does the recruit have what it takes to enter and successfully complete police academy training?

The entry stage is characterized primarily by bonding the recruit to the profession and to his or her peers. The entry phase defines the time spent enduring the written application process, interview upon interview, background checks, and medical and psychological testing. At this point, the recruit learns the attitudes and behaviors of the group while trying to avoid trouble through minimizing his or her activity. According to Van Maanen, veteran officers discourage overzealousness. Simply stated, veteran officers want rookies to be seen and not heard, to watch, listen, and learn. Commitment and establishing trust is highly encouraged.

Within the entry stage, applicants endure a lengthy screening process in anticipation of fulfilling a dream: becoming a police officer. Next, the recruit must enter, endure, and successfully complete the "dreaded" academy.

Phase Two: The Police Academy and the Beginning of Police Cultural Exposure

The idea of the police academy originated with August Vollmer in 1908 in Berkeley, California. Vollmer was a progressive criminologist. He was adamant in his belief that police departments must be "education centric," with academy training the first step in an officer's career-long educational journey. Vollmer also coined the term *college cops*, because during his tenure as police chief, he implemented off-duty and summer college-level courses for his officers, forwarding their journey toward excellence and professionalism. Academy training is also a means of passing along the traditional police culture. At this stage, recruits begin to identify with police and police culture, slowly acquiescing toward informal socialization into traditional ideas. Academies stress the importance of obedience to authority through a structure of shame and honor. Discipline teaches recruits merely to obey the authority of the police hierarchy while conforming to acceptable standards. As recruits begin to internalize the norms of the academy, they start to evaluate themselves and their peers based on the perspective of the senior staff. Most academy instructors are experienced officers, and this allows for traditional culture to be passed from one generation to the next. Further, the curriculum of the police academy indoctrinates recruits into police culture.

Haarr (2000) found that academy training reinforced the traditional model of policing. Conti and Nolan (2005) found ethics training that focused on stress and conformity helped recruits relate to their ethical ideas and, by extension, their ideas about their journey toward a policing career. For most recruits, their first sustained contact with the police subculture occurs at the academy. Absolute obedience to departmental rules and rigorous physical training is unavoidable. The training staff actively promotes solidarity through the use of group rewards and punishments. The staff encourages the use of identifying clothing, symbols, and flags for each recruiting class. At every conceivable opportunity, it is drilled into the mind of the recruit to show some unity; after all, as the saying goes, "United you stand, divided, you all fall." Ranking departmental personnel conduct the majority of instruction. Those of higher rank and authority give an air of superiority. The idea of superiority helps the recruit understand that a police department's authority is far reaching, a big brother sense of accountability and of "watching" the recruit. Critically, when "war stories" are conveyed with their graphic and heroic images, discipline within the recruiting class becomes relaxed, and a general atmosphere of camaraderie prevails.

E. The Female Recruit: Separating the Men from the Boys and Girls

According to Woolsey (2010), being a female in a predominantly male profession is a formidable challenge. The notion of the aggressive, macho crime fighter is synonymous with American policing. Women do not easily fit that mold or mind-set. Studies have shown that women in policing are less likely to use excessive and deadly force and are also less likely to be involved in fights or acts of aggression. Female officers rely more on interpersonal skills than physical force. Women are known to deescalate potentially violent situations more often than their male counterparts do. This emphasis on communication goes a long way in the modern approach to policing known as "community policing." Police departments are leaning more toward community partnerships and proactive problem solving versus the "tough guy" reactive approach popular in years past. Nonetheless, female police officers experience unique workplace stressors and issues, such as hearing sophomoric and sexually explicit language intended to shame and embarrass, being subjected to varying degrees of sexual discrimination, and often suffering a lack of mentors and role models. In a general sense, police work is a profession for men: the strong, rough-and-tumble, aggressive urban soldier. Women, who are considered by their male peers to be weak and too soft for dangerous and aggressive police encounters, are not welcome, are considered dangerous, and more importantly, are not seen as willing or able to back up their partner when "things hit the fan." Women face certain psychological pressures not encountered by men. Peer acceptance is one of the greatest constraints operating within police organizations. The desire to be known as a "good and competent officer" is a strong motivating factor, and failure to achieve that status can be very demoralizing and devastating. Unlike their male counterparts, women must overcome the societal prejudice of being the "weaker sex."

Phase Three: Encounter, Field Training, and Environmental Criminology

The encounter phase is the on-the-job training period, the "I'll learn something" from this real-world immersion phase. The encounter phase begins with the field training officer.

Field Training Officer

According to Warners (2000), field training is the most critical stage to becoming an independent police officer. During this period, FTOs present recruits with two challenges: to learn the practical aspects of law enforcement and community service and to assimilate into the professional culture of a particular agency. The second skill set learned makes the rookie an artisan; the idea is to turn the rookie into a jack-of-all-trades, comfortable in his or her skin and ready for just about anything.

After successful academy training, a recruit is introduced to the realities and complexities of policing through his or her FTO. It is through the eyes of the FTO that the newcomer begins to learn the subtle nuances of the police function. The FTO will tell tales and stories of all kinds: gruesome tales of death and violence, urban legends about old-school officers and their brand of street justice.

The encounter stage is often characteristic of field training or probationary periods for rookies. Field training is the first phase that offers a rookie a glimpse of the culture and climate of his or her department. During this period, rookies often experience a "reality shock" due to the demands and responsibilities of real-world police work. It is at this stage that rookies begin to become emotionally involved in their roles. Field training equates to the first practical exposure to more formal methods of socialization. These formal methods include officer safety, arrest procedures, and a wide variety of situation-based "street" scenarios. Interaction with veteran officers happens more regularly as the new officer begins to learn the ropes and to mimic those officers who exhibit behavior that coincides with the rookie's moral and ethical framework. It is during this phase of training that the rookie starts to observe and begins to understand the rules, policies, and regulations of his or her department.

On the Road: Reality Training

The first words out of an FTO's mouth might be that the academy was simply the test that got you to field training. It is here that real life and "the job" intersect with street life and human behavior. Field training officers are veteran patrol officers who will instruct you, chastise you, embarrass you, and teach you the right way of doing things. When discussing your process with other police officers, you might be called an "umbilical cord" or a useless "boot"; the list of degradations is too long to reckon. This type of jarring and insolence is part of the process; the FTO will make it very clear that to earn your badge, and the respect it symbolizes, is a journey. Nevertheless, over the next 6 to 12 months (training time is agency specific, depending on workforce and financial constraints), the rookie will be slowly indoctrinated into the community's street climate. Police culture has a mythical quality and is unique to each agency, although public opinion often paints police culture with a disparaging big brush. Call it conditioning, indoctrination, or acculturation, this tutelage happens slowly, but the progression is continuous. Subtly, over time, the FTO conveys certain information as cautionary tales of interactions to come. Rookies tend to assimilate into the philosophy of the training officer. Often, the FTO's point of view becomes the basis for the rookie's early perception of his or her peers and the beginning of his or her working personality. According to Bouza (1990), new officers soon discover that their role is to control fractious and rebellious souls who resent their very presence. Humbled by the discovery that their ministrations are not welcome and finding themselves challenged to maintain control, young officers make another disheartening discovery: Nobody understands them, not their friends and not their loved ones. Bouza continued by declaring that rookie cops are rarely told to be silent about departmental secrets. There are no written policies or standing orders upholding the code of silence. There is no need to be explicit. The reactions, body language, whispered suggestions, and other rites of initiation speak for themselves. Cops rarely seek counsel from anyone outside their ranks.

Inside the Mind of the Rookie Officer

Am I tough enough? Am I strong enough? Am I big enough? Am I smart enough? Am I as brave as I think I am? These subconscious questions represent a rookie's internal monolog, that little voice inside his or her head. This monolog is very personal, subjective, and often self-edifying. It is a powerful tool for new officers as they think about the causes and effects of their decisions. It is a place where they store and filter evil thoughts and secretly keep their fears and insecurities hidden from the world. Rookies, filled with hope, ambition and idealism, believe they will do great things for society. This Superman syndrome is more romantic than practical. Rookie officers usually begin their careers possessing one of the two psychological mind-sets. Idealism is the first; the idealistic idea that there is good in all people and criminal activity is a stress reaction that can be treated. This view may set the tone or be the basis for an on-the-job personality that attempts to solve every problem.

The second mind-set contains the power and authority inherent with the uniform and the badge. In this belief system, the police officer will make a quick and final determination for the solution to any situation, based on the police officer's initial understanding or impression of circumstances. As experience fine-tunes judgment calls, situational control becomes more rational as theory-to-practice decision making allows the rookie to view a bigger picture of society, not unlike a real-life chess game.

A Prelude to Danger, Anxiety, and Situational Focus

Before a rookie officer begins on-the-job, real-life training, there is a concept that contains both generational and historical roots. Some call it a hunch, a sixth sense, or a déjà vu warning from the collective experiences of officers about impending danger. It is a strong feeling that something bad is going to happen. Understanding and recognizing the varied aspects of patrol danger is considered a fundamental imperative for officer safety. Officers worldwide stress the significance of understanding the real and imagined danger as an important "perceptual" defense against those who threaten police and menace good people.

This perceptual phenomenon is what Skolnick and Fyfe (1994) called the "**symbolic assailant**." In an attempt to reduce or control the uncertainty associated with dangerous and unpredictable working environments, officers become suspicious actors. Skolnick and Fyfe noted, "It is the nature of the policeman's situation that his conception of order emphasizes regularity and predictability. It is, therefore, an understanding shaped by persistent suspicion" (p. 46). According to Brown (1988), police work can be tedious and monotonous, or it can explode with intense life-and-death situations. Brown added that "what must be recognized is that patrolmen lead something of a schizophrenic existence: they must cope not only with the terror of an often hostile and unpredictable citizenry, but also with a hostile—even tyrannical—unpredictable bureaucracy" (p. 9).

It is not easy for an FTO to impress upon the rookie particular psychosocial clues or hunches about a second sense. An FTO can give a rookie many truthful and tangible ideas and performance methods, but the FTO cannot teach a rookie to think. As rookie officers assimilate into the street culture of their communities, large and small, urban and suburban, their understanding of the danger, isolation, and solidarity affect their "cognitive lens." In the back of every police officer's mind, existing in the place inhabited by the very worst of worst-case scenarios, is fear. It is the fear of being a little too slow on the draw, that a situation might become too intense or frenzied, and that all the experience and training will not be enough. It is the fear of not seeing the cues that scream danger, and the fear that the power of the badge and the authority it represents will be rendered useless.

Shoot or Don't Shoot: The Most Frightening Dilemma

During basic academy, training recruits are exposed to the very worst of police work. Training films, lectures, and real images of a police officer being ambushed, beaten, tortured, and killed are shown and discussed for two reasons. One, they embed into the recruit that danger is everywhere, and cops die. Two, they are intended to impress upon the student that training is a career-long endeavor. The Space Shuttle *Challenger* exploded on day 2 of this writer's police academy experience. The lesson of the day was that no matter how much training and preparation is done, in an instant, a blink of an eye, life can take a lethal turn. A harsh reality is that practice and training cannot adequately prepare a police officer for the unpredictable, the unknown factors in life, and the impulse and volatile circumstances of the human condition. The rookie will learn that there is nothing more perplexing or dangerous to a police officer than when to shoot and when to hold fire. In a heartbeat, officers must sort through their emotions, fears, thoughts, and suspicions. They must lucidly recall their perception of the words immediately and imminently: Shoot or don't shoot. Life or death. In theory, an encounter that ends in deadly force happens quickly. Deadly force is met with deadly force, but police officers are trained to avoid lethal reactions.

F. The Use of Force

Skolnick and Fyfe (1994) outlined the ascending scale of force. There are the actions and reactions that police officers can utilize to quell a disturbance, affect an arrest, or react to a dangerous or violent situation or encounter. Deciding to use force is not only a matter of life and death for the officer and, by extension, the public, but also a feared ethical and moral dilemma. This dilemma is addressed in the police academy and remains ever present throughout an officer's career. The use of force continuum is a series of self-defense exercises that are designed to control a volatile situation. The continuum's goal is to deescalate a situation without causing harm to the police officer, the suspect, or the public. However, circumstances arise that become exponentially dangerous. Weapons add an air of immediacy and urgency to any situation, and a weapon in the possession of an unstable individual can have dire and lethal consequences. Use of force training is a constant throughout a police officer's career because there is always that unknown factor, that X-factor of human behavior that is not predictable. The old police adage—when the time to act arrives, the time to prepare is past—is considered sacrosanct in police work. According to Lentz and Chaires (2007), in 1829 Sir Robert Peel stated, "Police use physical force to the extent necessary to secure observance to the law or to restore order only when the exercise of persuasion, advice and warning is found to be insufficient." This statement was a corner stone of Peel's Principals of Policing (p.69)

Soft Hands, Strong Hands

The ascending scale of the use of force continuum contains seven stages:

1. Presence: the mere existence of an officer is not enough to handle the situation.
2. Persuasive verbalization: talking in firm tones but not yet commanding.
3. Command verbalization: sharp tones; the inflections of a "command." STOP now!
4. Firm grips: grabbing parts of a body with a warning to remain still and motionless.
5. Pain compliance: forcible contact, causing pain to control with lasting physical injury.
6. Impact techniques: clubs, batons, chemical spray, forcible but not life threatening.
7. Deadly force: a force capable of killing or likely to kill. Firearms. Any weapon that makes contact with a vital organ part.

An Example from this Writer's Experience

A suspect was holding a knife. He was standing against a wall screaming and threatening to kill anyone and everyone. He was pointing the weapon in my direction but remained stationary. His threats became loud and disconnected. In theory, someone standing alone, across the room, brandishing a dangerous weapon and threatening to kill is not, at that instant, an immediate threat. *Threat* is an ambiguous term. As the responding officer I was, of course, threatened, but in the context of this situation, threat would have a deeper meaning if civilians were present. However, my police training kicked in, and it focused my thoughts on the 21-foot rule (Tueller, 1983). Simply stated, it takes a police officer about 1.6 second to draw, point, and shoot a firearm. However, a suspect holding a knife and charging from a distance of 21 feet or less will reach the officer before his or her gun is drawn. The fatal flaw is an equation of distance and reaction time. Deciding and understanding the difference between making a threat and posing a threat gives the experienced officer options. That means that a police officer should react according to the use of force continuum. The continuum is an ascending scale of force, the force necessary to control an individual or situation. More often than not, the "continuum" can be monitored. The situation can deescalate before excessive or lethal force is warranted. However, time is crucial. In reality, the use of force continuum is nothing more than a rapid-fire mental checklist of immediate alternatives. Finding none, the officer can exercise the option of eliminating the threat; that is, stopping the target by shooting to kill if necessary.

The suspect standing against the wall began to move forward, across the room, not charging but advancing, the knife pointed in my direction. I steadied myself, believing that physical contact was imminent. Now, I was in immediate danger of bodily harm. The knife is a close-contact weapon, a deadly cutting instrument of death. Using my command voice and tone, I ordered the knife-wielding suspect to stop and drop the knife. I sidestepped backward and on an angle, putting a large piece of furniture between me and my assailant. I pulled and pointed my firearm at center mass—the closest and largest "point of bullet contact." If I shoot, the threat is eliminated. The suspect is dead. Is this justifiable?

The suspect became distracted by the sudden appearance of other police officers and retreated. He was cornered and disarmed. A later review found that I acted appropriately, according to the force continuum and immediacy of the situation. The investigation would have been more intense, and bureaucratic, had I shot the suspect. Use of force investigations are often complex and may be conducted by outside judiciary agencies. The court of public opinion and the general media are often quick to find fault with the police side of the use of force equation.

Wrongful death charges suggest that an officer's actions were inappropriate, unnecessary, extremely abusive, or complicit, as defined by criminal statutes. The media often uses the word *craven* to report police involvement in a lethal situations; the word is defined as contemptibly lacking in courage or being cowardly, as in an "officer's craven abdication of his moral duty." In this context, the police department as a whole suffers. The city where the incident occurred suffers. Families are shocked and unforgiving, demanding justice and transparent, full disclosure of the facts. Communities—and by extension, any racial, ethical, and philosophical subsets therein—as well as the entire country agonizes and writhes in confusion, finger pointing, and grief.

Society's Lens: Current Events, Old Wounds

The FTO will school the rookie on the many different and unique areas of public perception. The rookie will be told about enforcement ideas and strategies based on racial cues and bias; that is, how some officers form opinions about a person by skin color, speech, or dress. When police officers shoot unarmed civilians of color, they may be responding to racial cues that link Black people to criminality and violence. All of us are influenced by such racial cues, but police officers, more than private citizens, find themselves in situations in which they have to respond quickly without thinking. In the field, police officers may not have time to evaluate whether they are responding to actual danger or assumptions based on a person's race. Addressing the problem of racial stereotypes influencing a police officer's perception of criminality and risk is a difficult task for several reasons. First, all police work requires some amount of stereotyping or generalizing about people based on external characteristics. Police officers in the field must quickly size up a suspect and make decisions about how to handle a situation. In making split-second decisions, officers often must rely on external cues, such as dress, demeanor, location, and race. Because some stereotyping is necessary, it is easy to think that any and all stereotyping is permissible. The "color of suspicion" idea runs deep within police culture.

Minority Assailants, Deadly Consequences

Police officers are held to a higher standard than ordinary public citizens. But officers are human. They judge people according to their personal beliefs and familial attitudes about people, places, and things learned in childhood. Police academy training and police socialization add to an officers understanding of criminal behavior, racial bias, and patterns of deviant activity. In this writer's experience, no one ethnic group constitutes or contains an apex criminal. No one ethnic group automatically triggers danger or the psychological, symbolic assailant. However, the idea of the criminal Black man existed as the focus of much media attention in the 1980s. The idea lends itself to misunderstanding as thoughts about the possible risk and danger enter a police officer's mind. This idea is more symbolic than realistic, but the experienced officer is on guard for any dangerous or unpredictable encounter. Police responding to emergency and nonemergency calls for service are given the facts as interpreted by the dispatcher. Often police officers are dispatched using absolutes, meaning if a suspect is presumed to be armed, the officers must prepare for an armed confrontation. If a suspect is threatening violence or is acting "crazy," the officers must prepare for an encounter with an unbalanced, violent individual. This is how police officers develop a plan: a battle plan, a rescue plan, an escape plan, or an arrest. This mind-set translates to heightened awareness and caution, a response scenario, and the officer recalling the use of a force continuum: officer safety first, the threat eliminated, and the public safeguarded.

Minority Assailant, Lethal Fear

On February 25, 2012, Trayvon Martin, an unarmed, 17-year-old African American teenager wearing a hoodie, was shot and killed in Sanford, Florida. Martin was walking back to his father's home from a store. A neighborhood watch volunteer, George Zimmerman, shot him. Martin died at the scene. Zimmerman was a private citizen and a member of a neighborhood watch group. He was not a trained police officer and had no legal authority. The concept and design of any neighborhood watch, community policing program is for concerned citizens to observe and report suspicious behavior to the police. They are not trained to approach a suspect, detain, investigate, or confront a person they consider suspicious. Zimmerman called 911 and reported a suspicious person. He was told to stay away from the individual and to wait for police to respond. He likened Martin to a gang member due to his "arrogant" strut and emblematic clothing. Ostensibly, Zimmerman's suspicion and paranoia quickly identified the teenager as dangerous and aggressive, although at that moment in time, Zimmerman had only a visual impression of Martin. There had been a recent string of burglaries in the neighborhood, and Zimmerman claimed that his confrontation with Martin was in self-defense because he felt threatened and Martin appeared to be "up to no good." Zimmerman told police that as he confronted the teenager, push came to shove, and Martin, younger and apparently stronger, knocked him to the ground and repeatedly "bashed" his head against the pavement. In Zimmerman's mind, Martin was his fears personified, his symbolic assailant.

Zimmerman's fear ultimately caused Trayvon Martin's death. His behavior was accelerated to lethal force because of his attitudes and beliefs about Martin's ethnicity, personality, and intentions. That accentuated concern lies at the heart of **racial profiling** in law enforcement. There is no reason to think that profiling among citizen watches and patrols would be less prominent. The fact that the idea of a symbolic minority assailant was part of Zimmerman's thought process is disturbing; the transference of police legitimacy is not extended to private citizens. Zimmerman acted from a fear-based mind-set in which Martin was an instant enemy. It is disturbing that an untrained citizen would act with the authority inherent in police work. He had no legitimate authority to confront Martin in the first place.

G. Racial Profiling: A Presumption of Guilt

Rookies will be exposed to all the prejudices associated with the minority assailant. They will internalize the toxic ideas about race and danger from their FTO. Stories about the criminal Black man, as perpetuated by Goldberg (1999), fueled these bigoted beliefs. Goldberg's article appeared in the New York Times and centered on the attitudes of patrol officers and their use of racial profiling. He asked two city police officers the reasons why they were stopping and "overly investigating" a vehicle driven by a Black male. The passenger was also Black. Probable cause for the car stop was a broken taillight. The officers maintained that from the front seat of a police cruiser, racial profiling is not racism. It is an investigative tool—and cops have no intention of giving it up. Goldberg's interaction with multiple pairs of New York City patrol officers, those in-the-trenches of street life and crime, fortified his belief that Skolnick's (1994) symbolic assailant was alive and well in the minds of these street cops.

Keeping in line with Turk's (1969) predictions, we suspect that the combination of Black, young, and male enhances the likelihood of perceived threat—they are the perceptual shorthand of the symbolic assailant. The majority of the public does not understand the extent of profiling, racial or otherwise. Racial profiling—that is, making negative (police) assumptions about criminal behavior by race, color, or creed—is ideological, morally, and legally wrong. As we enter a new investigative technological age of information processing and reception, computers linked to a variety of criminal data sites are commonplace. Police routinely conduct criminal record checks and search for wanted or missing individuals with the tap of a keyboard. All of this information is processed, sorted, and received before an officer exits his or her vehicle to confront the operator.

H. The Relevance of Spatial Policing: Space Matters

Crawford (2010) talked about **spatial policing** as a neighborhood, community, or high-crime zone of a particular space. This is a place where police are very active and where there exists a continuous battle between the neighborhood and those who wish to control it by criminal means. These spaces may appear welcoming to some but may send waves of fear to others who have to enter. Good citizens avoid these spaces, especially at particular times of the day. However, although the areas are considered dangerous to law enforcement, those who live and survive in these spaces call them home. Police, on the other hand, actively patrol these areas. The FTO will help the rookie officer understand how conditions and interactions between citizens and police are at the heart of spatial policing. Ultimately, the rookie will learn that space matters. Moreover, the rookie will soon realize that police do not surrender their territorial space to anyone, least of all those who will destroy it, both figuratively and literally. These destroyers of space are the criminal element. As the rookies develop their "working personality" and learn about space and the potential criminal dangers within those, they will also become acquainted with typically less stressful patrol activities, such as the service call. Under this "situational umbrella," the rookie may experience low levels of perceived danger. This call is all about public service, accomplished with problem solving, attentive listening, negation techniques, and compromise.

Environmental Criminology

Environmental criminology focuses on criminal patterns within built environments and analyzes the impacts of these conditions on people's cognitive behavior. A veteran FTO may not be able to explain the many theories of crime. However, the FTO will be able to describe to a rookie how to gauge personal safety through a criminal landscape. These illegal spots will be the rookie's patrol sector, his or her defensible space, where he or she keeps the public safe from any criminal element. The FTO will attempt to transfer a theory-to-practice understanding of events and policing in relation to the things that make each patrol sector unique and ever changing. The FTO will talk about spatial policing, linking the presence of fear of crime to the amount of crime. Good people fear the loss of their territory, meaning their house, sidewalk, and those spaces that they call home; the areas where they feel protected. In addition, many people, ingrained in their space by culture or monetary restraints, often ignore the deviant behavior. The potential is real for a motivated individual to prey upon the weak in an attempt to control or secure space for continued criminal activity. If criminals covet what they know, then it is within this crime theory that the police and criminals interact. The rookie does not need to understand the theories or sub theories of crime, but he or she does need to understand the danger of the space and the territorial boundaries it contains. For the rookie on solo patrol, the identification and whereabouts of known criminals, the usual suspects, or in police vernacular, "frequent flyers," becomes common knowledge passed on from veteran officers. It is within these areas that a rookie's most frequent encounters will occur. It is not difficult for the patrol officer to understand the boundaries of neighborhood control. Gangs mark their territories, or turf, by graffiti and reinforced by the **aural graffiti** of the occupied zones. Aural graffiti was a term coined by Wooden (2001) to identify unique speech, symbols, and actions of particular groups in particular areas. Places like junkyards that convert stolen metal into cash are regularly patrolled. Easy targets are constantly on a patrol officer's radar, along with stores where shoplifting happens. These are the places where encounters take place.

I. Police Corruption: The Snake in the Grass

When FTOs release a recruit from their care and tutelage that is not the end of training. It is the beginning. Training, and by extension, learning, is a lifelong journey. Moreover, for the rookie officer each day is an exercise in endurance: emotional and visceral. However, for many vulnerable and naive rookies, the real dangers do not only exist on the street; the bad people and the deviant are not their most dangerous foe. That foe is often the veteran cop eager to share his or her corruptible perceptions of what is right and what is wrong. Just as it takes a village to raise a child, it takes other officers to introduce **corruption**. Modern thinking has nudged the idea of police corruption away from the traditional individually corrupt "bad apple." However, new ideas about organizational and occupational flaws are embodied within the traditional veil of silence and are reinforced by the fellowship of the thin blue line. A tolerance for the formation of corruption comes from inside a police organization. This suggests a corrupt culture. A corrupt officer and the rookie, like the hardened convict and his "fresh meat," have honed their crafts and possess the skills to teach or "turn out" a rookie or a new inmate.

Corrupt veteran police officers are shifty, scheming, and unscrupulous, and they are eager to pass on their knowledge to the new generation, the "new kids on the block."

As a veteran police officer, corrections official, and maturing academic, it would be easy to offer the reader, the student of everything "criminal justice," a vocabulary list of key words and theories, citing examples of police corruption. Corruption is often synonymous with greed and entitlement, spiced with a toxic mix of secrecy, retribution, and fear. Nevertheless, there are many faces behind a tarnished badge. The stress and anxiety for acceptance and trust are extraordinary for many rookies. This "another brick in the wall" syndrome represents a cultural foundation that is ripe for indoctrinating the corruptible; a foundation built upon, according to Newburn (1999), preference, power, payment, and privilege. Others call it perversion by favoritism, tribute, authority, and competence. Pick your poison. Nevertheless, corruption is deviance. The types and forms of police corruptions can be big or small, major crimes or misdemeanors, as the saying implies. However corruption is defined, it is an affront to the public trust and a slap in the face to good and honest police officers everywhere.

Deviance: The Thief of Souls

Pogregin and Atkins (1982) believed that (a) if a recruit of high ideals but little exposure to the realities that challenge naive expectations of police work (b) enters the world that exposes the worst in people and is (c) trained, influenced, and mentored by senior officers with tales of heroism, power, and greed, not understanding that these officers have lost all faith in police work and long for the days of sanctity and respect afforded to the old-time crime fighter; and (d) if the rookie or young officer must establish some mutual trust and reliance with fellow officers who use their employment to "line their own pockets" and to get their share of what others are "grabbing" as fast as they can; and (e) if their supervisors or those of higher rank and responsibility are unlikely to support efforts to behave honestly with some measurement of integrity; then (f) corruption is likely to happen without correction or oversight, the likelihood of sanctions negligible; then (g) the young "cop" experiencing cynicism or administrative indifference for the first time will probably test the waters and accept the status quo. This status quo may be accompanied initially by feelings of shame, but with the support of the greater brotherhood, corruption and bad acts grow without remorse.

Studies suggest that the remedy for attacking corruption at its source is not complex. The difficulty arises when cynical officers on both sides of the law profit from an alliance. And when the ability of supervisory staff to investigate the alleged corruption is obstructed or constrained, those officers under investigation will employ any means possible to preserve the status quo. In this context, attempts for reform or transformation are thwarted, and systemic change becomes an illusion.

Phase Four: Metamorphosis and Acceptance

During the final stage of socialization, metamorphosis, officers undergo a significant shift in attitudes and values. Rookies become integrated into the police culture and completely identify with the department; at this point, many ideals of the traditional model are expressed. New officers identify emotionally with veterans. It is this emotion that creates a bond and an important distinction. In the beginning the rookie simply had knowledge about the police. Now the rookie shares knowledge. The metamorphosis is almost complete. New officers first must evaluate all of their training, as well as the collective wisdom transferred from their FTO and other members of their department. New officers evaluate all the discussions, stories, and parables about staying safe; lessons learned about control and grace under pressure; and the motor vehicle stops, domestic disputes, and other potentially dangerous interactions. Rookies must also allow the evolution of their "working personality."

According to Wilson (1968), one of three general categories will dictate an officer's model of policing. In addition, individual police departments may create their mission statement to encompass one of the styles proposed by Wilson. In this context, three policing styles are identified to help balance the competing goals of protecting the community without disrupting or interfering with the lives of residents. These genres are:

1. The watchman style,
2. The legalistic style, and
3. The service style.

In simple terms, the watchman style, sometimes called the neighbor approach, emphasizes the maintenance of order. People and happenstance, those considered disorderly and disruptive, threaten order and peace. Keeping neighborhoods and high-crime areas safe, the residents feel protected. Police are viewed as neighbors who are helpful and resourceful in providing a visible deterrent to unwanted behavior. Within this style, community policing develops. The legalistic style, sometimes compared to a soldier on watch, focuses more on the enforcement of law than on maintaining order. This idea represents reactive policing; the police are responding to calls for service and act upon probable cause if any legal action is required, such as an arrest or an investigation. The service style, often referred to as the teaching style, approaches law enforcement from a problem-solving perspective. This teaching style strives to address and manage the variety of social problems through direct intervention or referral to an appropriate social agency. An officer's personality plays a significant role in the use of discretion, regardless of the style of policing characteristic of the department.

Flying Solo Metamorphosis Complete: Autonomy

After months of on-the-job street patrol, listening and learning, and playing a secondary role to the veteran training partner, the end of this training phase is near. After handling real-life benign and emergency situations without understanding the rules of the game or the rules of engagement; after countless conversations and parables about ethics and empathy and integrity; after dealing with citizens who became excited, agitated, rude and violent, the rookie has learned that police work is more about safety, compromise, and concession than it is about the romanticized man in blue. After all the simulations and situations in which an officer may be hurt or killed; after all the advice about interacting with citizens during routine service calls; after all the talk about suspects, victims, and bystanders in emergency or criminal encounters; after all the evaluations and homework and pass or fail examinations; after learning about the brotherhood, the thin blue line, and codes of silence; after getting in touch with personal bias regarding people, places, and things; after seeing the cause-and-effect results of addiction, violence, poverty and tragedy; and after laughing with citizens on good days and sharing their pain on bad days, the rookie is primed for solo patrol. These "hard and hazardous" calls elevate the rookie into his or her new status and role within the department and denotes to his or her immediate colleagues that the new officer is a member of the working police.

J. Conclusion

For the rookie, the allure of law enforcement and the power and prestige associated with the police and other enforcement agencies has been the aspiration of young and old alike. However, police work is anything but an adolescent's fantasy, and it takes a unique dedication to be successful. Law enforcement is a career that requires specialized training, a unique understanding of human behavior, and a resolve to maintain physical and mental fitness. Individuals also need a moral compass that points to all the intangible qualities—like integrity, character, and a caring outlook about the needs of people in a crisis—to be successful. Rookies must learn what veteran officers have already mastered. Veteran officers know how to balance their personal feelings of fear, anxiety, and retribution. They know how to temper their human frailties and frustrations with an understanding of their power and that of our Constitution. It is the understanding of social and restorative justice, interpreting the law without bias, and handling each unique situation with focused professionalism, with the paramount goal of helping the victims of society's worst. Moreover, police officers must keep themselves safe so that they can accomplish their prime directive: public safety. The person behind the uniform and badge inherits a great responsibly—not simply a sense of duty to help the injured, browbeaten, and disenfranchised, but to bring to justice those who break the law. That is a rookie's call to honor. It is a call that comes from the sacrifices of a police officer's past and the hope of new generations to carry the torch wherever it burns—to patrol, to serve, and to protect.

DISCUSSION QUESTIONS

1. Explain the ideas behind Skolnick and Fyfe's "symbolic assailant." What drives an officer's perception of people, places, and things?
2. For the rookie police officer on solo patrol, what is meant by defending territory within the concept of spatial policing?
3. Police culture is described as mysterious and secretive. Why is police culture so difficult to define?

REFERENCES

Bouza, A. (1990). *The police mystique: An insider's look at cops, crime, and the criminal justice system*. New York: Plenum Press.

Brown, M. (1988). *Working the street: Police discretion and the dilemmas of reform*. New York: Russell Sage Foundation.

Conti, N., & Nolan, J. (2005). Policing the platonic cave: Ethics and efficacy in police training. *Policing and Society, 15*(2), 166–186.

Crank, J., & Caldero, M. (2010). Police ethics: The Corruption of Noble Cause (3rd ed.). Burlington: Elsevier Science.

Crawford, C. (2010). *Spatial policing: The influence of time, space, and geography on law enforcement practices*. Durham, NC: Carolina Academic Press.

Haarr, R. (2000). *The impact of community policing training and program implementation on police personnel*. Washington, DC: US Department of Justice, National Institute of Justice.

Lentz, S. A., & Chaires, R. H. (2007). The invention of Peel's principles: A study of policing "textbook" history. *Journal of Criminal Justice, 35* (1), 69–79.

Newburn, T. (1999) Understanding and preventing police corruption: Lessons from literature. In Policing in Reducing Crime Unit: Police Research Series, European Journal on Criminal Policy, 2000.

Pogrebin, M., & Atkins, B. (1982) The Invisible Justice System: Discretion and the Law. Cincinnati: Anderson Publishing Company

Reuss-Ianni, E. (1983). *Two cultures of policing: Street cops and management cops*. New Brunswick, NJ: Transaction Books.

Skolnick, J., & Fyfe, J. (1994). *Above the law: Police and the excessive use of force*. New York: Free Press.

Sparrow, M., & Moore, M. (1990). *Beyond 911: A new era for policing*. New York: Basic Books.

Tueller, D. (1983). The 21-foot rule. How close is too close? *SWAT Magazine*, 03.

Turk, A. (1969). *Criminality and the legal order*. Chicago: McNally.

Van Maanen, J. (1975). Police socialization: A longitudinal examination of job attitudes in an urban police department. *Administrative Science Quarterly, 20*, 207–228.

Warners, R. (2010) "The Field Training Experience: Perspectives of Field Training Officers and Trainees," *The Police Chief,* vol. 77 (November 2010): 58–64,

Westley, W. (1970). *Violence and the police: A sociological study of law, custom, and morality.* Cambridge, MA: MIT Press.

Wilson, J. Q. (1968). *Varieties of police behavior.* Cambridge, MA: Harvard University Press.

Wooden, S & Blazak, R. (2001) Renegade Kids, Suburban Outlaws: From Youth Culture to Delinquency. Wadsworth Publishing-University of Michigan Press.

Woolsey, S. & Bertacchi, D. (2010) *Female Police and Sexual Harassment.* Town and Country Patch, Manchester, MO. Reprinted, March 27, 2012

05

The Courts

Mia R. Ortiz

KEY TERMS

- BAIL
- BEYOND A REASONABLE DOUBT
- EXCLUSIONARY RULE
- FELONY
- GRAND JURY
- MIRANDA WARNINGS
- MISDEMEANOR
- PLEA BARGAINING
- TRIAL
- VOIR DIRE

Equal justice under law is not merely a caption on the facade of the Supreme Court building; it is perhaps the most inspiring ideal of our society. It is one of the ends for which our entire legal system exists ... it is fundamental that justice should be the same, in substance and availability, without regard to economic status.

—Lewis Powell Jr., U.S. Supreme Court justice

A. Introduction

The judicial branch of American government is responsible for interpreting laws as they pertain to the Constitution, state, or local laws. The U.S. court system is a multilayered, multi-tiered institution governed and directed by the Constitution, rules of evidence, and the local jurisdiction. Its foundation is based on reviewing and evaluating evidence based on a mandate of justice and fairness. Thus, the decisions made by courts have a direct impact on the accused, the victims, and the community at large. This chapter provides an overview of the court system, which includes the development and organization of the federal and state court systems, a discussion on the constitutional rights of the accused, a description of the courtroom work group, as well as detail of the trajectory of how criminal cases are processed. Woven into these sections are historical and contemporary court cases as well as discussion on the impact that the U.S. court system has on matters of social justice and ethical concerns among disenfranchised communities.

B. Development and Evolution of the Courts

The initial development of the U.S. court system emerged from the Constitution, specifically through the first acts of Congress under the Judiciary Act of 1789 as part of maintaining checks and balances with the legislative and executive branches of government. Court system began on the principle of federalism, which is the idea of having a central or federal government. Over time, with the emergence of states (and state government), federalism evolved to include the recognition of autonomous state governments and therefore dual court systems: the federal courts and the state courts. Although these systems have for the most part distinct jurisdictions, the court of last resort for both is the Supreme Court of the United States. The description of

the federal court system is discussed in the next section.

Federal Court System

District Courts

The structure of the federal court system consists of district courts, appellate courts, and the Supreme Court. The federal district courts consist of 94 judicial districts and the U.S. bankruptcy courts. There is at least one district court in each state as well as in the U.S. territories of American Samoa, Guam, Northern Mariana Islands, Panama, U.S. Virgin Islands, and Puerto Rico. An important question to ask is what cases do the federal courts have jurisdiction over (what types of cases are heard)? The federal court system has jurisdiction over matters that include "the constitutionality of the law, cases involving U.S. laws and treaties, disputes between two or more states, maritime law, and bankruptcy cases" (United States Courts, 2015, nd).

One of the most recent high-profile cases in the federal court system was the matter of the *United States v. Dzhokhar Tsarnaev, 2013*. Tsarnaev was arrested, indicted, and convicted for manufacturing and detonating two pressure cooker bombs near the finish line of the Boston Marathon in 2013, which resulted in the deaths of four people (an act that he did with his deceased brother, Tamerlan Tsarnaev). Additionally, he was convicted of carjacking and killing a university police officer during a shootout. Among many charges, Tsarnaev was charged in the federal system because the bombs were considered a weapon of mass destruction (U.S.C. § 2332a) and the bombing occurred in a place of public use (U.S.C. § 2332), which resulted in malicious destruction of property (U.S.C. § 844).

An important question to raise is why was Tsarnaev charged in federal court instead of the Massachusetts state court? The prosecution can charge a defendant on the federal level if it can be determined that the crime committed impacted interstate commerce. In Tsarnaev's case, the charges of mass destruction and malicious destruction of property had a direct impact on the role of commerce on marathon Monday. Each year, the Boston Marathon attracts millions of runners, and spectators from around the world who rely on the hotels, restaurants, and other businesses that offer special services for marathon participants. The prosecution argued that the bombing significantly interrupted interstate commerce in Boston.

In addition to these offenses, Tsarnaev was also charged with conspiracy (the planning and commission of the bombings). On April 8, 2015, he was found guilty of 30 counts of federal crimes, and on May 15, 2015, the jury recommended death by lethal injection. Tsarnaev's conviction or death sentence will likely be sent to the U.S. Court of Appeals for the First Circuit—the same court where the trial took place—on grounds that he did not have a fair trial (the defendant's request to have the trial outside of Boston for purposes of having a fair jury and trial was denied during pretrial motions). The First Circuit includes the districts of Maine, Massachusetts, New Hampshire, Puerto Rico, and Rhode Island.

U.S. Courts of Appeals

When cases heard in district courts are appealed, they proceed through one of 12 appellate courts. In 2013 there were nearly 60,000 appeals filed on the appellate level (United States Court of Appeals, 2014). The majority of the cases involve petitions from prisoners to seek sentence reductions or appeals of trial convictions. In criminal cases, the losing party of the initial court matter, known on the appellate level as the appellant, will either present written legal grounds (known as a brief) or engage in oral argument against the appellee (the side arguing to uphold the initial court decision). The briefs or arguments are heard by a panel of appellate judges, and their ruling is final. At the appellate level, it is usually the defendant who challenges the conviction (the prosecution may never appeal an acquittal but may contest the sentence) (Administrative Office of the U.S. Courts, 2015). If one of the litigants is unsatisfied with the judgement of the appellate court or the highest state court, he or she may file a petition to the U.S. Supreme Court for review (known as a writ of certiorari).

One federal court case that proceeded to the appellate court involved Boston attorney Simon Glik, who was arrested in 2007 for videotaping an arrest by police officers in Boston Commons. The police charged Glik with illegal wiretapping, aiding the escape of the prisoner, and disturbing the peace.

Although all criminal charges were eventually dropped, Glik sued the city of Boston and the police officers in district court for violating his civil rights. Glik was awarded $170,000 for damages and legal fees. The appellants (the city and the police officers) contested the settlement because the police officers argued that they had *qualified immunity*, in that by their public office status, they could not be held responsible. However, the decision by appellate court judge Kermit Lipez upheld Glik's civil rights; here is an excerpt of his opinion:

> *The filming of government officials engaged in their duties in a public place, including police officers performing their responsibilities, fits comfortably within these principles. Gathering information about government officials in a form that can readily be disseminated to others serves a cardinal First Amendment interest in protecting and promoting "the free discussion of governmental affairs" (655 F.3d 78).*

The Supreme Court

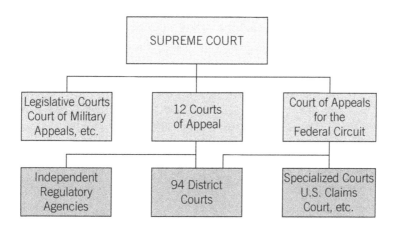

The Supreme Court was created through a provision under Article III of the Constitution. In addition to executing its responsibility of maintaining checks and balances as the head the judiciary branch of government of the United States, the role of the Supreme Court is to operate as the final court for both state and federal jurisdictions and to review cases over concerns of constitutionality. The decisions of all of these matters not only provide a sense of justice in the immediate case, but also provide a precedent (a rule) for decisions in future court cases.

Currently there are nine Supreme Court justices. Justices are nominated by the president, and then vetted through extensive congressional hearings. Once confirmed by Congress, justices are appointed for life. Although the Supreme Court operates as an independent branch like the executive and legislative branches, presidents typically nominate potential justices with political ideologies that are similar to their own, which may affect court decisions on criminal or civil proceedings in the future. Over the years, the composition of the Supreme Court has changed from solely White men to the inclusion of female and minority justices. In 1967 Thurgood Marshall, an accomplished lawyer who successfully challenged racial segregation in public schools in *Brown v. Board of Education of Topeka* (1954), was appointed as the first African American justice of the Supreme Court. Fourteen years later, Sandra Day O'Connor was the first female justice appointed to the high court. Currently on the bench are three female and one African American justice. With the exception of Justice Ruth Bader Ginsburg (who attended Columbia University's Law School), current justices have graduated from either Harvard or Yale Law Schools.

The State Court System

In most states, the state court system is typically divided into three levels: trial courts, appellate courts, and the court of last resort (typically called supreme courts). It is within the state court system that most of the criminal and civil court cases are processed.

Trial Courts

Trial courts are typically the court where most criminal and civil matters enter after arrest. Depending on the state, trial courts may be further divided into courts of limited or special jurisdiction, where the court only hears certain cases (such as **misdemeanor**, family court, community courts, or other specialized court). Courts of general jurisdiction oversee a variety of criminal and civil matters.

The organization of state court structure varies from state to state. In New York State, the highest court in the state is the Court of Appeals, followed by the Appellate Terms of the Supreme Court, which is followed by Supreme Courts, District Courts, and then City Courts. In the state of North Dakota, the Supreme Court is the highest court, followed by the Temporary Court of Appeals, the District Court, and Municipal Courts. Every state court system is designed to fit the needs of its state jurisdiction.

Court of Appeals

The purpose of the court of appeals is to challenge the ruling of the lower trial court. The court of appeals does not hear new cases, but rather makes rulings as to whether to affirm the lower court's rulings (that is, agree), remand (return to the lower court for retrial), or overturn (reverse the court's decision). Some of the reasons that cases are brought to the state appellate court include the inclusion of inadmissible evidence or testimony (which should have been excluded) or incorrect jury instructions by the judge. The majority of appeals brought by the defendant are rarely successful. In California, only 6 percent of criminal appeals are considered for further appellate action (Judicial Council of California, 2013).

Wrongful Convictions

The greatest miscarriage of justice occurs when a defendant has been wrongfully incarcerated or worse, put to death. In the United States, there have been a number of defendants who have been wrongfully convicted based on misidentification, unreliable testimony, or racial bias. The Innocence Project, an organization that has used DNA evidence to challenge wrongful convictions since the early 1990s, has been pivotal in addressing these injustices. To date, the organization has been successful in exonerating more than 300 wrongfully convicted persons.

State Supreme Court

In the majority of state case matters, the state Supreme Court is the court of last resort. The Supreme Court on the state level, as on the federal level, is composed of the justices who decide the merits of the decisions from the lower and appellate court. Unlike the U.S, Supreme Court, which does hear new cases, the state Supreme Court does not oversee trials. The state Supreme Court will consider cases that were not settled on the appellate level to determine if judicial or other court error in the original court of jurisdiction occurred. There are many notable cases that have been settled on the state Supreme Court level. In California, under *Jones v. Chappell*, the state justices found that chemical elements used in lethal injections were found to be cruel and unusual; this was the impetus toward establishing a moratorium on capital punishment in the state in 2014. In 1783 in the *Commonwealth of Massachusetts v. Nathaniel Jennison*, the court found that slave masters could be held criminally responsible for assaulting runaway slaves in free states.

C. Due Process Rights of the Accused

In the United States defendants are afforded certain rights outlined by the Constitution to ensure that they are treated fairly during the judicial process. Specifically, certain rights (known as due process rights) are outlined within the 4th, 5th, 6th, and 14th Amendments of the Bill of Rights in the

Constitution. Due process is the foundation for justice and fairness and is afforded to every defendant who comes before the courts (even for the most egregious of alleged acts or the most notorious of offenders). Moreover, there have been a series of landmark Supreme Court cases that have reaffirmed the significance of these amendments.

Fourth Amendment

Under the Constitution, the Fourth Amendment states the following:

> *The right of the people to be secure in their persons, houses, papers, and effects, against unreasonable searches and seizures, shall not be violated, and no warrants shall issue, but upon probable cause, supported by oath or affirmation, and particularly describing the place to be searched, and the persons or things to be seized.*

Mapp v. Ohio

The right against unlawful search and seizure is invoked prior to arrest and subsequent court involvement and requires law enforcement (in most cases, footnote exceptions) to obtain warrants prior to searching or seizing a defendant's property. However, since such obtained evidence entered into court can affect the liberty of the defendant, it is essential that the evidence be obtained justly as required by the law. One landmark case that tested the constitutionality of search and seizure was *Mapp v. Ohio* (367 U.S. 643). In this case, Cleveland police entered the home of Dollree Mapp without a warrant on a tip that a bomb suspect was in her home. After handcuffing Mapp, the police obtained a gun, communist propaganda, and obscene material in her basement. Mapp was subsequently charged with possession of obscene material. In 1961, in a 6–3 ruling in the Supreme Court, despite the illegal contents that were in the home, the court decided that Mapp's arrest was unlawful because the police failed to enter her home on a valid warrant. This is defined as the *exclusionary rule*, in which evidence that was unlawfully obtained by the police cannot be admitted into evidence against the defendant.

Fifth Amendment

Several important components of the Fifth Amendment are relevant to the criminal justice system. These include the right against self-incrimination and double jeopardy, as well as protection against disclosing privileged communication. In many respects, the Fifth Amendment protections serve as a safeguard against coercive practices that have occurred during police interrogations in which confessions were obtained.

The Right Against Self-Incrimination

The most well-known constitutional right involves what the police are required to say to suspects and detainees at the time of arrest and questioning. These statements, called the **Miranda warnings**, generally consist of the following:

> *You have the right to remain silent. Anything you say can and will be used against you in a court of law. You have the right to speak to an attorney, and to have an attorney present during any questioning. If you cannot afford a lawyer, one will be provided for you at no cost to you.*

The Miranda warnings stem from the landmark Supreme Court case *Miranda v. Arizona* (384 U.S. 436, 1966). In this case, Ernesto Miranda was charged, convicted, and sentenced for rape and kidnapping after confessing to the crime during interrogation, in which he had no attorney, nor was he advised that he could remain silent during questioning. In 1966 the Warren court ruled that the police had violated Fifth Amendment rights due to their neglect of Miranda's rights, and accordingly the conviction was reversed. Additionally, illegally obtained confessions or evidence that has been entered into court can be stricken from consideration in future court actions. The right against self-incrimination extends from any onset of any police involvement. Additionally, Fifth Amendment protects the accused from being required to testify against themselves in court. Should a defendant voluntarily testify, the defendant may invoke his or her Fifth Amendment rights at any time to avoid self-incrimination (that is, "I plead the fifth").

In addition to the Fifth Amendment's protections against self-incrimination, there are also other persons with a direct relationship to the accused who may not be compelled to testify in the effort to incriminate the accused. These persons include spouses, doctors, psychiatrists, the accused's attorney, and clergy.

While *Miranda* has far-reaching implications in the criminal justice system, there are many examples that reflect illegal police practices imposed on suspects. In *Brown v. Mississippi*, police officers whipped and hung defendants in order to obtain a confession to murder. In the case of the Scottsboro Boys, eight young Black men who were accused of raping two White girls were not allowed to consult with an attorney (despite being charged with a capital crime that would lead to a death sentence) and were denied the ability to waive their right to a speedy trial. In fact, the court wanted to try the entire case in and one and a half days. The trial (and subsequent trials) were heard by all-White juries since

Alabama had highly discriminatory practices, which prevented African Americans from serving. (For more information on this compelling case, see Carter, 1979.)

The Right Against Double Jeopardy

Another component of the Fifth Amendment is the right against being tried for the same crime twice (also known as double jeopardy). Essentially, a defendant may not be punished for the same conviction twice and may not be retried after an acquittal. Double jeopardy violations do not include grand jury deliberations or mistrial. Additionally, double jeopardy violations do not include criminal cases that are tried at the state and federal level. Because the state and federal courts, in many respects, are separate entities, a defendant may be tried in both courts for the same offense. For example, a person could send child pornography through the mail and be charged with a state offense of possession of child pornography and a federal offense of sending child pornography through the U.S. mail. In addition, double jeopardy has not been violated if the defendant is held to answer in criminal court and is sued in civil court for the same offense. For instance, former football star O. J. Simpson was acquitted of the murder of his ex-wife, Nicole Brown Simpson, and her friend Ronald Goldman but was sued (and was held responsible) in civil court for wrongful death.

Sixth Amendment

Rights of the accused under the Sixth Amendment involve several important matters within court proceedings specifically as it relates to trial. Within the Constitution, the Sixth Amendment states the following:

> In all criminal prosecutions, the accused shall enjoy the right to a speedy and public trial, by an impartial jury of the State and district wherein the crime shall have been committed, which district shall have been previously ascertained by law, and to be informed of the nature and cause of the accusation; to be confronted with the witnesses against him; to have compulsory process for obtaining witnesses in his favor, and to have the Assistance of Counsel for his defence.

There are several fundamental rights that defendants have. First, the defendant has a right to be informed of the criminal charges placed on him or her. This must occur upon arrest and at arraignment when formal charges are filed by the prosecution. Additionally, defendants have the right to view and/or challenge any evidence or testimony against them in court.

Right to an Attorney

The Sixth Amendment affirms that defendants have the right to have an attorney represent them in criminal proceedings regardless of their ability to pay. In *Gideon v. Wainright* (1963), the Supreme Court held that the state of Florida had violated Clarence Gideon's constitutional rights because it had denied Gideon's request to have an attorney represent him in court. As such, the high court overturned Gideon's state conviction (since he was forced to represent himself).

In today's courts the public defender is responsible for providing representation for defendants who are unable to secure their own defense due to their inability to pay. Indigent defense is the most commonly used defense for defendants. According to the Bureau of Justice Statistics, nearly $3 billion were spent for indigent defense in 2012 (Herberman & Kyckelhahn, 2014). Moreover, only 1 in 4 county public defender offices have enough lawyers to properly manage the caseload as set by the National Advisory Commission on Criminal Justice System Standards and Goals (Farole, 2010). In other words, the majority of the country's indigent defense systems are tremendously overwhelmed by growing caseloads

Right to a Jury Trial

Another constitutional right afforded through the Sixth Amendment is the right to a jury trial. Although this is a constitutional right, it is rarely used (only 10 percent of criminal cases go to trial). The majority of defendants will have their matters resolved during a stage within the criminal court process, typically through a practice called **plea bargaining**. Plea bargaining occurs when the prosecution and the defense come to an agreement on the case that will result in the defendant pleading guilty to the agreed upon charges. For attorneys and the courts, there are benefits to this practice: It reduces the volume of cases that go to trial (which can be extremely costly and time consuming); it can also guarantee conviction rates (for district attorneys) and can be a benefit to defense attorneys (particularly indigent defense attorneys with large caseloads). Although there are direct benefits for the court work group, it has been criticized over several concerns. One concern is that defendants may be under pressure to plea bargain, especially if they are currently in custody, with the agreement that they will be able to be released immediately. In some cases, the pains of pretrial detention may be significant enough that defendants may plead guilty to crimes they may not have committed, thus leading to legal, social, and financial consequences that may affect them for the rest of their lives.

Another criticism of plea bargaining relates to the issue of whether the practice circumvents the intentions of the due process rights of the defendants—specifically their right to a jury trial. Though defendants are informed prior to pleading guilty that they are waiving their constitutional rights to a trial and to the right to appeal, the reality is that plea bargaining was never the intention of (nor explicitly stated by) the framers of the Constitution. Due process rights as stated in the Constitution affirm that defendants who are accused of a crime have the right to trial, the right to testify (if they so choose), as well as the right to challenge the evidence and the witnesses against them. Many critics suggest that plea bargaining bypasses this very important legal process (Lynch, 2003, p. 27).

Eighth Amendment

The Eighth Amendment relates to the rights against cruel and unusual punishment and the rights against excessive bail. The Constitution requires that punishment be proportional to the crime for which the defendant was convicted. For example, an individual convicted for a petty, low-level crime should not have the same punishment as someone convicted of murder. A landmark Supreme Court case that tested the cruel and unusual punishment provision included *Furman v. Georgia* (408 U.S. 238), in which a man was sentenced to death for attempted burglary. The Supreme Court struck down this sentence because of the violation to the defendant's constitutional rights.

A Discussion on Bail

While there is no constitutional right to bail, clauses within the Eighth Amendment of the Constitution affirm that when bail is assigned, it must not be excessive. In determining bail, the judge takes the following into consideration as stated in the Eighth Amendment:

> *The court takes into consideration several factors: (1) the seriousness of the offense; (2) the Weight of Evidence against the accused; (3) the nature and extent of any ties, such as family or employment, that the accused has to the community where he or she will be prosecuted; (4) the accused's ability to pay a given amount; and (5) the likelihood that the accused will flee the jurisdiction if released.*

Absent of capital offenses (such as capital murder) and certain criminal violations (for example, violation of parole, probation, or bench and arrest warrants for failing to appear in court), most defendants will be assigned bail, and in fact, two thirds of defendants will be released on bail prior to trial. Bail refers to the financial or nonfinancial condition of being released from custody. Most courts yield to a bail schedule that has a bail amount assigned for each charge for which the defendant is arrested or arraigned. Bail is divided into two categories: those with financial conditions and those with nonfinancial conditions. Financial conditions include surety bail (defendants pay 10% of the total bail plus secure their release with property collateral); deposit bail (defendants pay 10% of the total bail with the amount refunded at the conclusion of the case); full cash bond (defendants pay the full amount of the bail to the court with the total amount refunded at the conclusion of the case); and property bond (property, usually a home or business, is put up as collateral).

In the 1960s critics argued that financial conditions of bail created significant disparities between affluent and disadvantaged defendants in that those who could not afford bail had to remain detained at pretrial. Further, it was argued that bail bond agents (a for-profit entity) were largely becoming the decision makers in determining release conditions—solely on the basis that the defendant could pay for the bond and thus circumvent the justice system. In 1961 Vera Institute of Justice conducted the Manhattan Bail Project, a research project designed to test whether defendants who were released without paying a financial bail are likely to skip their court appearances (Kohler, 1962). The results showed that fewer than 2% of defendants released without paying a financial condition of bail failed to appear to future court dates. The results of this research proved to be a watershed moment for the bail reform movement and helped inform courts across the country on ways to implement nonfinancial conditions to bail.

In addition to the noted social class disparities that are present in pretrial release decisions, research has also studied the impact that the race of the defendant has on the conditions of bail. Findings show that Black defendants were least likely to be released from the least restrictive pretrial conditions as compared to White defendants (Demuth, 2003; Schlesinger, 2007).

Fourteenth Amendment

The 14th Amendment affords each defendant equal protection the law. This is of particular importance, since there has been an extensive history of the denial of equal justice among defendants from underrepresented communities within the court of law. Specifically, 14th Amendment to the Constitution affirms the following:

> *All persons born or naturalized in the United States and subject to the jurisdiction thereof are citizens of the United States and of the State wherein they reside. No State shall make or enforce any law which shall abridge the privileges or immunities of citizens of the United States; nor shall any State deprive any person of life, liberty, or property, without due process of law; nor deny to any person within its jurisdiction the equal protection of the laws.*

Loving v. Virginia

In *Loving v. Virginia* (1967), the Supreme Court ruled that laws which banned interracial marriage violated the equal protection clause of the Constitution. The case was brought forward by Richard and

Mildred Loving (a White man and a Black woman), who were sentenced to jail for getting married; under Virginia's Racial Integrity Act of 1924, such marriages were deemed illegal. Similarly, in B*rown v. Board of Education* (1954), the Supreme Court determined that school segregation was in fact unequal and therefore violated the equal protection under the law clause of the 14th Amendment.

Consequences of Convictions

Recently, there has been greater discussion about the impact that misdemeanor and violations have on the defendant, the courts, and the community. These convictions bring many consequences for those convicted of lower level crimes. Certain misdemeanor convictions can lead to deportation, denial to hold certain professional licenses, loss of employment, eviction, and required registry into state sex registries. Moreover, police practices such as "broken windows" (where police are required to arrest or issue summons for minor infractions) increase the volume of misdemeanor cases in the court system as well as the cost to prosecute and defend each of these cases.

D. A Profile of Criminal Defendants

Although there is a high volume of cases that are going through the nation's courts, the reality is that the majority of the defendants come from disenfranchised communities. More than a third of the cases that enter the courts are drug related (that is, possession or intent to sell/trafficking). Violent crimes (murder, robbery, and sexual assaults) make up approximately one quarter of the cases, and the remaining cases involve property offenses (that is, burglary, larceny, and auto theft) (Reaves, 2013). Over the course of 2 decades, Black males represent the bulk (45%) of defendants entering the **felony** criminal courts. White defendants reflect a third of the population, and Hispanic defendants represent a fourth. Black males under age 18 represent more than half (55%) of the juvenile population (Reaves, 2013).

Female defendants are less than a quarter of those who enter the court system; this has remained consistent over the past 20 years. Most crimes that female offenders are charged with tend to be lower level offenses or incidents in which they are accessories to violent crimes (such as robbery) (the Cohen & Reaves, 2007). The average age at arrest is currently 32, as compared to 20 years ago, when it was 28. In fact, 1 in 4 defendants are 40 years old or older. This may reflect the revolving door of the criminal justice system in that once a person has been identified through conviction and incarceration, it may be difficult to earn legitimate employment, access to quality housing, and relocating to productive and safer communities; thus, many will return to criminal involvement. Because of the limitations that criminal convictions can have on opportunities for desisting from future criminal behavior, policy stakeholders in the court system have begun to rethink the role of courts and to consider innovative ways in which to address social ills that lead to crime through the use of problem-solving courts.

E. Problem-Solving Courts

Specialized courts are designed to address the defendant's specific criminal, social, or mental health needs more effectively than the traditional criminal court, with the goal of reducing future criminal involvement. Toward the end of the 20th century, there was an emergence of several specialized courts across the country to address specific criminal behaviors and quality of life matters that affect many defendants who come before the court.

Drug Courts

In the past 30 years, the increase in the volume of court cases has largely been attributed to drug-related offenses (for example, possession and distribution). In 1989 the first drug court was enacted in Miami–Dade County, Florida, as a response to the number of drug-related cases that were clogging the criminal courts (National Association of Drug Court Professionals, 2014). Nearly 30 years later, there are close to 3,000 drug courts across the country, with at least one court situated in each state. The purpose of the drug court is to divert defendants away from the traditional criminal court processing so that they may participate in rehabilitation related to their substance abuse. The commitment to the drug court is typically 18 months and requires defendants to attend regularly scheduled meetings where they submit to regular drug testing. Defendants who continually test positive for illicit substances or are charged with new crimes during their drug court involvement may be returned to the regular criminal court processing, where they could be subject to harsher penalties. Participants who successfully complete drug court will have their conviction sealed or the charges dropped entirely. Results from several major studies have concluded that not only are defendants who participate in the drug courts (compared to defendants charged with similar drug charges) more likely to desist from future drug use, they are also less likely to engage in future criminal behavior (Rempel, Green & Kraelstein, 2012).

Domestic Violence Courts

For nearly a decade, domestic violence has accounted for nearly a fifth of all violent crime in the United States (Truman & Morgan, 2014). Domestic violence cases make up a significant portion of criminal court processing. Domestic violence courts have emerged as another problem-solving court to address this issue. In 2009 there were more than 200 domestic violence courts implemented within the United

States and 150 that had been developed internationally (Labriola, Bradley, O'Sullivan, Rempel, & Moore, 2009). Although there is variation, domestic violence court revolve around two goals: (a) to provide greater safeguards in securing the victims' safety, which can include access to victims advocate programs internal and external to the courts; and (b) to ensure offenders' accountability in the alleged crime (Labriola et al., 2009). Additionally, there are integrated domestic violence courts that also incorporate family court matters, which include child custody and child protective service matters (Labriola et al., 2009). Leading experts of domestic violence courts are quick to admit that the success of these courts is not tethered to the rates of recidivism, since there have been no results that show that this particular problem-solving court reduces this crime as compared to domestic violence defendants in traditional court setting (Mazur & Aldrich, 2003). However, the major distinction between the two courts is that there are greater supports for victims in the domestic violence court.

Mental Health Courts

According to the National Alliance on Mental Illness, there are 2 million people arrested every year with a serious mental illness with an additional half a million are being treated while incarcerated. The purpose of mental health courts is to engage defendants in participating in treatment. Similar to drug courts, defendants are assigned a case manager, who conducts a psychosocial assessment, and must participate in periodic case meetings in court during their treatment.

Assessment of Problem-Solving Courts

These specialized courts provide many benefits not only to the defendant, but also to the community at large. Such courts provide a new view on the purpose of justice—that is, identifying the quality of life and low-level crimes that can plague a community and a society. In many respects, these courts offer individualized treatment that is distinct from the typical criminal court experience. Moreover, for many the participation in these specialized courts is the first time that defendants have had access to treatment or social services. Although these benefits are significant, critics have argued that there are concerns related to this approach. One concern relates to the fact that in order to receive services (like counseling, rehabilitation, and other social services), a person must be identified in the criminal justice system (arrested, charged, or incarcerated). A second concern is that most defendants have to plead guilty to the offense charged (often through a plea bargaining agreement) in order to be diverted to the specialized court. In addition, such problem-solving courts also call into question the historical purpose of the court system, since judges in these particular courts have dual roles as social worker and dispenser of justice (Neyfakh, 2014).

F. Courtroom Professionals

Though the professionals in the courtroom have very distinct roles, they operate as a well-functioning work group with the ultimate goal of carrying out justice to defendants, victims, and society at large. Each of these professionals must deal with the tension between administering justice and the ethical concerns they are confronted with on a daily basis. The following section discusses each professional's responsibility.

Judge

The judge is the sole authority of the courtroom and is responsible for overseeing cases, informing defendants of charges, and determining what evidence or testimony is allowed to be considered during trial. Specifically, as a neutral party, the judge is ultimately an essential arbiter in the administration of justice. Judges are also responsible for overseeing the jury selection process and instructing juries on the law prior to deliberating. Finally, they are also responsible for sentencing convicted defendants. There is a variety of ways in which judges are selected to the bench. On the state level, judges are generally appointed by the governor; however, in subsequent elections, appointed judges will have to be reelected to remain on the bench. Their terms of service can vary depending on the state. For instance, in California the term for judges to serve on the superior court level is 6 years; in Massachusetts judges—regardless of the level at which they serve—are appointed by the governor for life (National Center for State Courts, 2014).

Although judges lead the court's processes, they are not without ethical dilemmas. One ethical issue is in the selection of judges. Judges are generally appointed by governors (or presidents, at the federal level) or are elected by the local constituency. Although judges are charged with neutrality, they are typically elected or appointed by those who assume similar political leanings, which may impact the manner in which justice is administered.

District Attorney

The district attorney (DA) is the chief criminal prosecutor of the jurisdiction (generally situated on a county or city level). The DA is generally an elected official and is typically responsible for personally trying the jurisdiction's most high-profile criminal cases and providing consultation to local mayors and police departments. In their day-to-day responsibilities, DAs are charged with managing the deputy and assistant districts attorneys who are responsible for prosecuting defendants in courts. Cities such as Los Angeles and New York employ thousands of assistant district attorneys.

There are key ethical considerations that DAs face. In many jurisdictions, promotions in the DA's office are based on the conviction rate (the rate of convictions that each DA has prosecuted). Accordingly, plea bargaining becomes a convenient way to ensure conviction; however, DAs are required to uphold ethical standards (in the interest of justice) to ensure that there is sufficient evidence to charge a defendant with a crime before the defendant pleads guilty, because the consequences of conviction can be extreme.

Another ethical dilemma involves the DA's relationship with the police. Similar to what you have seen on television shows, the police are responsible for investigating crimes, and the district attorney is responsible for prosecuting the defendants in court. An important question to consider is what happens when it is the police who are being charged with criminal offenses? Recently six Baltimore police officers were indicted on second-degree murder charges of Freddie Gray for failing to secure him in a lockup van after arrest and then driving recklessly to cause his death. As with any other defendant, it is the responsibility (as well as ethical obligation) of the DA's office to prosecute any defendant (regardless of relationship with the office) to the full extent of the law if there is evidence to support it.

Defense Attorneys

The defense attorney is responsible for representing the defendant and ensuring that his or her due process rights are being upheld from arrest to sentencing. The Sixth Amendment guarantees the right of the defendant to be represented by counsel. There are several types of defense attorneys.

Private Defense Attorneys

Private attorneys generally have smaller caseloads, which provide the opportunity for greater attention to the client. However, they are significantly more expensive. Since such attorneys are at a premium, this prevents many indigent defendants access to this resource; such people are likely to be represented by public defenders, who may not provide the same amount of attention for each client.

Court Appointed Attorneys

In certain situations where the defendant is ineligible to receive the services of the public defender's office or where there may be a conflict of interest (where there are codefendants in the case that are being represented by the public defender's office), a private attorney is appointed by the court as defense attorney.

One of the most discussed ethical issues pertains to criminal defense attorneys representing defendants where it was clear that the defendants are guilty of the crime charged. Recall from the discussion of due process rights that every defendant is entitled to representation under the Fifth and Sixth

Amendments, regardless of guilt or innocence. It is also important to remember that the burden is on the prosecution to prove that the defendant is guilty of the crime charged. Finally, it is the responsibility of the defense attorney to show that the prosecution failed to prove its case, regardless of whether the defendant actually committed the crime.

G. The Trajectory of the Accused into the Criminal Justice System

Immediately upon arrest, the accused begins the path into the court system. The American court system is a series of many routes that lead to several final outcomes, including acquittal, dismissal, diversion, conviction, and sentencing.

   After arrest, the police will send the arrest report to the county district attorney's office for consideration of filing formal charges. The district attorney will dismiss either some or all of the charges. Those charges that will be filed require the defendant to proceed through the next court phase. In some states defendants who have been arrested on felony charges or are involved in high-profile cases will be subject to a **grand jury**. A grand jury is responsible for considering the evidence and/or witnesses to determine if there is sufficient evidence to formally charge (or indict) the defendant.

Arraignment

The next step in the court process after charges have been filed is **arraignment**. Arraignment is the court hearing where the judge informs defendant of the charges as well as his or her constitutional rights to due process. This is also the stage of the process where the defendant enters a plea (guilty or not guilty) to the charges. The court will set the **bail** (either a monetary or nonmonetary guarantee to return for future court dates) and impose protective orders (those that require the defendant to stay away from the victim or location) or other conditions (for example, a curfew or being required to stay away from codefendants who are also charged in this case) on the defendant while the case is being considered in court.

Preliminary Hearings

At the preliminary hearing the district attorney, the defense attorney, and the judge have the opportunity to assess the status of the case to determine if there is a sufficient basis to proceed with a trial. There is no set number of hearings. In the criminal courts, the burden is on the prosecution to bring forth evidence and witnesses against the defendant to establish that there is probable cause (which is a lower standard than beyond a reasonable doubt at trial) that the defendant committed the crimes alleged. In these hearings, the defense attorney is responsible for ensuring that the defendant's' rights

What is the sequence of events in the criminal justice system?

Bureau of Justice Statistics / Copyright in the Public Domain.

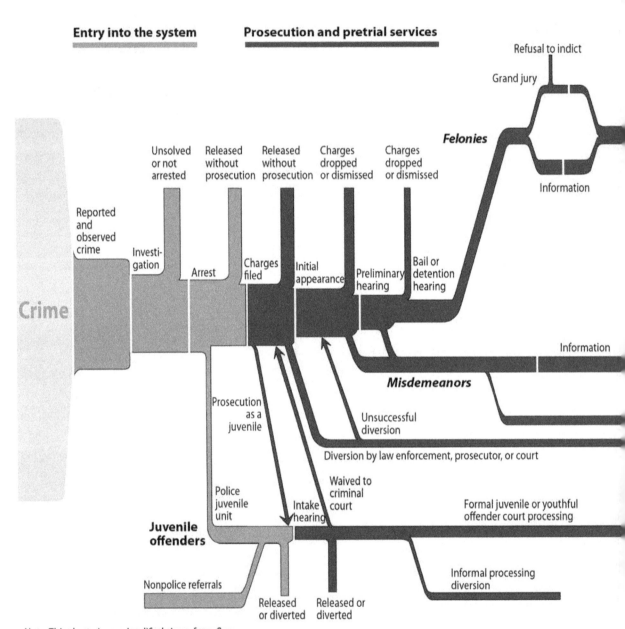

Entry into the system

Prosecution and pretrial services

Note: This chart gives a simplified view of caseflow through the criminal justice system. Procedures vary among jurisdictions. The weights of the lines are not intended to show actual size of caseloads.

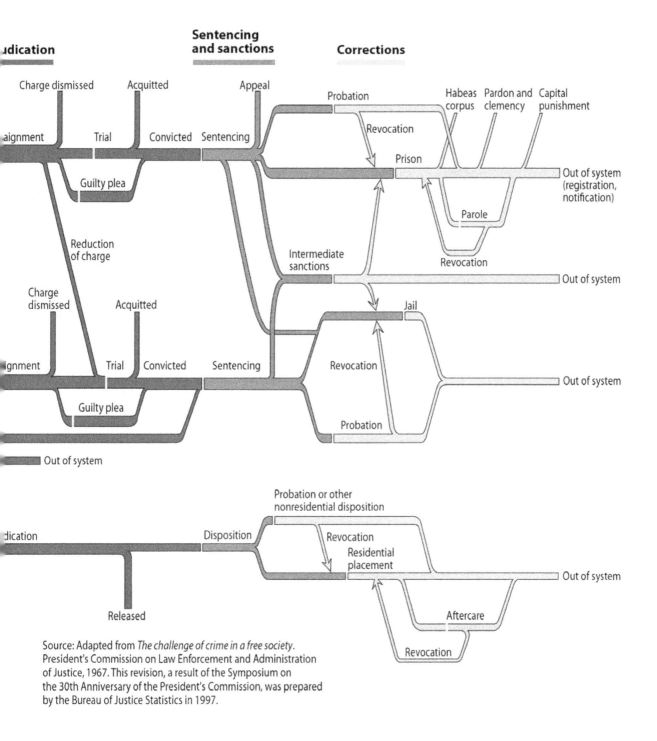

Adjudication

Sentencing and sanctions

Corrections

Charge dismissed   Acquitted   Appeal   Probation   Habeas corpus   Pardon and clemency   Capital punishment

Arraignment   Trial   Convicted   Sentencing   Revocation   Prison

Guilty plea

Reduction of charge   Out of system (registration, notification)

Charge dismissed   Acquitted   Parole

Arraignment   Trial   Convicted   Sentencing   Intermediate sanctions   Revocation

Guilty plea   Out of system

Jail

Revocation

Out of system

Probation

Out of system

Adjudication   Disposition   Probation or other nonresidential disposition

Revocation

Residential placement

Out of system

Released   Aftercare

Revocation

Source: Adapted from *The challenge of crime in a free society*.
President's Commission on Law Enforcement and Administration
of Justice, 1967. This revision, a result of the Symposium on
the 30th Anniversary of the President's Commission, was prepared
by the Bureau of Justice Statistics in 1997.

are being upheld, specifically in relation to concerns of violations of the Fourth Amendment (unlawfully obtained evidence by the police) and/or Fifth Amendment rights (failure to read rights or unlawful confessions). Reliant on the rules of evidence, the judge's responsibility is to determine what evidence is sufficient to proceed with trial.

Trial

In the instances where the prosecution and the defense cannot agree to resolve the case, the matter will be held for trial. A **trial** is a legal event in which the prosecution is responsible for proving that the defendant was responsible for committing the crime charged. In criminal proceedings, the burden is on the prosecution to prove the case **beyond a reasonable doubt** (a level of certainty that the defendant did in fact commit the crime). In a civil trial, when the case that is tried is about legal responsibility, the legal standard for responsibility is based on the **preponderance of the evidence** (which assumes that more likely than not, the defendant was legally responsible). Trials can consist of two approaches: jury trials (a group of citizens who will determine guilt or innocence) or trial by judge (in which the judge is solely responsible for determining the outcome).

Jury Selection

Although jury service is typically viewed as an inconvenient obligation, it is a civic responsibility (absconders can face fines and possible jail time) and a critical component to the trial stage as well as a constitutional right for the accused. Selecting the jury has tremendous ramifications for both the prosecution and the defense. During jury selection, large pools of potential jurors are vetted based on their background (by completed juror questionnaires as well as attorney oral questions at the time of selection), attitudes on the criminal justice system, and possible allegiances to either the prosecution or the defense. This process (called **voir dire**) allows for judges and attorneys to challenge potential jurors in the effort of having a fair and impartial jury.

Stages Within the Trial

In most trials a typical format is followed. In the criminal court setting, since the burden is on the prosecution, it is always first to present in each stage. In **opening remarks**, the prosecution provides an introduction to the case, an overview of the evidence in the case, and an explanation of why the defendant should be found guilty. This is followed by remarks from the defense, whose role is to cast doubt on the defendant's culpability to commit the alleged offense. During **direct examination**, each side will ask its own witnesses questions related to the case. Additionally, the prosecution and the defense will have the opportunity to challenge the testimony of the witnesses from the opposite side through **cross-examination**, as well as opportunities to recall past witnesses through **redirect examination**. At the conclusion of the trial, each side will surmise its position to the juror pool through **closing remarks**.

In today's courts the use of technology (namely the use of DNA, fingerprinting, ballistics, and other forms of physical, scientific evidence) has become a significant part of trials and has been further bolstered by popular culture television shows such as *CSI*. However, the inclusion of such physical evidence in terms of determining guilt or innocence serves as a mixed blessing. In one sense, physical evidence can either place the accused at the scene of the crime or eliminate the accused as the suspct (organizations such as the Innocence Project have used DNA evidence as a justification to release the wrongfully convicted from incarceration). However, there is an argument that jurors are becoming too dependent on such evidence to convict. In other words, there is a growing interest among jurors to have scientific certainty rather relying on beyond a reasonable doubt. Such a dependency on certainty may result in acquittals and arguably an injustice.

At each stage of the proceedings, the judge is charged with ruling over objections from the attorneys. During these objections, the judge may either **sustain** the objection (that is, there was an error committed either in the phrasing of a question or in the answer of a witness) or **overrule** the objection (that is, no error has been made and the trial may continue). The judge is also responsible for instructing the jury on the law as well as giving deliberating instructions prior to deliberation.

Verdict

After the jury deliberates, the jury foreperson will deliver the verdict form to the court clerk, who will then read the verdict aloud in court. If the defendant is found not guilty, the defendant's involvement in the criminal portion of the case is over. If the defendant is found guilty, in most cases he or she will be immediately **remanded** (detained) to county jail until sentencing.

H. Summary and Analysis of the American Court System

The American judicial system is, without question, one of the best court systems in the world. Its system and processes have withstood the shifting political identities of presidencies and members of Congress for more than 2 centuries. The institution has been the executor of social change and equality. Beyond that, it subscribes to an essential mandate in which all accused persons who enter the legal process are entitled to due process and equal treatment under the law. Although this institution serves as a model to other countries around the world, it is certainly not without criticism or limitations.

A criticism to consider is the role of the victim in criminal court proceedings. Typically, the main parties in a criminal case involve the jurisdiction (represented by the prosecution) and the defendant (represented by a defense attorney). Until the past 20 years, victims (with exception to eyewitnesses or subpoenaed testimony) were rarely integral to this process. Victims' rights movements and funds for victims' assistance from the federal government have provided financial assistance for victims. Restorative justice (a system of criminal justice that focuses on the rehabilitation of offenders through reconciliation with victims and the community at large) has been implemented in many courts, but many crime victims still remain disconnected from the court process and feel a sense that their victimization is not taken into account during sentencing. This is a particular concern for survivors of violent crime and survivors of murder victims.

It is also important to recognize that the American judicial system has largely contributed to the largest prison population in the world as a result of draconian and publicly charged sentencing policies such as mandatory minimums, truth in sentencing, three-strikes laws, and harsh sentencing policies for those convicted of drug possession. Not only do these policies increase the state and federal prison rate, they remove the right of the sentencing judge to use discretion in determining a custom punishment.

Connected to the rate of high incarceration is the overrepresentation of minority and economically disenfranchised offenders who proceed through the nation's court system. Although such involvement begins prior to the court process (that is, at arrest), the reality is that poor defendants and defendants of color are more likely to suffer stricter pretrial and bail conditions, remain incarcerated while their case is being processed, and suffer the "pains of incarceration" (that is, employment and family interruption) than their White and/or affluent counterparts. As mentioned earlier in this chapter, the pressure to plea bargain their case remains very high for such defendants, who desire to end the court process quickly regardless of their guilt or innocence. Finally, it is important to consider that the American court system (as with other institutions within the criminal justice system) continues to magnify the growing root problems that exist within our society today, particularly in relation to the lack of access to educational and employment opportunities (especially to those with criminal records), family involvement and reunification, and financial investment in struggling communities. As mentioned in an earlier section, problem-solving courts focus on addressing these root cause issues; however, services are provided to those who are identified in the criminal justice system.

DISCUSSION QUESTIONS

1. In your opinion, what group of defendants is most impacted in the criminal justice system—African Americans, women, or economically disenfranchised people?
2. How can victims be better served throughout the court process?
3. What consequences may be associated with the popular culture portrayal of courtroom proceedings?

REFERENCES

655 F.3d 78

(2014). U.S. Courts of Appeals-Judicial Business 2014. United States Courts. Accessed at: http://www.uscourts.gov/statistics-reports/us-courts-appeals-judicial-business-201

(2015). Administrative Office of the Court of Appeals. United States Courts. Accessed at: http://www.uscourts.gov/about-federal-courts/types-cases/appeals

(2015). United States Courts. *Court Role and Structure. Accessed at: http://www.uscourts.gov/about-federal-courts/court-role-and-structure*

(2014). History, Justice Professionals pursue a vision. National Association of Drug Court Professionals. Accessed at: http://www.nadcp.org/learn/what-are-drug-courts/drug-court-history

(2014). National Center for State Courts. Judicial Selection in the States. Accessed at:

Carter, D. T. (1979). *Scottsboro: A tragedy of the American South* (rev. ed.). Baton Rouge: Louisiana State University Press.

Cohen, T. D. & Reaves, B. A. (2007). Pretrial release of felony defendants in state courts (NCJ 214994). Bureau of Justice Statistics. U.S. Department of Justice. Retrieved from: http://www.bjs.gov/content/pub/pdf/prfdsc.pdf

Demuth, S. (2003) Racial and ethnic differences in pretrial release decision and outcomes: a comparison of Latino, Black, and White felony arrestees. Criminology, 41:873-907.

Farole, D. (2010). A national assessment of public defender office caseloads. Bureau of Justice Statistics. Presented at Justice Research and Statistics Association Annual Meeting. Retrieved from http://www.jrsa.org/events/conference/presentations-10/Donald_Farole.pdf

Herberman, E., & Kyckelhahn, T. (2014). State government indigent defense expenditures, FY 2008–2012. Bureau of Justice Statistics. Retrieved from http://www.bjs.gov/content/pub/pdf/sgide0812.pdf

Judicial Council of California. (2013). Court statistics report: Statewide trends 2002–2003 through 2011–2012. Retrieved from http://www.courts.ca.gov/documents/2013-Court-Statistics-Report.pdf

Kohler, S. (1962). Case 29: Vera Institute of Justice: Manhattan Bail Project. Ford Foundation. Retrieved from https://cspcs.sanford.duke.edu/sites/default/files/descriptive/manhattan_bail_project.pdf

Labriola, M., Bradley, S., O'Sullivan, C. S., Rempel, M., & Moore, S. (2009). *A national portrait of domestic violence courts*. New York: Center for Court Innovation.

Lynch, T. (2003). The case against plea bargaining. Regulation. Cato Institute. Retrieved from http://www.cato.org/sites/cato.org/files/serials/files/regulation/2003/10/v26n3-7.pdf

Mazur, R., & Aldrich, L. (2003). What makes a domestic violence court work? Lessons from New York. *Judges' Journal*, American Bar Association. Retrieved from http://www.courtinnovation.org/pdf/what_makes_dvcourt_work.pdf

Neyfakh, L. (2014, March 23). The custom justice of 'problem-solving courts': A new kind of court is reshaping the American legal system—with little oversight. *Boston Globe*. Retrieved from https://www.bostonglobe.com/ideas/2014/03/22/the-custom-justice-problem-solving-courts/PQJLC758Sgw7qQhiefT6MM/story.html

Reaves, B. (2013). Felony defendants in large urban counties, 2009–Statistical Tables. State Court Processing Statistics, Bureau of Justice Statistics. Retrieved from http://www.bjs.gov/index.cfm?ty=pbdetail&iid=4845

Rempel, M., Green, M., & Kralstein, D. (2012). The impact of adult drug courts on crime and incarceration: Findings from a multi-site quasi-experimental design. *Journal of Experimental Criminology, 8*(2), 165–192.

Schlesinger, T. (2005). Racial and ethnic disparity in pretrial criminal processing. *JQ: Justice Quarterly, 22*(2), 170-192.

Truman, J. L., & Morgan, R. E. (2014). Nonfatal domestic violence, 2003–2012 (NCJ 244697). Bureau of Justice Statistics. Retrieved from http://www.bjs.gov/content/pub/pdf/ndv0312.pdf

United States v. Dzhokhar Tsarnaev, 2013 (13-cr-10200)

US Const. amend. IV

US Const. amend. VI

US Const. amend. VIII

US Const. amend. XIV

U.S.C. § 844

U.S.C. § 2332

U.S.C. § 2332a

06

Community Corrections

Francis Williams

KEY TERMS

- COMMUNITY CORRECTIONS
- COMMUNITY SERVICE
- ELECTRONIC MONITORING
- FORFEITURE
- HOME CONFINEMENT
- HOUSE ARREST
- INTENSIVE PROBATION SUPERVISION
- INTERMEDIATE SANCTIONS
- RESIDENTIAL COMMUNITY CORRECTIONS
- RESTITUTION
- SHOCK PROBATION
- SPLIT SENTENCES

A. Introduction

Corrections is a significant segment of the criminal justice system. At any given time there are approximately 2.2 million inmates housed in U.S. jails and prisons. The American corrections system is a $74 billion annual drain on state and federal government budgets. According to the Vera Institute of Justice (2012), the cost of the American corrections system has increased 700% over the past 4 decades at a cost of $39 billion annually to the taxpayers. A cost savings alternative to incarceration is **community corrections**.

This chapter discusses community corrections as part of a group of intermediate sanctions that are handed down by the court in order to punish primarily those convicted of nonviolent offenses. There is a brief section on the history of community corrections before the chapter describes the types and goals of the various community sanctions, from fines through probation and parole. The chapter reports on information about whether intermediate sanctions actually work or whether they are effective as measured by rates of rearrests. In addition, and most importantly for this text, the chapter delves into some of the more important moral implications associated with the use of community sanctions. It's important to remember that morals and ethics both represent right and wrong and are sometimes used interchangeably. However, ethics typically come from an external source, whereas morals are more internally individual. It is not unusual then for those working in corrections and the criminal justice system as a whole to sometimes experience clashes between personal morals and professional ethics in the performance of their daily duties.

B. What Is Community Corrections?

Community corrections is the most common form of punishment in the U.S. criminal justice system today. Community corrections, also referred to as **intermediate sanctions,** includes *sentences* that consists of a diverse array of *alternatives* to incarceration that includes programs, specialty treatments, and sanctions. Each provides convicted offenders opportunities to remain within the community while completing court-ordered conditions in lieu of jail or prison. Although probation remains the number one community sentence given convicted offenders, additional probation requirements such as restitution, fines,

forfeiture, home confinement, and/or electric monitoring give the court more opportunities to monitor and control these individuals.

Typically, intermediate sanctions range between probation and prison across a spectrum of punishment alternatives. In addition, the designation of a number of other intermediate sanctions has become part of the landscape of community corrections. These sanctions, which include other versions of probation such as shock probation and **intensive probation supervision** (IPS), are split sentences, house arrest, and residential community programs that can provide the court more cost-effective alternatives that help reduce the number of offenders serving time in overcrowded jails and prison. *Restorative justice* programs are another form of intermediate sanctions that stress restoration of the victim and the community while seeking to reintegrate the offender back into the community without the emphasis on punishment and ostracism. Traditionally, these alternative community sentences are primarily for nonviolent, first-time, or low-risk offenders who are under some variation of structured supervision and would be considered a minimal risk or threat to public safety

Conceptually, the use of community sentencing provides a number of benefits, both economic and social, that correctional administrators favor. These benefits include but are not limited to:

- lowering costs of jail or prison sentences by helping reduce the number of inmates serving time in a correctional institution,
- providing opportunities for the offenders to maintain important family and community ties,
- giving offenders a second chance while providing opportunities to be productive citizens,
- promoting maximization of public safety,
- allowing for flexibility in sentencing based on severity of crime and individual circumstances, and
- ensuring that many current programs are about restoration and reintegration.[1]

Not surprisingly, these sanctions work more seamlessly with youth offenders, rendering the practice of community sentencing fairly standard with juvenile cases.

Although judges are much more willing to use these alternatives, research shows that "the public's desire for safety, as opposed to punishment, is swinging corrections back toward the goal of providing meaningful interventions that change offenders' behaviors. Strong public support exists for programs that return offenders to society as law-abiding citizens" (Dillingham, 1994, p. 84). Some people consider most forms of community sentencing today to be nonpunitive in nature, in that it is not so much about punishing the offender as it is about assisting the victim. The use of additional requirements of probation and other intermediate sanctions help leverage the idea that convicted criminals are not being punished harshly enough. What the public doesn't recognize is that the majority of convicted offenders are nonviolent, and punitive correctional policies are not beneficial but rather are costly additions to state and federal budgets (Meyer & Baker, 2004). Nevertheless, DeMichele and Paparozzi (2008) point out that community corrections agencies should be mindful that punitive correctional practices alone do not reduce recidivism; programs that focus on education, vocation, and employment training have been proved to reduce recidivism. In fact, a meta-analysis conducted by Wilson, Gallagher, and McKenzie (2000) of corrections-based education and vocation and work programs for adult offenders found that participants of the programs recidivate at a lower rate than do nonparticipants. However, the researchers did point out that because of weak methodological characteristics of the 33 studies they examined, they were prevented from attributing the rates specifically to the programs. Also, programs designed to alter criminogenic thinking patterns (that is, cognitive–behavioral treatment, or CBT) improve community supervision.[2] For example, one program,

> Project STOP, provides assessment and treatment for adults with intellectual disabilities (ID) who have been convicted or identified as being at risk for sex offending behavior. Treatment is based on a multi-component CBT model,

---

1   For more on the reasons why community corrections matter, see Evans, 2004.
2   This document can also be viewed at https://www.ncjrs.gov/App/Publications/abstract.aspx?ID=248295.

and employs an individualized case formation approach. (as cited in Nezu,
Greenberg, & Nezu, 2006, p. 97)

The authors found that over the 3-year evaluation period of this program, recidivism rates were as low as 4%. However, over the course of the past 2 decades or so, many fear that community corrections has become a dumping ground for drug abusers, the mentally ill, and even violent felons; ultimately pushing the very fabric of ethical and moral decision making by the criminal justice system.

Morality within the context of criminal justice is complex. The issue of morality presents itself within all components of the criminal justice system, whether the milieu is law enforcement, courts, corrections, or victimology. Public views of how the criminal justice system should function are based primarily on individual ideals and principles or morals. Morals play a significant role in how one feels the police should enforce the law, how the courts should dispense the law and provide for justice, how those who are convicted should be punished, and how correctional facilities should administer punishment. Yet it is an axiom that much of the public view on the criminal justice system is shaped by individual personal experiences both directly and indirectly with the system; invariably it is just as highly influenced by the media (see Robinson, 2014). This suggests that the vast majority of the public has both a narrow and skewed perception of the criminal justice system as a whole that is based on limited personal interactions and misperceptions perpetuated by the media (Robinson, 2014).

C. History of Community Corrections

Community corrections has its roots in English common law dating back to the Middle Ages (500–1500), when judges began assigning convicted offenders to other forms of punishment separate and distinct from many of the harsh and crueler penalties that then existed. During the Middle Ages, European *secular law*, organized according to the feudal system, subjected lawbreakers to all variants of torture, corporal punishment, and death. The church as the dominant social institution during this time maintained its rights to provide for ecclesiastical punishments for those who violated the laws of the church and in many cases protected those who claimed *benefit of clergy* from secular punishments. *Judicial reprieve* was a common law practice that allowed judges to suspend punishments. Offenders could seek pardons or provide the court time to gather further evidence because they deserved an opportunity to reform their behaviors. Typically, these particular individuals were released on personal recognizance, and various methods were created in order for these offenders to pay back the debts owed to the state or to the victims. In some cases certain citizens acted as sureties, enabling them to take responsibility for the offenders' behavior.

In 1841 a Boston shoemaker, John Augustus, convinced a Boston judge to release a convicted offender, a drunkard, into his custody; 3 weeks later Augustus returned with his charge now clean and sober and seemingly reformed. Thus began an 18-year career for Augustus that resulted in his supervision of more than 2,000 probationers, helping them locate jobs and reestablish themselves as contributing citizens in their communities. The term *probation* comes from the Latin word *probare*, meaning "to prove, to test" (Sieh, 1993). Thus began what was to become the chief form of community corrections: probation overseen by probation officers. Today probation is the primary form of community corrections and is the most widely used alternative to incarceration in the U.S. correctional system.

It wasn't until 1878 that the Massachusetts legislature passed a law authorizing the appointment of the first paid "probation officer" for the city of Boston. The birth of community corrections spread to superior courts in Massachusetts (1878) for those who were convicted of more serious crimes (felonies) and eventually to other states (Missouri, 1887; Vermont, 1898), which copied the Massachusetts model. Probation as a system found its way into the federal court system in 1925, when the U.S. district courts adopted it (Sieh, 1993).

Parole found its way to the United States by a different route, though the English roots are consistent. As explained by Wodahl and Garland (2009):

> *Parole originated in Europe in the 1840s (Cromwell, Killinger, & Kerper, 1974; Dressler, 1969). Cromwell et al. (1974) noted that "parole, as a practice, originated almost simultaneously with three European prison administrators: a Spaniard, Montesinos, a German, Obermaier, and an Englishman, Maconochie" (p. 235). It is Maconochie, however, with his ticket-of-leave system, who is generally recognized as the father of parole (Cromwell et al., 1974). Maconochie was named the superintendent of the British penal colony of Norfolk Island. In addition, he established a "mark system" that allowed inmates to progress through graduated levels of confinement as well as earn time off their sentences through good behavior and steady employment (Morris, 2002Harrus). Once enough marks were earned, inmates became eligible for a ticket of leave (Dressler, 1969). A ticket of leave was an order signed by the "colonial governor" excusing the inmate from further service. Once released, the inmate was required to remain in the jurisdiction; however, there was no formal supervision or further conditions of release (Dressler, 1969). (as cited in Wodahl & Garland, 2009, p. 85S).*

In the early 1970s community corrections acts were developed and passed by many local communities. These acts were seen as part of a larger commitment to involve local communities in handling offenders. The acts came at a time when both conservatives and liberals lost trust and faith in state governments to uphold rehabilitative efforts. These acts specifically attempt to address the needs of local communities and the value of partnerships between state and local governments (Cromwell et al., 1974; Harris, 1996).

Community corrections as an alternative to incarceration became more of an option in the United States in the latter part of the 1970s. It was primarily used for released offenders who were moved to residential services and halfway houses. Oregon, Colorado, and Minnesota were the first states to establish pilot projects sans government funding support. These "front-end" sentencing programs provided judges with community-based options and were used primarily for rehabilitation purposes. Subsequently, as correctional facilities began experiencing even more overcrowded conditions in the 1980s, legislation was increasingly introduced to make community corrections acceptable as punishment for even more convicted offenders (Nieto, 1996).

D. Types and Goals of Community Sentences

Probation

Probation is a criminal sentence given to certain individuals who have been convicted of a crime. Probation seeks to rehabilitate without the need to incarcerate. The goal of probation is basically to rehabilitate the offender while protecting the safety of the general public. Probation demonstrates several philosophies of the criminal justice system; rehabilitation, incapacitation, punishment, deterrence, reintegration, and crime control (Wilson & Petersilia, 2002). A probation sentence requires court-ordered supervision of an offender by an assigned probation officer in lieu of jail or prison time. It is designed to punish convicted offenders and ensure they receive enough monitoring to successfully complete conditions of probation. Probation is a contract between the state or federal court and the probationer. As required by law, the court must apply explicit conditions of probation, or contractual requirements with an option to provide discretionary conditions (U.S. Code § 3563-Conditions of Probation).

Probation contracts usually consist of both mandatory and discretionary conditions. Mandated conditions include things such as the payment of fines, fees, and/or restitution, including not leaving the jurisdiction without prior approval by the court, making regular reports to probation officers, and staying out of further legal trouble. Examples of more discretionary or special conditions of probation will vary and are based on the individual offenders' circumstances and the type of crime committed. These may include job or school participation, drug or alcohol abuse treatment (sex offenders receive more specific treatment conditions such as mandated sexual offender registration), counseling, anger management, stay away orders from victims and/or places, and so on. Violations of any of these conditions are serious matters and may subject the probationer to a revocation of the probation contract, which is outlined in the Federal Rules of Criminal Procedure by Rule 32.,1 whereas the revocation is governed by 18 U.S. Code § 3563-Conditions of Probation.

A violation of probation or violation of the conditions of probation results in a revocation hearing where if the probationer is found in violation, his or her probation is revoked; depending on the nature of the violation, he or she may be incarcerated or additional sanctions may be imposed. Probationers do have procedural safeguards in place that guarantee them certain due process rights if there is a move to revoke their probation. For example, the Supreme Court has ruled that probationers are constitutionally entitled to counsel (*Mempa v. Rhay*, 1967); the requirement of an informal inquiry to determine whether there is probable cause to believe the defendant violated parole or probation, and that they are entitled to a hearing (*Morrissey v. Brewer*, 1972); and the clarification of what is considered a fair sentence when the revocation of a community sentence occurs (*United States v. Granderson*, 1994).

Types of Probation

There are several variations in which probation can be administered. *Straight probation* is when the sentence imposed by the judge does not carry a specific prison sentence. With a straight probation sentence, a violation of the conditions of probation or another arrest gives the court the option to impose a sentence that is more commensurate with the type of violation. Alternatively, a judge may order a specific sentence that is consistent with the law and suspend this sentence for the duration of the probationary period. For example, the judge may impose a 1-year sentence and suspend it for a 2-year probationary period. This means that a violation of the conditions of probation within that 2-year period could result in a revocation of that probationer's contract and result in his or her serving the 1-year sentence.

IPS is a variation on traditional probation programs that targets higher risk offenders and provides closer supervision, smaller caseloads, and more effective monitoring of activities. There are several strategies involved with IPS, which typically begins with electronic monitoring and/or house arrest and includes restrictions on where the probationer can live, curfews, restitution, mandatory drug and alcohol testing, and treatment if necessary (Morris & Tonry, 1990). Typically, liberals see IPS as a way to divert offenders from jails and prisons without being soft on crime; whereas conservatives view it as being tough on crime without increasing correctional costs (Byrne, 1990).

These programs came into existence in the early 1980s after Georgia's IPS program claimed to reduce recidivism rates and costs. By 1989 all 50 states had adopted IPS programs, and in 1991 the U.S. Department of Justice provided nationwide funding to demonstrate and evaluate intensive probation programs.

The evidence of the effectiveness of IPS overall is inconclusive, however. The earliest study in Georgia found that IPS was effective; however, it relied on the small caseloads for probation officers. Georgia also has one of the highest percentages of incarceration rates in the nation; thus, many of these offenders put on probation may not have been high risk and slated for prison. Those who were put on IPS where effectively chosen because they represented the greatest potential for success with the program (Morris & Tonry, 1990). Another study found that effectiveness for reducing recidivism is possible if IPS maintains a high level of treatment integrity by using a human service philosophy, especially one that does not have an orientation toward deterrence (Lowenkamp, Flores, Holsinger, Makarios, & Latessa, 2010). Certainly, the imposition of IPS on a defendant presupposes some moral questions. Setting aside the above mentioned studies of effectiveness of IPS, it can be argued that IPS sets rigid requirements for a population of chronic offenders, who have never completed any task or program with any consistency or success, thereby giving them little to no chance of meeting IPS requirements. Is it morally acceptable to have these individuals at liberty in any community? If an IPS participant reoffends, who should suffer the fault of his or her failure? Do we blame it on the individual or on the system?

Shock probation is a variation in which the probationer "gets a taste" of prison life (deterrent) for a relatively short time, typically amounting to 1 to 6 months, before serving the rest of the sentence on probation. These are also examples of **split sentences** handed down by judges, where the shock is the result of a defendant receiving a lengthy or maximum sentence, but he or she is released early under community supervision.

Who Gets Probation?

Who is awarded probation depends on a number of factors. There are some crimes for which the law mandates that prison sentences be given, so granting probation is not an option. Federal and state district courts and state superior courts can all award probation. Jury cases in some states may also allow recommendations of probation if the case meets certain eligibility requirements. An example of this is those cases that are eligible by federal or state statute based on offense category. Judges always have the final say and fairly wide discretion, whether it is a jury or nonjury case where granting probation is solely by judicial mandate. Serious chronic and violent adult offenders who commit repeated crimes like murder or rape are not usually eligible for probation sentences; however, it is not uncommon to find first-time or even second-time felons granted probation sentences. It is fairly common that in most states juvenile cases always hold the option of probation, since the primary task is to divert youthful offenders away from the criminal justice system.

Probation appears to be a common sanction imposed on many celebrities, who also tend to violate it. Actress Lindsay Lohan, after being arrested twice within a matter of months for possessing cocaine, transporting narcotics, and driving under the influence of drugs, was given 3 years' probation. However, Lohan violated her probation on May 20, 2010, when she chose to go yachting in Cannes instead of attending her mandatory court hearing. On July 6, 2010, Lohan was charged with missing nine mandatory court-ordered alcohol classes during her probation period and began serving 90 days in prison as well as a 90-day inpatient rehabilitation program starting July 20, 2015. The actress went on to become a regular in the court system with additional trips to rehab, stints in jail, house arrest, and the felony necklace theft debacle. Another less recent example is Robert Downey Jr. "Before he was Iron Man, he was "Jail Man." He was sentenced to 3 years' probation for driving drunk and possessing cocaine, heroin, and a Magnum revolver. However, once he violated his parole, he got put in the slammer for 6 months" (http://www.ranker.com). These celebrity examples provide just a very small sampling of who gets probation.

According to the most recent statistics compiled by the Bureau of Justice Statistics, in 2012 there were 3.94 million offenders under probation supervision in the United States. This represents a decline in the total correctional population (probation, parole, prisons, and jails) for the fourth consecutive year, with almost the entire decline (38,000) coming from the probation population (Bonczar, & Maruschak, 2013). Although probation remains the number one sentence given convicted offenders, a number of other intermediate sanctions have become part of the landscape of community corrections. Many people confuse probation and parole, but they are two distinctly different alternatives. Essentially, whereas probation is a sanction imposed by the court, parole is a reward of early conditional release given administratively by corrections officials (parole board) when a convicted offender serves a portion of his or her sentence successfully.

Parole

Parole is an early conditional release of prisoners from a correctional facility into the community; such prisoners have served a portion of their sentence successfully and been deemed worthy enough to reenter mainstream society. Parole decisions are made by a parole board, which is typically made up of a group of citizens who have some experience in the criminal justice or related field and are appointed by the state's governor, though there is some variation in states. Parolees traditionally have been convicted of more serious crimes than those individuals you might find on probation; though a growing trend has been to use probation as a way to lessen the overcrowding in jails and prisons. Released inmates are thus reintegrated back into society under the supervision of a parole officer. Parole comes from the French word *parole* meaning "word," or to give one's word of honor or promise. Parole has two primary goals: (a) to reward inmates for good behavior while incarcerated, and (b) to provide a more cost-effective way to supervise offenders in lieu of incarceration. A 2012 study released by the Vera Institute of Justice reports that the average cost of incarceration to taxpayers per year for one prisoner in the states covered by the study ranges between $31,307 and $60,000. The average cost of supervising a parolee is $2,727, which proves to be a significant reduction from incarceration.

Historically, parole has generally leaned more toward enforcement as opposed to treatment. For parole officers the question of treatment versus enforcement is less of a moral dilemma. Parole officers have legal rights to carry firearms, to search parolees, to order arrests without probable cause, and to confine without bail (Rudovsky, Brownstein, Koren, & Cade, 1988). However, the moral question that must be asked is: Can we expect parole officers to wield such power and authority without the danger of corruption creeping in? Petersilia (1999) argues that parole officers are "walking court systems" (p. 505) who are hampered by large caseloads, lack of time and resources, and increased paperwork, and who are performing a quasi-policing role rather than one concerned with rehabilitation.

U.S. adult residents on community supervision, probation, and parole, 2000–2013			
Year	Community supervision population	Probation	Parole
2000	4,565,100	3,839,500	725,500
2001	4,665,900	3,934,700	731,100
2002	4,748,300	3,995,200	753,100
2003	4,847,500	4,074,000	773,500
2004	4,916,500	4,140,600	775,900
2005	4,946,800	4,162,500	784,400
2006	5,035,200	4,237,000	798,200
2007	5,119,300	4,293,200	826,100
2008	5,095,200	4,271,100	828,200
2009	5,017,900	4,198,200	824,100
2010	4,887,900	4,055,500	840,700
2011	4,814,200	3,971,300	853,900
2012	4,781,300	3,942,800	851,200
2013	4,751,400	3,910,600	853,200
Average annual percent change, 2000–2012	0.4%	0.2%	1.3%
Percent change 2012–2013	–0.6%	–0.8%	0.2%

Notes. Counts rounded to the nearest 100. Detail may not sum to total due to rounding. Counts based on most recent data and may differ from previously published statistics. Reporting methods for some probation agencies changed over time. See Bureau of Justice Statistics, Probation and parole in United States, 2013, *methodology section.*

Source: Bureau of Justice Statistics (2013), Probation and Parole in the United States, 2013

Table reprinted from Bulletin *revised January 21, 2015 – Probation and Parole in the United States, 2013. U.S. Department of Justice, Office of Justice Programs,* Bureau of Justice Statistics. *www.ojp.usdoj.gov*

E. Moral Implications

What are the moral obligations of those who monitor and supervise (that is, probation and parole officers, treatment professionals, and so on) community sanctions? Morality discussions for many tend to revolve around whether or not community sanctions is treatment or punishment, or perhaps both. Do they provide service or surveillance or some measure of both? Community corrections emphasize the relationship between the offender and the community. Helping the offender become a "better" person is a morally ethical position because it suggests that a caring and committed relationship evolves from treating offenders in a less punitive manner. Alternatively, Deigh (2014) points out that there are arguments for

> regarding as morally more defensible sentencing policies whose goal is preserving social order than sentencing policies whose goal is that of classical deterrence theory, which is to achieve the smallest incidence of crimes consistent with not diminishing the overall welfare of society. (p. 185)

As community sanctions continued to flourish in the 1990s, von Hirsch (1990) questioned the ethics of whether such sanctions were proportionate to the gravity of the crime and whether they were unduly intrusive on the defendants' human dignity or privacy. He asserts that the use of community-based sanctions may create a mechanism for further humiliation and damage to offenders' lives. Where do we draw the line between punishment and treatment, or is community corrections morally obligated to provide both? To illustrate, Adrian Peterson, a star running back for the Minnesota Vikings, was required to report monthly to Montgomery County, Minnesota, probation officials and submit to drug testing after plea bargaining a felony child abuse charge down to a misdemeanor reckless assault for whipping his 4-year-old son with a switch in 2014. In January 2015 Peterson was ordered to do **community service** in Texas and undergo counseling to determine whether the exiled Vikings running back has a drug problem, according to court documents obtained by the Pioneer Press. District Court Judge Kelly Case cataloged 17 conditions Peterson must fulfill within 2 years to have his criminal conviction expunged from his record, including to refrain from using or consuming controlled substances, avoid persons and places of disreputable or harmful character, work faithfully at suitable employment as far as possible, and support his dependents.[3] In this situation the offender is being punished for his actions while receiving an opportunity to get treatment for his personal afflictions that may or may not have contributed to the criminal act. There are many cases where the judicial

---

3   Murphy, 2015.

system provides a combination of punishment and treatment. Does this mean that the court is morally obligated to provide treatment as part of the disposition?

Another controversial moral issue is the arming of probation and parole officers. Most of this dissonance comes from within the service ranks of probation and parole rather than externally. If probation and parole are morally defensible in regards to preserving the social order, as Deigh (2014) argues, then arming them should also be morally acceptable. No question that what constitutes the role of probation and parole has changed over the years. Probation officers in particular see it as a more philosophical or moral argument. Some say:

> these claims are typically framed in relation to the increased threat in the job, and the resulting need for safety due to both the more violent nature of probationers, as well as the increased expectations of proactive enforcement on the part of probation (Abadinsky, 2003; Brown, 1989, 1990). (as cited in Roscoe, Duffee, Rivera, & Smith, 2007, p. 17)

The authors point out that the decision to arm is more related to the enforcement versus treatment preference of the probation staff, rather than those who actually make policy. Therefore, the arming has influenced a "philosophy toward enforcement rather than an enforcement-oriented philosophy" (Roscoe et al., 2007, p. 18). Proponents for arming probation officers point to their right for self-protection rather than the use of such weapons for taking probation violators into custody, thus nullifying the enforcement aspect; whereas opponents argue that it gives probation officers a law enforcement mentality and diminishes the social work aspect of probation. Given the convoluted role of probation officers in the criminal justice system (enforcement versus treatment), part of the moral dilemma is whether they are forcing behaviors on individuals who are not necessarily agreeable to such change, which puts them at odds with the moral principles of doing the job. Behavioral change is best accomplished voluntarily, not through use of force. How do we reconcile that?

House Arrest

House arrest or **home confinement** is an intermediate sanction that requires convicted offenders to stay in or close to their home when not working or otherwise engaged in a court approved activity. In some cases it is used in lieu of bail while a defendant is awaiting trial. Many are monitored by probation departments, whereas others are monitored by judicial surveillance officers. The obvious benefit of this sanction is to allow individuals an opportunity to maintain employment and support themselves and/ or their family while restricting the offenders' movements. Although some view it as an avoidance of deserved prison or jail time, important benefits to the correctional system are that it reduces costs and overcrowding in prisons and jails. The evidence is mixed on the effectiveness of house arrests to act as a crime deterrent or reduce recidivism, but more often than not house arrest is coupled with **electronic monitoring**, or what may be referred to as electronic house arrest (Marion, 2002). Electronic monitoring requires a transmitter to be placed on the ankle of the offender; the transmitter sends a continuous signal to a monitoring station, and if the signal is interrupted, the offender's whereabouts are checked. As mentioned above, evaluation studies are mixed; for example, one study found that 10% of the sample population's probation was revoked within 18 months for technical violations (Baird & Wagner, 1990). Other studies that measured recidivism with or without electronic monitoring have shown no statistical differences (Gable & Gable, 2005).

Moral Implications of House Arrest

House arrest uses radio frequency and Global Positioning System (GPS) technologies to monitor the movements of high-, medium-, and low-risk offenders, both juvenile and adult. GPS and other tracking technology agencies rely on GPS and other tracking technology to monitor offenders in the community. With the expansion of the offender reentry initiatives, the importance of these technologies has increased. GPS technology is not necessarily used for tracking inmates but is used extensively in monitoring higher risk offenders, such as sex offenders being supervised in the community. Does this type of monitoring violate individual rights?

Although privacy issues abound when the discussion focuses on the government's ability to electronically monitor an individual's activities, when it comes to high-risk offenders, opposition is lessened. For example, sex offenders carry a significant negative connotation in society. The issue of dangerousness in regard to reoffending tends to be more prominent in the minds of the public than with many other types of offenders. Most people would argue that it is in the best interest of the public for authorities to closely monitor these offenders. In this view, no measures are too extreme to protect the public and deter offenders from further crime. Meloy and Coleman (2009) assert that the only way to ensure that sex offenders "do not recidivate is through lifetime incarceration or the implementation of the death penalty" (p. 247) for commission of serious sex crimes. Certainly such measures present problems on fiscal, legal, and moral grounds. Although some might argue that convicted sex offenders' gives up their rights by such offending behavior, probation officers who monitor these individuals must tread a thin line when it comes to how closely to supervise them. Is it morally right to supervise sex offenders more stringently than other probationers who may actually have committed more violent crimes? Or should they be less stringently supervised, especially in light of the fact that many sex offenders score lower on risk factors?[4] Do the individual privacy rights of high-risk offenders like some

---

4 Typically, the level of supervision is determined by scores on a risk/need assessment form completed by probation officers. For more information on risk/need assessments for probation services, see http://www.ncsc.org/~/media/Microsites/Files/CSI/RNA%20Guide%20Final.ashx.

sex offenders matter less than those of lower risk offenders? Is it morally right to pick and choose which individuals' privacy is more acceptable to violate than others? These questions and others are best addressed in individual cases.

Residential Community Corrections/Reentry Programs

Residential community corrections, or reentry programs, were previously established to assist convicts who were nearing the end of their sentences and almost ready to be released from prison into the mainstream population. These facilities are also referred to as halfway houses, community correctional centers, and community treatment centers. Residential community corrections facilities are considered the most secure intermediate sanction outside of prison that a judge might impose. Typically, inmates spend the last few months of their prison sentences in these facilities. Such facilities offer an opportunity for these individuals to seek employment or to work, obtain educational services, and perhaps even participate in continued substance abuse or other treatment services. They provide a way to integrate released convicts back into society while they reside in a place that is less expensive overall than trying to support themselves. These facilities are less secure than prisons but do provide supervision of activities and movements.

Reintegration has become an integral part of the corrections process over the past few years. Offender reentry and postrelease supervision programs (that is, work release) are now more readily supported than they have historically been. Of the 7 million people under some form of correctional supervision, approximately 5 million are supervised by community corrections. In 2005 the Re-entry Policy Council—a bipartisan assembly of almost 100 leading elected officials, policy makers, corrections leaders, and practitioners from community-based organizations around the country—released a report on offender reentry titled *Charting the Safe and Successful Return of Prisoners to the Community*[5]. According to this report, 2 out of 3 of the 650,000 individuals released from jails and prisons annually will be rearrested within 3 years of their release. The significance of this report in regard to reoffending rates of released offenders brought to light the many barriers created by the complex issues of reentry. Some of these issues include facts like three quarters of those released have a history of substance abuse; high percentages of those released are suffering from physical and mental disabilities (almost 3 times the rate of the general population); two thirds of them do not have a high school diploma and were earning less than $600 per month prior to incarceration, consequently they leave prison or jails with greatly reduced opportunities to find employment or are only likely to find employment with minimum wage levels sustainability[6].

---

5   www.reentrypolicy.org
6   www.reentrypolicy.org

Moral Implications

Inmates working in the community (that is, community service, work release, or work program) are a significant programmatic reality for many agencies. Budget cuts have required some agencies to reduce these programs. The need to balance public safety considerations and the benefits of community work programs are the crux of the priority issue among correctional agencies. Programs of this nature support the successful transition of offenders back into the community. Reentry programs in particular present significant challenges. It is immoral on society's part to release offenders back into the community without providing for appropriate supports to help ensure success. Certainly we have to be cognizant of the chronic serious violent offenders who are released and reintegrated into mainstream society, but what are the moral obligations of the system when it comes to releasing those perceived as less dangerous but perhaps even more needy; for example, elderly inmates, women, women with children, the poor and uneducated, or those who have diagnosable mental disorders? All of these special populations face significant challenges upon reentry, and they are not tracked as closely as are those chronic serious violent offenders. Finding the right balance between the inmate's risk and the level of supervision in the community is an ongoing challenge and in many circumstances occasions much more public scrutiny than usual, depending upon the nature of the offense.

One special population, sex offenders, is becoming increasingly difficult to place in the community. The general public tends to display much stronger opposition to the idea of reintegrating convicted sex offenders back into the community. Public attitudes toward sex offenders are more negative and are heavily influenced by media stereotypes, and it is likely that support for protective measures taken against sex offenders is high because of this media influence (Willis, Levenson, & Ward, 2010). Is this a moral obligation or misdirected public hysteria? Although sex offenders present the extreme lowest recidivist rate, the fact that the public shuns them and continues to express the "not in my backyard" culture means that securing housing for sex offenders is extremely difficult.

Community Service

Community service is traditionally a condition of probation for minimum- to moderate-risk offenders to provide unpaid service/labor to the community in order to account for their actions. It originally gained popularity for use with white-collar crime (Morris & Tonry, 1990). It isn't necessarily a sanction in and of itself that a judge would impose as a sentence. Celebrities like Chris Brown, Naomi Campbell, Lindsay Lohan, Boy George, Snoop Dogg, and Kanye West have all had community service imposed as part of their sentence.[7] Community service has since grown to a standalone program in many

---

7   http://www.theguardian.com/world/2014/apr/15/famous-community-service-silvio-berlusconi

communities. The problem is that community service suffers from a vague understanding of what it is actually supposed to accomplish with the offender. Although community service does provide the opportunity for the offender to serve the community in various ways and help reduce the cost of their own supervision, does it act as a deterrent, rehabilitate offenders, or reduce recidivism? And if community service is not completed, how then do we punish the violators?

Fines, Restitution, and Forfeiture

Fines are monetary payments that are imposed on offenders by the court that go to the state and not the victim, usually to fund courts and other programs. Monetary sanctions were a commonly used penalty in common law practice in early England and Europe. Fines are usually imposed for minor offenses and misdemeanors and may be used as the sole sanction; however, they are more commonly combined with other punishments. Fines may also be imposed in felony cases where there was a financial benefit by the offender. A primary problem with fines is that although they seek to punish fairly, they tend to punish the poor more than the affluent. It is much more of a penalty for a poor person to pay these fines and doesn't carry the same impact for those who are better off financially. So are fines really fair? Is it morally right to impose fines on those less fortunate, for whom they become an even greater burden and constitutes a harsher penalty than for those who are more fortunate? In an attempt to rectify the inequity of fines, some jurisdictions are employing the concept of *day fines* or *structured fines*; a concept drafted from some European countries that takes into account an offender's daily net worth. Using a formula that includes severity of crime, weighted by a chart-based daily-income value and the number of dependents the offender has, an appropriate fine is determined (U.S. Department of Justice, 1996; Eriksson & Goodin, 2007).

Restitution orders are typically monetary sanctions that provide recompense or equity to victims. Restitution provides for payments of debts owed to the victim and is separate and distinct from state monies. Restitution in some cases can be an alternative to incarceration. The concept of restitution extends back to the Code of Hammurabi (c. 1750 BCE). The Twelve Tables of Roman law (c. 449 BCE) also prescribed restitution as a way for convicted thieves to pay for the goods they stole. In the case of violent offenses, Middle Eastern codes, such as the Sumerian Code of Umammu (c. 2050 B.C.) and the Code of Eshnunna (c. 1700 B.C.) required restitution (Van Ness & Strong, 1997). In ninth century Britain, offenders were required to restore peace by making payments to the victims and the victim's families (Karmen, 2010)[8].

Forfeiture proceedings require that goods and instruments gained from the commission of a criminal act may be seized or confiscated by both state and federal authorities and used to compensate

---

8 Reprinted with permission from www.restorativejustice.org (copyright 2001–2014, Prison Fellowship International Centre for Justice and Reconciliation).

victims or later sold to the general public with the proceeds going to the state or local government. Criminal forfeiture came about as a result of the Racketeer Influenced and Corrupt Organization Act (RICO) Act, Title 18, U.S. Code, Sections 1961–1968. When it was passed by Congress in 1970, its goal was to eliminate the ill effects of organized crime on the nation's economy. In addition, the Continuing Criminal Enterprise Statute, 21 U.S.C. 848, was enacted as part of the Comprehensive Drug Abuse Prevention and Control Act of 1970. The statute is aimed at any person who "occupies a position of organizer, a supervisory position, or any other position of management"[9] in a drug-producing and drug-distributing enterprise. This legislation provides for one of the most severe penalties of any federal criminal statute.

Is the Risk of Community Corrections Moral?

Criminal justice professionals also have views of what is or is not morally acceptable within the scope of their official duties. Their views are perhaps shaped more by their experiences within the reality of performing these tasks on a daily basis and less by media influences. However, it is also true that criminal justice professionals have an ethical obligation to their profession that doesn't necessarily always align with their moral views. Although ethics and morals are both related to right and wrong, one would assume that criminal justice professionals' views fully reflect the ethics of their professional role, rather than their individual morals.

Given that ethics are defined by external groups whereas morals are more internalized and may be more deeply embedded within an individual's psyche, it might be reasonable to assume that some criminal justice professionals may find themselves attempting to suppress or situate their morals within the ethical constraints of their tasks at times. In other words, they may compromise or ameliorate their morals in order to do their job. For example, a trial court judge may be morally opposed to capital punishment yet may find him- or herself in a position where a death sentence is legally mandated for a particular offense. Since ethics are dependent on others for definition, it is not unusual for them to vary between contexts, because unless a person's beliefs change, morals usually stay consistent.

One of the central moral issues is the inquiry of the reason or mission of probation, parole, and different sorts of community corrections. Many people are calling for use of corrective methodologies to the supervision of offenders. This extremely fundamental clash of thoughts is conspicuous in probation and parole, and it influences different issues; for example, privatization and corruption (Pollock, 2014). Questions arise about whether these community sentences are too soft or perhaps even unfair, given who is actually eligible for these sentences. Even further, how should we think and feel morally about criminals (Reiman & Leighton, 2014)? Think about it for a moment. If you have

---

9   as cited in Legal Theory, n.d.

ever been a victim of a crime or had a family member or good friend who was a victim of a crime, how does that affect your morals when it comes to crime and punishment? Reiman suggests that in order to determine how we feel and think morally about a criminal, we must first look at the moral nature of crime. In his view this will tell us "what the criminal who commits it is responsible for" (Reiman & Leighton, 2014, p. 3). This is not as easy as one might think. It is simplistic to say that because a person broke the law, he or she should be punished accordingly. However, what if the process of convicting the individual was unjust? It might be just as easy from the outside looking in to say that community sentences are too soft and don't sit well with our morality regarding punishment. However, would it be even more moralistically unacceptable had this person been incarcerated due to an unjust or unfair process?

F. Do Community Sanctions Work?

This is not a simple question to answer. The research seems to be mixed on this question. Some might say that it depends on who you ask and what you are measuring. For example, in one study, Marion (2002) attempts to answer this question by studying three primary measures of effectiveness for community corrections, recidivism, cost, and overcrowding of jails and prison. In this case study, which she admits is not wholly generalizable but valuable nonetheless, the findings indicate that for effectiveness in lowering recidivism, these programs are not successful but are no worse than prison for protecting society; and for costs, community corrections is not necessarily more cost effective than prison. However, in regard to overcrowding, community corrections effectively succeeds at this. In so doing, Marion points out that the state "widens the net in people it controls" (p. 494).

How effective have these alternatives been, according to data that typically focuses on rearrest rates? According to the National Institute of Corrections Community Corrections Collaborative Network, which represents community corrections professionals, "Community corrections is changing lives, reducing harm, and helping build communities, and it has strong public support" (Ziedenberg, 2014 p. i). A position paper published in August 2014 finds "that community corrections is a critical part of the public safety system that supervises individuals under the legal authority in the community to reduce crime and victimization" (Ziedenberg, 2014, p. i). However, according to an April 2014 report from the Bureau of Justice Statistics of the prisoners released in 2005 in 30 states, 3 in 4 were rearrested within 5 years of their release.[10] Although this is not broken down by specific sanctions, keep in mind that probation and parole are the primary community corrections sanctions.

10 Cooper, Durose, & Snyder, 2014.

Finally, keep in mind that sex offenders are becoming increasingly difficult to place in the community. The general public tends to display much stronger opposition to the idea of reintegrating convicted sex offenders back into the community. Public attitudes toward sex offenders are more negative and are heavily influenced by media stereotypes, and support for protective measures taken against sex offenders is high probably because of this media influence (Willis et al., 2010).

G. Conclusion

Community corrections has a long history as an alternative to incarceration in Europe and the United States and has grown to be the most commonly used punishment in the criminal justice system. Also commonly referred to as intermediate sanctions, it gives the courts authority to impose a variety of punishments such as probation, which is the most common of all the sanctions but also, parole (though this sanction is not typically part of court dispositions); restitution, fines, forfeiture, home confinement and/or electric monitoring, therefore expanding opportunities to control these individuals while keeping them in their communities. More recently, a focus on concepts such as reintegration and restoration has begun to meet the challenges of public safety, recidivism, costs, and overcrowding, while taking into account the needs of the victims. Public attitudes typically see community sanctions as being too soft on crime, especially when they are used as punishment with serious offenders; however, the fact remains that they are a valuable alternative for juveniles and less serious crime offenders. Sex offenders present a special challenge to community corrections service providers. The public views these offenders as especially predatory, and specific laws demand closer scrutiny of those released into the community. Community corrections walks a fine line when it comes to aspects of punishment and treatment. The success of community sanctions is debatable, however. Depending on what variable is used to measure effectiveness—whether it is recidivism rates, the cost of imprisonment, or overcrowding of prisons and jails—the evidence is mixed. Morality within the context of criminal justice is complex. Public views of how the criminal justice system should function are based primarily on individual ideals and principles or morals. The government, or more specifically the criminal justice system, has a moral obligation not only to protect public safety but also to insure that those who commit crimes are punished appropriately and victims are fairly compensated. Given the mission of community corrections, moral obligations do not fall just within the purview of the criminal justice system or directly on the service providers from probation and parole officers through treatment providers, but also indirectly on members of the various communities in which the offenders reside.

1. Criminal justice professionals have an ethical obligation to their profession that doesn't necessarily always align with their moral principles. Although ethics and morals are both related to right and wrong, one would assume that their views fully reflect the ethics of their professional role, rather than their individual morals. Discuss how issues in community corrections could potentially cause those who are obligated to supervise and monitor these individuals may compromise their morals in order to uphold ethical obligations. Provide some examples from the news.

2. Some may argue that the arming of probation officers is a moral issue in that it encourages a law enforcement mentality in probation officers, rather than a social work or "helping" mentality. In regard to the issues discussed in the chapter, what are your views on this topic, and can you think of other issues or concerns either way?

Baird, S. C., & Wagner, D. (1990). Measuring diversion: The Florida community control program. *Crime and Delinquency, 36*, 112–125.

Bonczar, T. P., & Maruschak, L. M. (2013), *Probation and parole in the United States, 2012*. Bureau of Justice Statistics NCJ 243826 www.bjs.gov/index.cfm?ty=pbdetail&iid=4908

Bureau of Justice Statistics. (2013). Probation and parole in the United States, 2013. Washington, DC: US Department of Justice, Office of Justice Programs.

Byrne, J. (1990). The future of intensive probation supervision and the new intermediate sanctions. *Crime and Delinquency, 36*(1), 6–41.

Cooper, A. D., Durose, M. R., & Snyder, H. N. (2014). Recidivism of prisoners released in 30 states in 2005: Patterns from 2005 to 2010. Press release, Recidivism of Prisoners Released Series, Bureau of Justice Statistics, Washington, DC. Retrieved from http://www.bjs.gov/index.cfm?ty=pbdetail&iid=4987

Cromwell, P., Killinger, G., & Kerper, H. (1974). The history and concept of parole. In G. Killinger & P.F. Cromwell (Eds.). *Corrections in the community: Alternatives to imprisonment selected readings* (pp. 233–241)/ St. Paul, MN: West.

Deigh, J. (2014). Punishment and proportionality. *Criminal Justice Ethics, 33*(3), 185–199.

DeMichele, M., & Paparozzi, M. (2008). Community corrections: A powerful field. *Corrections Today, 70*(5), 68–72.

Dillingham, D. (1994). New attitudes toward corrections determine programs and policies. *Corrections Today, 56*(1), 84.

Dressler, D. (1969). *Practice and theory of probation and parole*. New York: Columbia University Press.

Eriksson, L., & Goodin, R. (2007). The measuring rod of time: The example of Swedish day-fines. *Journal of Applied Philosophy, 24*, 125–136.

Evans, D. G. (2004). Why community corrections matter. *Corrections Today, 66*(6). 18–19.

Gable, R. K., & Gable, R. S. (2005). Electronic monitoring: Positive intervention strategies. *Federal Probation,* 69(1). Retrieved from www.uscourts.gov/file/document/federal-probation -journal-june-2005?doc=/uscourts/FederalCourts/PPS/Fe

Harris, M. K. (1996). Key differences among community corrections acts in the United States: An overview. *Prison Journal.* (76)2. 192–239.

Karmen, A. (2010). *Crime victims: An introduction to victimology.* Belmont, CA: Cengage Learning.

Legal Theory. (n.d.). Continuing criminal enterprise. Retrieved from http://legaltheory.tripod.com/id6. html

Lowenkamp, C. T., Flores, A. W., Holsinger, A. M., Makarios, M. D., & Latessa, E. J. (2010). Intensive probation supervision: Does program philosophy and the principles of effective intervention matter? *Journal of Criminal Justice, 38*(4), 368–375.

Marion, N. (2002). Effectiveness of community-based correctional programs: A case study. *Prison Journal, 82*(4), 478–497.

Meloy, M. L., & Coleman, S. (2009) GPS monitoring for sex offenders. In R. G. Wright (Ed.), *Sex offender laws: Failed policies, new directions* (2nd ed.) (pp. 243–266). New York: Springer.

Mempa v. Rhay 389 US 128 (LexisNexis 1967)

Meyer, F., & Baker, R. (2004). Punitive correctional policy: The impact of the state legislature. *Conference Papers—Midwestern Political Science Association*, 1–47. doi:mpsa_proceeding_25455. PDF

Morris. N. (2002). *Maconochie's gentlemen: The story of Norfolk Island and the roots of modern prison reform.* New York: Oxford University Press.

Morris, N., & Tonry, M. (1990). *Between prison and probation: Intermediate punishments in a rational sentencing system.* New York: Oxford University Press.

Morrissey v. Brewer, 408 U.S. 471 (1972)

Murphy, B. (2015, January 29). Adrian Peterson probation: Drug testing, counseling, 15 other conditions. *Twincities.com Sports.* Retrieved from http://www.twincities.com/sports/ci_27418878/ vikings-adrian-petersons-probation-begins-wednesday-includes-drug

Nezu, C. M., Greenberg, J., & Nezu, M. M. (2006). Project STOP: Cognitive behavioral assessment and treatment for sex offenders with intellectual disability. *Journal of Forensic Psychology Practice, 6*(3), 87–103. doi:10. I 300/J I 58v06n0306

Nieto, M. (1996). *Community correction punishments: An alternative to incarceration for nonviolent offenders.* California Research Bureau, California State Library. Retrieved from https://www.ncjrs.gov/ App/publications/abstract.aspx?ID=165255

Petersilia, J. (1999). Parole and prisoner reentry in the United States. In M. Tonry & J. Petersilia (Eds.), *Prisons* (pp. 479–529). Chicago: Chicago University Press.

Pollock, J. M. (2014). *Ethical dilemmas and decisions in criminal justice.* Belmont, CA: Wadsworth, Cengage Learning.

Reiman, J., & Leighton, P. (2014). *The rich get richer and the poor get prison: Ideology, class and criminal justice* (11th ed.). Boston: Pearson/Allyn & Bacon.

Robinson, M. B. (2014). *Media coverage of crime and criminal justice* (2nd ed.). Durham, NC: Carolina Academic Press.

Roscoe, T., Duffee, D. E., Rivera, C., & Smith, T. R. (2007). Arming probation officers: Correlates of the decision to arm at the department level. *Criminal Justice Studies, 20*(1), 43–63.

Rudovsky, D., Brownstein, A., Koren, E., & Cade, J. (1988). *The rights of prisoners.* Carbondale: Southern Illinois University Press.

Sieh, E. (1993). From Augustus to the progressives: A study of probation's formative years. *Federal Probation, 57*, 67–72.

US Department of Justice. (1996). *How to use structured fines (day fines) as an intermediate sanction.* Washington, DC: Office of Justice Programs, Bureau of Justice Assistance, NCJ 165242. Retrieved from http://www.ojp.usdoj.gov/BJA

Van Ness, D., & Strong, K. H. (1997). *Restoring justice.* Cincinnati: Anderson.

Vera Institute of Justice. (2012). *The price of prisons: What incarceration costs taxpayers.* Report, Center on Sentencing and Corrections, New York. Retrieved from http://www.vera.org/sites/default/files/resources/downloads/price-of-prisons-updated-version-021914.pdf

Von Hirsch, A. (1990). The ethics of community-based sanctions. *Crime & Delinquency, 36*(1), 162–173.

Willis, G. M., Levenson, J. S., & Ward, T. (2010). Desistance and attitudes towards sex offenders: Facilitation or hindrance? *Journal of Family Violence, 25*, 545–556.

Wilson, D. B., Gallagher, C. A., & MacKenzie, D. L. (2000). A meta-analysis of corrections-based education, vocation, and work programs for adult offenders. *Journal of Research in Crime & Delinquency, 37*(4), 347–368.

Wilson, J. Q., & Petersilia, J. (2002). *Crime, public policies for crime control.* Oakland, CA: Institute for Contemporary Studies Press.

Wodahl, E. J., & Garland, B. (2009). The evolution of community corrections: The enduring influence of the prison. *Prison Journal, 89*(S1). 81S-104S. http://dx.doi.org/10.1177/0032885508329775

United States v. Granderson (92-1662), 511 U.S. 39 (1994).

U.S. Code: Title 18 Part II Chapter 227, Subchapter B § 3563-Conditions of Probation.

Ziedenberg, J. (2014). Community corrections collaborative network: Safe and smart ways to solve America's correctional challenges. National Institute of Corrections, US Department of Justice. Retrieved from http://nicic.gov/library/028317

07

Institutional Corrections

Carolyn Petrosino

KEY TERMS

- BIG HOUSE
- COMMUNITY MODEL
- CONVICT LEASE SYSTEM
- NEW YORK (CONGREGATE) SYSTEM
- NEW PENOLOGY
- PENNSYLVANIA (SEPARATE) SYSTEM
- SECURITY LEVELS
- SUPERMAX FACILITY

A. Introduction

The primary mission of the correctional component of the criminal justice system is to carry out the sentences received by convicted offenders. Sentences can range from probation to short-term jail sentences and fines to lengthy terms of imprisonment, and even the death penalty. Accordingly, there are several different corrections agencies that oversee this objective. Since most convicted offenders are under probation supervision, (more than 50%),[1] probation offices are involved with the bulk of offenders.

However, institutional corrections refers to those facilities designed to detain or imprison offenders who are either awaiting court actions or who have been convicted and sentenced to jail or state or federal prison. Offenders who receive a sentence of up to one year or less typically serve time in a local county jail; longer sentences are typically served in a state prison unless stated otherwise. Those convicted of federal crimes serve time in the federal

---

1   Bureau of Justice Statistics, 2014a.

correctional system, known as the Federal Bureau of Prisons. There are approximately 1,800 state and federal correctional facilities in the United States. Local jails and county facilities outnumber prisons, at approximately 3,100.

Institutional corrections receives a good deal of notoriety due to the startling fact that the United States imprisons more people than any other nation. The Bureau of Justice Statistics reports that as of December 31, 2013, there were 2.2 million people locked up in jails, state, and federal prisons.[2] It is difficult to fully comprehend the meaning of this statistic until it is compared to the incarceration rate of other nations. The International Centre for Prison Studies reports the following data[3] in Table 7.1.

Table 7.1. Incarceration rate by nation

Country	Incarceration rate
United States	2,217,000
China	1,657,812
Russian Federation	667,546
Brazil	607,730
India	411,992
United Kingdom (England and Wales)	85,743
France	66,761
Germany	61,872
Canada	37,864
United Kingdom (Northern Ireland)	1,715

Why are the numbers as large as they are in the United States? During the 1970s crime in the United States increased significantly. Much has been written about the causes of this rise; some of the major explanations include: the criminal justice system is too soft on criminals and thus does not deter crime; drug trafficking is a growing problem which feeds addictions; and there is simply more opportunities for crime. Conservatives and liberals, both displeased with the justice system but for different reasons, agreed that changes were necessary. The result was the popularity of determinant sentencing policies that would cause more people to be incarcerated for longer periods. Determinant sentencing not only substantially decreased judicial discretion, it also limited the discretion of parole authorities. By definition, determinant sentences are designated by a fixed term that is only reducible by earned "good" time (credit given for good behavior) and time already served before sentencing. Thus, the time of parole release is not subject to the discretion of parole authorities. Examples of determinant sentences include Truth in Sentencing, mandatory sentences for drug possession and or firearms, and Three-Strikes laws. The frequent use of these and other determinant sentencing models helped to exponentially grow the incarceration rate and a corresponding increase in the number of prisons in the United States. Some have referred to this expansion period as the onset of the "prison–industrial complex," which

2   U.S. Department of Justice, 2014.
3   International Centre for Prison Studies, n.d.a.

emerged from a "confluence of special interests"[4] comprising political and economic entities. The term *prison–industrial complex* suggests that there were business and profit interests intertwined with the government's crime policy, which incentivized the buildup of prisons throughout the United States for economic gain rather than to effectively addressing crime.

B. The Role of Institutional Corrections in the Criminal Justice System

Jails

Jails play a vital role in institutional corrections. Recall that most crime is primarily defined by jurisdiction and that in every state there are at least two levels of criminal law enforced within the state (that is, state and local). Individuals who violate local laws and are sentenced to terms of 1 year or less will serve their time in the local jail as stated earlier. According to the American Jail Association, there are about 3,100 jails in the United States.[5] Lockups are not the same as a jail. The former is a temporary holding area that is commonly located in and controlled by the local police department, whereas jails are correctional facilities where jail (not state prison) sentences are served. Jails are usually managed and staffed by county sheriff departments or other county correctional personnel. In addition to housing individuals serving shorter sentences, jails provide other functions. Persons who are awaiting various court actions such as bail, arraignment, trial, sentencing, or other hearings are frequently held in jail. Parolees who are arrested and are pending a parole revocation hearing are also held in jail. All of these needs are critical and are integral to the function of the criminal justice system. It is estimated that jails hold 5% of the 2.2 million persons incarcerated.

Cook County Jail in Chicago, Illinois, is reported to be the largest jail in the United States.[6] In 2012 it had an average daily population of more than 9,400.[7] It has an operating budget of $226 million and a staff of 3,800.[8] Besides housing pretrial and sentenced persons, this jail offers an array of offender programs that include an electronic monitoring program, a day reporting center, a prerelease center, a vocational rehabilitative impact center, the women's justice program, and the female furlough program. Of course the average jail has far fewer offenders to house, as well as fewer program options.

Prisons

---

4   Schlosser, 1998.
5   American Jail Association, n.d.
6   Ford, 2015.
7   Moser, 2013.
8   Olson, 2013.

Prisons are correctional facilities that are designed to hold offenders who are sentenced to terms of incarceration that exceed a year. The number of these prisoners increased from 2012 to 2013[9]. Most states have several prisons to house state prison inmates (see Table 7.2). Even though the public may view prisons as places for dangerous criminals, just a little over half of state prison inmates are there for violent crimes. Federal prisons are located in various locations in the United States and are not found in each of the 50 states.

Table 7.2. Number of prisons by state*

Alabama	15
Arizona	10
California	25
Colorado	23
Delaware	4
Florida	48
Maine	6
Massachusetts	12
Mississippi	14
Texas	50
Vermont	7
Wyoming	3

*State prisons are also referred to as correctional facilities. (Source: Adapted from List of U.S. State Prisons. Available at: **https://en.wikipedia.org/wiki/List_of_United_States_state_prisons**).

Privatize Facilities and Accountability

What are private prisons? Charles H. Logan defines private prisons as "a place of confinement that is privately owned, operated, or managed under contract by the government," (pg. 292).[10] Private prisons held 8% of the total U.S. prison population at the end of 2013 (Bureau of Justice Statistics, 2014b). There is a good deal of controversy surrounding the use of private facilities. What issues of concern come to your mind? One of the most worrisome aspects is that private prisons are for profit. The corporations that own them have an interest in financial gain from running these facilities. Today there are approximately 18 corporations involved in the business of guarding offenders in private facilities. Where do their profits come from? Housing more inmates? Hiring correctional personnel for lower salaries and benefits? Limiting institutional programs such as health care services and educational/

---

9   Bureau of Justice Statistics, 2014b.
10   as cited in Vyas, 1991.

vocational or drug treatment programs? What are the possible consequences from these inadequacies? Other areas of concern include state monitoring and the manner of accountability to government authorities. Finally, is the public safer when offenders are housed in private prisons?

C. History of Punishment (Corrections) in America

The early penitentiary illustrates the nature of punishment in colonial America after many became disillusioned with public corporal punishment. The new focus became changing character rather than inflicting bodily harm. The early penitentiary also served as a model for the modern prison.

One of the primary objectives of the early penitentiary was to subject the criminal to what Robert Johnson referred to as disciplined isolation.[11] Isolation was meant to protect the offender from the corrupting influences that existed in an ever-changing society. The heavy emphasis on discipline was to retrain the offender in the ways of constructive, moral, and prosocial habits. If successful, a rehabilitated individual would emerge who would be sufficiently disciplined and morally retooled to do well upon release.

There were two models of penitentiaries that developed: the **Pennsylvania, or separate, system** (estab. 1790) and the **New York, or congregate, system** (estab. 1821). The Pennsylvania model was heavily shaped by the Quaker religious perspective. Emphasizing the importance of self-reflection and repentance, the complete solitary confinement of the offender was the prominent feature of this model. Each offender was held in a single cell first in the Walnut Street Jail and later in the Eastern State Penitentiary, where self-examination and remorse should occur. The Bible was the only book permitted for the offender. The offender also did manual labor in the cell. Offenders were segregated from one another and kept away from the negative influences of society. However, authorities would discover that a terrible price was paid for this regimen. Many inmates became psychologically unstable, erratic, and mentally unhealthy, and some became suicidal. Human beings are social creatures and do not normally do well completely cut off from human contact. The Pennsylvania model unfortunately facilitated mental illness.

The New York model took note and structured a different penitentiary system. Congregation of inmates was permitted during work and meal times. Therefore, inmates were not placed in total solitary confinement. The concept of one man per cell was maintained, but work time was conducted in groups. This method preserved mental well-being, allowed for self-reflection, and also achieved more effective work regimens. But even though there were congregate times throughout the day, inmates were not permitted to speak to one another. Thus, the New York model was known as the silent

---

11   Johnson, 2002.

congregate system. One of the major criticisms of this model was the idea that inmates were being groomed to meet society's need for disciplined manual laborers rather than being encouraged toward self-direction and growth as individuals with potential.

Despite the noble intentions of the two penitentiary systems, both fell short of their desired goals. The New York model became the preferred system, but it would become more known for the brutalization of inmates and the inability to maintain its original goals.

The Pennsylvania and New York models were developed in the northeastern part of the United States. These models did not take hold in the southern states. Keep in mind that the institution of slavery was in full effect during the time of the competing solitary and congregate systems until 1863, when the Emancipation Proclamation was signed. However, slavery continued illegally in Texas until 1865. The early manifestation of the criminal justice system in the South occurred with the slave patrols; the slave patrollers were also referred to as "paddy rollers." These groups would hunt and capture runaway slaves and developed a system of harassing, interrogating, intimidating, and beating of Black people (whether they were runaway slaves or free). Blacks captured by paddy rollers were promptly handed over to slave owners.

But how did this lead to the southern correctional system? The southern penal farm would replace the southern plantation with the use of the convict lease system. To extend profit interests, the *leasing* of inmates to private contractors (businesses) became institutionalized in penal farms. With slavery ending, there grew a need to find inexpensive labor for economic gain—the basic motivation for Black slavery.

Newly freed Blacks were subjected to baseless arrests and sentenced to prison, where they would become free labor for contractors in the convict lease system. In a relatively short span of time, African Americans made up 90% of the incarcerated in the South.[12] Alabama implemented the convict labor system longer than any other southern state, beginning in 1846 and ending in 1928.[13] It was a vital part of Alabama's economy, with 73% of the state's total revenue coming from the state's **convict leasing** program in 1898. Alabama's system was particularly immoral and brutal. The death rates of leased inmates were 10 times that of nonleased inmates incarcerated in other states.

The **Big House** era (1930s–1940s) replaced the failed penitentiary system. These facilities were built to be large intimidating dreary structures. Their primary objective was to warehouse inmates. The thinking of the time was that in order to help inmates, one had to break their spirits by requiring backbreaking manual labor mixed with unrelenting boredom. Submissiveness, conformity, and discipline were the ultimate goals. These facilities also mirrored the social norms of the day; therefore, Big Houses were racially segregated. Non-White inmates were provided starker living conditions within these immense entombments. Female inmates were housed in Big Houses but in separate facilities,

12   McShane, 1996.
13   Mancini, 1996.

apart from male inmates. As the numbers of female inmates grew, so did the need for standalone prisons to accommodate their housing needs. The federal prison at Alcatraz (1934–1963) and San Quentin State Prison (1852–present)—both in California—and Statesville Correctional Center at Joliet, Illinois (1925–present), all typify the Big House prison. Their popularity waned in the 1950s, opening the door for the rise of the modern correctional facility.

One of the most influential penologists to arise in the mid-1850s was Zebulon Brockway. Brockway was committed to prison reform and was drawn to the idea of permitting inmates to have some ability to impact their incarceration experience and eventual release. The Elmira Reformatory opened in 1876 and was administered by Brockway. He emphasized reform over punishment and utilized the indeterminate sentence to provide inmates incentives (marks) for good behavior and participation in individualized constructive activities such as academic study and vocational training. Marks earned were rewarded with privileges and moved up eligibility for parole. This **new penology** represented the first formal experiment with indeterminate sentencing, rehabilitation, and parole. Elmira was designed to house first offenders who were between 16 and 30 years of age. Despite good intentions, Elmira became enmeshed in a number of negative developments: overcrowding, a change in the population to more hardened criminals, formation of criminal rings among inmates, abuse (physical assaults) of inmates by inmate trustees as well as corrections staff, and the eventual resignation of Brockway himself. Still, Brockway left a legacy that served as an ideal for the next 100 years. It included the implementation of a classification process, emphasis on the reform of the inmate, individualized rehabilitation pursuits, the earning of privileges, and the use of the indeterminate sentence and discretionary parole. These developments were a marked departure from the regimentation and banality that characterized earlier correctional punishment. We now turn to briefly review the next major stage in correctional development: the Progressive era.

The start of the Progressive era began with Elmira but reached its pinnacle in the 1920s. The American landscape, particularly in urban centers, changed quickly due to increased industrialization. Immigrants arriving from Europe along with African Americans migrating from the South flocked to northern cities in search of employment and a better way of life. With urban centers becoming overpopulated, insufficient housing, less-than-desirable living conditions, and poverty, crime became more pervasive. The state of poor children in urban centers was dire. Children who became involved with crime were placed in custody with adult offenders. Child labor was unregulated, and children were placed in tough working environments that were unsafe and did not recognize the special needs of minors. Social reformers were intent on improving many of these conditions through advocacy.

One of the most important achievements of the Progressive era was the establishment of a separate juvenile justice system. Emerging research and science provided new insights on child development, noting that juveniles should not be punished like adult offenders; that they are recoverable and must be rehabilitated. The state's role would change and become the *protector* of the interests of youth through the policy of *parens patriae* (the state acting as parent or guardian). Reformatories for youth began to appear in the 1800s, but the first juvenile court occurred in 1899 in Cook County, Illinois. The second major establishment during the Progressive era was the expansion of parole. Since indeterminate sentencing was used for juveniles and appropriate adult offenders, parole became popular as the mechanism used for release. Recall that Brockway used parole for Elmira inmates in the late 1890s. But by 1925, 46 states had implemented parole. Parole would be the primary release mechanism for the incarcerated until the 1970s.

The 1960s were a turbulent time in the United States. Significant social change was urged by organized protests. Some of the more significant social movements included the civil rights movement, the anti–Vietnam War movement, the youth counterculture movement, the women's rights movement, and the gay rights movement. The civil rights movement in particular extended into the area of prisoners' rights. With that, attention was given to the problem of persistent crime, recidivism, and the meagerness of support that is offered to the ex-offender in the community. Out of this concern emerged the **community model** of corrections.

The focus of the community model was to put new emphasis on the importance of preparing inmates to successfully navigate the community environment. Prior to this perspective, reform efforts were limited to the individual offender, to fix his or her problem areas. The community model, however, recognized the need to connect reform to the environment in which the offender must live, work, and confront the temptation of crime. Reintegration of the offender into the community was the central aim. This included preparing the offender with practical living skills such as résumé writing, job interviewing skills, opening a bank account and meeting financial responsibility, and so on. But disillusionment with this approach was caused by the entrenchment of poverty for too many crime-ridden communities and the struggle for the ex-offender to have access to opportunities that matter. Conservative voices would shape the next period in corrections, the crime control era.

Just as the 1960s saw a number of social forces that would shape crime policy, so did the 1970s. The community model was well intended, but resources were insufficient to change the persistent criminogenic features of inner-city neighborhoods—home to many ex-offenders. In addition, a critical research study of the impact of correctional programs would further deflate expectations about rehabilitation. Robert Martinson's report, *What Works?* published in 1974, reported the effects of several program initiatives. Many of the effects were small or inconsequential, but some yielded positive outcomes. But the interpretation by policy makers was that *nothing works* and that rehabilitation programs were therefore of little use. During this period liberal voices expressed concern over the use of parole discretion, seeing it as arbitrary, confusing, and unfair to inmates. Conservatives argued that rehabilitation and judicial and parole discretion *coddled* the offender. A consensus formed around determinant sentencing, which diminished uncertainty and made punishment, not rehabilitation, the focus of modern correctional policy. Thus, the crime control era emphasized punishment—tougher sentences, decreased judicial and parole discretion, and reliance on incarceration and the prisons to deal with crime. Even community-based punishments, along with parole, became stringent and more about risk management.

The Nature of Incarceration

Have you ever heard someone say that inmates have it easy in prison? Somehow this perception has existed for decades—maybe longer! But is there some truth to that? Exactly what is it like to be incarcerated in prison? There is much written about the incarceration experience. Much of it describes anything but an easy or pleasant experience. Sociologists James Austin and John Irwin describe the prison environment in the following way:

> *Inmates in state and federal prisons must ... cope with an extremely aggravating and threatening set of conditions, brought on by crowding, racial conflict, new practices stemming from the punitive penological philosophy, and bureaucratic policies. The worst of these features is the potential for prisoner-to-prisoner violence. The other key dimension is idleness and boredom that dominants much of the prison experience today. ... In the high-security units ... violent acts occur on a regular basis.*[14]

The extent to which violence occurs in prison (or jails) depends a great deal on the effectiveness of correctional supervision. Poorly monitored jails could have incidents of violence just as maximum security prisons do. A recent news report[15] describes a $10 million lawsuit recently filed against the Mercer County Jail warden. A female inmate alleges that she was raped by a male officer while she was held in solitary confinement in the Mercer County facility. The lawsuit states that the rape occurred due to the lack of institutional control at the county jail.

It has been reported that "as many as 20%"[16] of inmates are raped or sexually assaulted yearly. According to the Bureau of Justice Statistics, there were 6,660 allegations of sexual victimizations reported in 2011; approximately 10% were substantiated by investigation.[17]

As a result of these disturbing accounts, Congress enacted the Prison Rape Elimination Act in 2003. This law requires that all correctional facilities (including public, private, adult, and juvenile

---

14   Austin & Irwin, 2012, pp. 79, 81.
15   Avilucea (2015).
16   Austin & Irwin, 2012, p. 82.
17   Bureau of Justice Statistics, 2014c.

facilities) develop a protocol for detecting, punishing, and preventing sexual assaults and implementing procedures for documenting and reporting sexual assault data.

Another aspect of the incarceration experience is the presence of prison gangs. Prison gangs have been part of prison life since the era of the Big House. Today there are dozens of prison gangs (also referred to as *security threat groups*) with street chapters as well. Among the most recognizable are the Aryan Brotherhood, Black Guerrilla Family, Mexican Mafia, La Nuestra Familia, and the Texas Syndicate. Most prison gangs are racial or ethnic specific. Each tends to control particular areas of the prison as well as areas of illegal activity both inside and outside the prison. All of this is problematic for unaffiliated and vulnerable inmates who find themselves needing to seek protection from a gang organization. Too often these groups require new members to show allegiance by committing an act of violence or becoming involved in the prison drug trade, contraband, or sex trafficking. Some inmates learn how to sidestep these problems by avoiding potential problem situations.

Although assaults, rapes, and thefts do occur in prisons in the form of inmate-on-inmate violence, perhaps even more difficult is for inmates to live day to day with the knowledge that an attack may occur against them in an instant and at any time. This is a tremendously stressful reality to adjust to.

Prisons are generally designated by four **security levels**: maximum security, medium security, and minimum security. Maximum security prisons have design features and procedures that are the most restrictive of the three. Surveillance towers manned with armed officers, barbed wire atop high formidable walls, roving patrols, and heavy use of cameras for 24-hour observation are typical. The movement of inmates in these prisons is strictly controlled, and day-to-day operations are extremely structured and regulated. Inmates assigned to maximum security prisons are classified as dangerous individuals—dangerous to other inmates and to correctional staff. They must be under the closest observation and control. It is not uncommon for these inmates to be shackled during movements.

Medium security prisons are most common in state correctional systems. They are less imposing structures than the maximum security prison, meaning there are fewer barriers between the inmates and the outside world. Still, medium security prisons will have some of the same features as maximum security prisons, such as roving patrols or watch towers. Inmate movements are not as tightly controlled but will occur with correctional officer escort and under the watchful eye of other guards as well as cameras. Inmates assigned to medium security are not classified as individuals who are a threat to others. They may be assigned to a dormitory setting or cells that are shared. Medium security prisons also have a common recreation area for television viewing and other activities within the housing areas of residents.

Minimum security facilities have the fewest restrictions. There are typically no high walls, towers, or barbed wire surrounding the facility. They are often referred to as honor camps or prison farms. The inmates assigned there do not usually go directly to minimum security but more typically earn their way there because of exemplary adjustment while in a medium security facility. These inmates pose the least risk to others. They are sometimes able to wear their own clothing and overall enjoy a more relaxed atmosphere. One may get the sense that these inmates could easily walk away from such facilities. But with careful selection processes at classification, escapes do not often occur. Inmates work under some supervision but are generally trusted to complete their assigned tasks. Minimum security inmates are expected to go on to prerelease status and prepare for parole by participating in work release or other preparatory programs.

There is a fourth level of security that is reserved for those inmates who are either persistently violent and present a danger in maximum security facilities or are deemed so dangerous that they are immediately housed in a **supermax facility**. Supermax facilities were designed to hold inmates who pose a very serious threat to others. These individuals may be involved in violent gangs or other organized criminal groups, committed domestic or foreign terrorist acts, deemed high escape risks, or viewed as violent individuals capable of killing or causing great bodily harm to others. For example, al-Qaeda-inspired Richard Reid, better known as the Shoe Bomber, and domestic terrorist Terry Nichols, who was involved in the bombing of the Alfred P. Murrah Federal Building in Oklahoma City, are both housed in a federal supermax facility. These prisons provide the most stringently controlled environment, with multiple levels of security and surveillance tools. Inmates housed in these facilities are exposed to very little human contact, due to their isolation.

As mentioned earlier, the United States has 2.2 million people incarcerated. The reality of mass incarceration has placed tremendous strain on all four security levels.

D. Mass Incarceration

The United States has the dubious distinction of having the highest incarceration rate in the world.[18] It has 751 people in prison or jail for every 100,000 in population. Russia, as a modern industrialized nation, is second, with 627 per 100,000. (China has numbers higher than Russia, but mingled in reported numbers are persons in administrative detention who are held for "reeducation."). The Netherlands' rate is 458 per 100,000.[19] The incarceration rate of other modern nations is much lower: England, 151 per 100,000; Germany, 88 per 100,000; and Japan, 63 per 100,000.[20] The United States has less than 5% of the world's population but almost 25% of the world's prisoners.

Various sociopolitical forces and crime policies facilitated the high level of incarceration found in the United States (see Table 7.3). An informative research paper issued by the Sentencing Project identifies factors that have driven incarceration. The most important one is the "get tough on crime"

---

18   Austin & Irwin, 2012.
19   International Centre for Prison Studies, n.d.b.
20   Liptak, 2008.

approaches, which utilize harsher sentencing policies. This punitive approach emerged from a number of developments that became apparent during the 1960s and 1970s, as mentioned earlier. Crime increased rather dramatically in the mid- to late 1960s and into the 1970s (see Table 7.4). Because the 1970s saw a turn away from rehabilitation efforts in corrections, as well as discretionary decision making by criminal justice professionals, policy makers embraced the idea of determinant punishment—lengthy sentences as the means to deal with the problem of crime. The appearance of crack cocaine in the 1980s and the devastating ease of addiction caused a moral panic that stimulated a strong response. Furthermore, crime had become politicized. As a topic, crime was elevated from a local problem to a national concern as interpreted by political candidates vying for national office. Policing strategies were also modified to respond to increased crime. Broken windows policing was introduced in the 1980s. It required police to focus on low-level crimes in an effort to stop the deteriorating neighborhood conditions that invite more serious crime. Additional sentencing models (that is, truth in sentencing, mandatory sentences for drug offenses, three-strikes laws, and so on) caused *more* people to go to jail for *longer* periods of time.

Table 7.3. Table of correctional populations by year in the United States[21]

Year	Correctional population
1910	68,735
1930	120,496
1940	165,585
1950	178,128
1960	226,344
1970	198,831
1980	302,377
1990*	745,000[22]
2000*	1,391,261[23]
2010*	1,605,127[24]

(Source: Bureau of Justice Statistics, December 1986.)

Table 7.4. U.S. crime rates

---

21 Cahalan, 1986.
22 Bureau of Justice Statistics, 1992.
23 Bureau of Justice Statistics, 2010.
24 Bureau of Justice Statistics, 2011.

Year	Total number of reported crimes
1960	3,384,200
1968	6,720,200
1970	8,098,000
1978	11,209,000
1980	13,408,300
1988	13,923,100
1990	14,475,600
1998	12,475,634

(Source: U.S. Crime Rates 1960–2013. Available at: http://www.disastercenter.com/crime/uscrime.htm. Accessed on July 20, 2015.)

The U.S. incarceration rate was created by policies that were intended to do just that: imprison more offenders for longer periods of time. Perhaps many would view this outcome as evidence of an effective crime policy. But there are additional effects that may not be considered so positive. There is significant racial disparity evident in the effort to forge mass incarceration. The typical inmate is a young African American or Hispanic male with little consistent work history and limited education. According to Austin and Irwin as cited in Pratt (2009), the incarceration rate of minority men is "two to six times higher than Whites"[25] (p. 3). Many of the crimes that are punishable by stiff penalties are those that are primarily committed by poor urban dwellers.

The number of women in prison increased by 646% between 1980 and 2010 and of the 2.2 million persons incarcerated in the United States, 205,000 of them are women.[26] Although their numbers are extremely low, women are incarcerated at a faster rate (1.5 times more) than are men. Oklahoma incarcerates more women per capita than any other state, at 130 per 100,000; and Maine reports the lowest rate (21 per 100,000).

The average incarcerated female is a 20- to 30-year-old African American who also has children, a poor education, minimal work experience, a substance abuse background, and a history of being physically and/or sexually abused.[27] Unlike the typical male criminal, women are often involved as accomplices to a boyfriend or husband who is involved in a criminal lifestyle. Their crimes often involve drug offenses, low-level property crime, prostitution, and other public order crimes, as well as domestic violence–related crimes.

A fact less known is that women enter the U.S. correctional system with more health issues than their male counterparts. Poverty alone brings its own set of health risks. These women often suffer from poor nutrition, hypertension, diabetes, and poor dental and gynecological health. Moreover, mental

---

25 Pratt, 2009.
26 Sentencing Project, 2012.
27 Krisberg, Marchionna, & Hartney, 2015.

health problems are more pronounced among incarcerated women. "In 2005, 73% of women in state prisons had mental health problems, compared to 55% of men in state prisons."[28] The challenge for correctional administrators is to provide adequate health care for all inmates but to be particularly aware that incarcerated women are less healthy than nonincarcerated women and have greater and different needs from that of incarcerated men.

E. Questions of Ethics in Corrections

Criminal Justice students who are learning more about institutional corrections and corrections in general, will discover many moral issues that are encountered by corrections personnel. An initial area confronting policymakers and the public is whether it is morally acceptable to spend millions of dollars to incarcerate offenders to the detriment of other public services that rely on tax dollars. For example, it has been reported that up to 75% of imprisonment spending occurs at the state level where dollars are drawn from the general fund—the source for many other public services including health care and education. With prison costs rising dramatically since 1970, what is the effect on the ability of state governments to sufficiently address other public needs? A 2012 report published by California Common Sense announced the following key findings:

- **Corrections' growing slice of the State budget, High Education's shrinking slice.** As California's Department of Correction's share of the State General Fund budget increased steadily through most of the last three decades, higher education's share declined consistently.
- **Corrections inmate population explosion driving higher costs.** Over the last 30 years, the number of people California incarcerates grew more than eight times faster than the general population. Our calculations show that 55% of the increase in the cost of the state prison system between 1980 and 2012 … can be traced to this rapid growth.
- **Annual salary increases for prison guards, stagnant faculty salaries over last decade.** Whereas prison guard salaries are subject to periods of sustained salary increases, faculty salaries have seen only weak growth over the years, falling in real terms over the past decade.[29]

These findings should not come as a surprise, but it is important for the public to be aware of the repercussions for vigorously pursuing mass incarceration. Of course, the experience of California

28 Krisberg, Marchionna, & Hartney, 2015 , p. 293.
29 Anand, 2012.

will be unlike most other states, but perhaps it does serve as the proverbial canary in the coal mine for other states. The greater moral question is whether it is right to not fully fund higher education or public education for the sake of incarcerating thousands.

Another issue involves how accessible prisons are for the family and friends of the incarcerated. We stated earlier that the typical inmate is a Black or Hispanic young man who is from an economically distressed urban community. We also know that strong family ties and connection with one's community are conditions that support reintegration. Yet many prisons are located in hubs that are located far from the social support systems of many inmates. In Florence, Colorado, there is 1 prisoner for every 3 citizens. The county of Fremont, where Florence is located, has 13 prisons,[30] many of which house inmates from states other than Colorado in order to ease overcrowding elsewhere. However, even if inmates are housed in a prison within their own state, they have no control over where they will be sent, which affects the ability for family to visit. If classification committees are able to keep inmates close to the communities where their family reside, would that not be helpful to all parties?

Another example of a moral dilemma involves the use of private prisons. Is it appropriate for the state to contract the supervision, management, and care of convicted persons to private corporations? Private prisons began to appear in the 1980s but caught steam in the 1990s after the Clinton administration restricted the federal workforce budget. It was the Justice Department and the Federal Bureau of Prisons that initially contracted private prisons for detaining illegal immigrants[31] and other categories of prisoners.

Private prisons are provided funds for each prisoner they house. It is clear that it is in the best interest of these facilities to maintain a high number of prisoners. If the administrators of these prisons have a say over how well or how poorly an inmate is adjusting, it is possible that their motivation could include *delaying* release by easily writing up charges. According to Global Research, Corrections Corporation of America (CCA) inmates housed in New Mexico lost "good behavior time" at a rate 8 times higher than those in conventional state prisons. Private prisons benefit from overcrowded state prisons that seek relief by contracting their services. Thus, there is a business interest in mass incarceration. Just as any group seeks to influence policy, private corporations utilize lobbyists to influence legislators. A recent report stated:

> *The three main companies have contributed $835,514 to federal candidates and over $6 million to state politicians. They have also spent hundreds of thousands of dollars on direct lobbying efforts. CCA has spent over $900,000*

---

30   Hallinan, 2003.
31   Global Research, 2014.

on federal lobbying and GEO spent anywhere from $120,000 to $199,992 in Florida alone during a short three-month span this year.[32]

The final example of a moral issue that we will offer concerns the use of supermax prisons. There is no doubt that secure facilities are needed to keep dangerous individuals away from anyone that they could possible hurt. But is segregation along with isolation the only means to gain safety? As far back as the 1990s, 34 states operated supermax prisons.[33]

As mentioned earlier, inmates held in supermax facilities are in almost total isolation. What are the psychological effects from this condition? We know from history, specifically the Pennsylvania model, that isolation produced destabilization of some offenders. Should we expect any different outcome today? Not enough research has been done in this area. The supermax facility is a black box of sorts in which too little, if anything, is fully understood regarding the impact of this experience. Is this morally right, despite the nature of the inmates subjected to this environment?

F. Conclusion

Institutional corrections has and will continue to be instrumental to the criminal justice system. As long as individuals commit crime and pose too high a risk to serve their sentences in the community, there will be a need for institutional corrections. We have more than 200 years of recorded observations of institutional corrections in the United States. Much has been learned, but clearly there is a long way to go. Some pivotal questions that must be answered include: What should be the primary purpose of corrections? How do we best go about achieving and maintaining it? How do we stay clear of political distractions and pressures and maintain a commitment to the purpose of corrections? Finally, how do correctional agents see the nobility and value in their tasks, maintain their humanity, and remain the utmost professionals in their work? You are students today, but you are also future leaders in criminal justice and corrections. How will you improve corrections in the United States?

---

32   Sanchez, 2011.
33   Kurki & Morris, 2001.

DISCUSSION QUESTIONS

1. We have seen our correctional system focus on rehabilitation and then on punishment. Which do you think is most effect in responding to crime? Why?
2. Female criminality differs in nature from male criminality. Should men and women therefore be punished differently as a result?
3. How can the correctional system mitigate racial disparities in jails and prisons?

REFERENCES

American Jail Association. (n.d.) Statistics of note. Retrieved from https://members.aja.org/About/StatisticsOfNote.aspx

Anand, P. (2012). Winners and losers: Corrections and higher education in California. California Common Sense. Retrieved from http://cacs.org/research/winners-and-losers-corrections-and-higher-education-in-california

Austin, J., & Irwin, J. (2012). *It's about time: America's imprisonment binge* (4th ed.). Belmont, CA: Wadsworth.

Avilucea, I. (2015, March 30). Mercer inmate suing county claims sexual assault routinely ignored. *Trentonian*. Retrieved from http://www.trentonian.com/general-news/20150330/mercer-inmate-suing-county-claims-sexual-assault-routinely-ignored

Bureau of Justice Statistics. (1992). Correctional populations in the U.S., 1990. Retrieved from http://www.bjs.gov/content/pub/pdf/cpus90.pdf

Bureau of Justice Statistics. (2010). Correctional populations in the U.S., 2009. Retrieved from http://bjs.gov/content/pub/pdf/cpus09.pdf

Bureau of Justice Statistics. (2011). Correctional populations in the U.S., 2010. Retrieved from http://www.bjs.gov/content/pub/pdf/cpus10.pdf

Bureau of Justice Statistics. (2014a). Correctional populations in the United States, 2013. Retrieved from http://www.bjs.gov/content/pub/pdf/cpus13.pdf

Bureau of Justice Statistics. (2014b). Prisoners in 2013. Retrieved from http://www.bjs.gov/content/pub/pdf/p13.pdf

Bureau of Justice Statistics. (2014c). Survey of sexual violence in adult correctional facilities, 2009–11 -statistical tables. Retrieved from http://www.bjs.gov/content/pub/pdf/ssvacf0911st.pdf

Cahalan, M. W. (1986). Historical corrections statistics in the United States, 1850–1987. NCJ-102529, Bureau of Justice Statistics. Retrieved from http://www.bjs.gov/content/pub/pdf/hcsus5084.pdf

Ford, M. (2015, June 8). America's largest mental hospital is a jail. *Atlantic*. Retrieved from http://www.theatlantic.com/politics/archive/2015/06/americas-largest-mental-hospital-is-a-jail/395012

Global Research. (2014). The prison industry in the United States: Big business or a new form of slavery? Retrieved from http://www.globalresearch.ca/the-prison-industry-in-the-united-states-big-business-or-a-new-form-of-slavery/8289

Hallinan, J. T. (2003). *Going up the river*. New York: Random House.

International Centre for Prison Studies. (n.d.a). Highest to lowest prison population total. Retrieved from http://www.prisonstudies.org/highest-to-lowest/prison-population-total?field_region_taxonomy_tid=All&=Apply

International Centre for Prison Studies (n.d.b). *World prison population list* (10th ed.). Retrieved from http://www.prisonstudies.org/sites/default/files/resources/downloads/wppl_10.pdf

Johnson, R. (2002). *Hard time.* Belmont, CA: Wadsworth/Thomson Learning.

Krisberg, B., Marchionna, S., & Hartney, C. (2015). *American corrections: Concepts and controversies* Thousand Oaks, CA: Sage.

Kurki, L., & Morris, N. (2001). The purposes, practices and problems of supermax prisons. *Crime and Justice, 28* 385–424.

Liptak, A. (2008, April 23). U.S. prison population dwarfs that of other nations. *New York Times.* Retrieved from http://www.nytimes.com/2008/04/23/world/americas/23iht-23prison.12253738.html?pagewanted=all&_r=0

List of U.S. State Prisons. (2010). Retrieved from https://en.wikipedia.org/wiki/List_of_United_States_state_prisons

Mancini, M. J. (1996). *One dies, get another: Convict leasing in the American South, 1866–1928.* Columbia: University of South Carolina Press.

McShane, M. D. (1996). Chain gangs. In M. D. McShane & F. P. Williams (Eds.), *Encyclopedia of American prisons* (pp. 117–144). London: Taylor & Francis.

Moser, W. (2013, April 1. Cook County Jail is America's biggest. *Chicago Magazine* Retrieved from http://www.chicagomag.com/Chicago-Magazine/The-312/April-2013/Cook-County-Jail-Americas-Biggest-Jail-By-the-Numbers

Olson, D. E. (2013). An examination of admissions, discharges and the population of the Cook County Jail, 2012. Retrieved from http://works.bepress.com/cgi/viewcontent.cgi?article=1016&context=david_e_olson

Pratt, T. C. (2009). *Addicted to incarceration.* Thousand Oaks, CA: Sage.

Sanchez, A. (2011, June 23). Private prisons spend millions on lobbying to put more people in jail. *ThinkProgress.* Retrieved from http://thinkprogress.org/justice/2011/06/23/251363/cca-geogroup-prison-industry

Schlosser, E. (1998, December). The prison-industrial complex. *Atlantic.* Retrieved from http://www.theatlantic.com/magazine/archive/1998/12/the-prison-industrial-complex/304669

Sentencing Project (2012). Incarcerated women. Retrieved from http://www.sentencingproject.org/doc/publications/cc_incarcerated_women_factsheet_sep24sp.pdf

United States Crime Rates 1960–2013. (n.d.). Disaster Center. Retrieved from http://www.disaster-center.com/crime/uscrime.htm

US Department of Justice (2014). Correctional Populations in the United States, 2013. Bureau of Justice Statistics. Retrieved from http://www.bjs.gov/content/pub/pdf/cpus13.pdf

Vyas, A. G. (1991). Book Review: Logan, C. H. (1990). *Private prisons: Cons and pros.* New York: Oxford University Press. *Social Forces, 70,* 1. Pg. 292.

08

Offender Reentry as a Moral Choice

Trevor Fronius, Anthony Petrosino & Sarah Guckenburg, Justice & Prevention Research Center, Learning Innovations Program, and WestEd

CHAPTER OUTLINE

KEY TERMS

- COMMUNITY CORRECTIONS
- PAROLE
- RECIDIVISM
- REENTRY
- REINTEGRATION
- RELEASE
- SUPERVISION

ACKNOWLEDGMENTS

The authors thank the editor, Carolyn Petrosino, and WestEd colleagues Claire Morgan, Jonathan Nakamoto, and Staci Wendt for their comments on the chapter.

A. Background

The United States incarcerates more persons than any other developed nation in the world.[1] The use of incarceration has four primary goals: to punish offenders for the harm they have caused; to incapacitate them from any further crime to the public by locking them up; to rehabilitate or treat them so they will no longer offend; and to deter them from future crime by punishment.

---

1 Although 9 million offenders cycle through jails each year, our focus in this chapter is on reentry of offenders from state or federal prison systems.

The evidence for achieving the latter two goals is admittedly weak. Indeed, research shows that 66% of all individuals will recidivate within 5 years after their **release** from prison (Kyckelhahn, 2012). By **recidivism** in this context, we mean that a released prisoner either commits a new offense (arrested or convicted for a new offense) or violates release or **parole** conditions. It is important to understand the reasons a released inmate may recidivate and the institutional structures that may facilitate the issue. For example, some of this recidivism is due to the released offender violating the conditions set for his or her parole (for example, not complying with a condition to attend treatment). Others may be arrested because of their proximity to other crime scenes or criminal actors upon release (Zara & Farrington, 2015). This is often due to the lack of supports that might otherwise lead one away from a criminogenic setting or lifestyle rather than drawing a person toward crime. Whether new crimes or parole violations, recidivism results in harm to society, with a new set of citizens being victimized by recidivists along with the costs of further criminal justice system involvement by the same individuals. Often overlooked is that recidivism places the offender in danger of ending up in prison again for a longer stretch, at great cost to both the individual offender and his or her family and the larger community in which the offender resides. Clear (1994), for one, has called the impact of incarcerating large numbers of African American men for nonviolent or drug offenses on the communities they come from as an example of "penal harm."

Further compounding the issue is the sheer number of prison releases. Except for those serving life sentences (or those who die in prison via execution, murder, or natural causes), a vast majority of prisoners will return to free society at some point, usually within 5 years (Travis, 2005). Figure 8.1 shows the annual number of prison admissions and prison releases from 1978–2012. Both were on an exponential climb until 2007 or so, when the numbers began to decrease. However, the number of releases in 2012 was more than 600,000. Reform due to dated federal sentencing guidelines and similar state-held laws (for example, California's three-strikes law, which enhances prison terms for a 3rd felony conviction) will continue to drive additional early releases and more appropriate sentences (that is, less lengthy). In addition to policy reform, the financial toll that mass incarceration is having on state budgets is forcing some jurisdictions to consider early release of nonviolent offenders if only to reduce costs and free up prison space. Proposition 47 in California is an example of one state action, supported by voters, that has mandated early release for thousands of state prisoners.

Figure 8.1. Sentenced state and federal prison admissions and releases and year-end sentenced prison population, 1978–2012

Bureau of Justice Statistics / Copyright in the Public Domain.

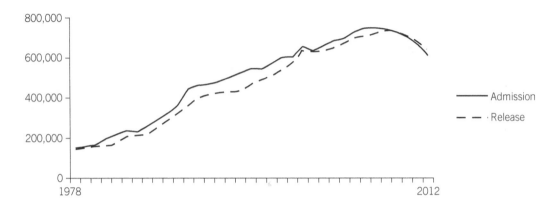

This mass migration of incarcerated individual back into the general public underscores the importance of offender **reentry**, or the **reintegration** of offenders from a period of incarceration into free society. From any moral perspective, it appears to be the right action for the United States and any other civilized country to have a solid plan for effective reentry. It would result in reduced harm to society, fewer victims, and offenders who can lead productive lives and contribute to their families and communities. Moreover, successful reentry comes at considerable cost savings to the public. The cost of parole is only about 10% of the cost of prison (Schmitt, Warner, & Gupta, 2010), and successful parole may result in even greater savings. This moral view, based on the utilitarian philosophy of the greatest good for the greatest number of people, was recently echoed by U.S. Attorney General Eric Holder, when he said: "Reentry provides a major opportunity to reduce recidivism, save taxpayer dollars, and make our communities safer." Backed by a groundswell from the populus, who have come to see reentry as a good and moral action that makes sense financially, the federal government (under both the Bush and Obama administrations) have funded several initiatives to support it. Although the term *offender reentry* is a relatively new phrase, the actual justice system work to help reintegrate offenders back into free society has been in play for many decades.

Research reviews of evidence on the effects of offender reentry indicate that some strategies are positive and reduce criminal recidivism. For example, Seiter and Kadela (2003) located 32 studies of reentry programs and concluded that a wide range of strategies reduced recidivism, including work release, vocational, and drug treatment programs. On the other hand, Visher, Winterfield, and Coggeshall (2006) located eight rigorous studies of employment training programs for ex-offenders and found little consistent evidence of a positive impact on subsequent recidivism. MacKenzie's (2008) review also did not report positive impact for employment training programs but emphasized the role of cognitive behavioral programs in restructuring offender thinking as a very effective reentry strategy. In general, the totality of the evidence, and the fact that 95% of all offenders will be released, does support the overall position that investing in offender reentry is necessary. And these reviews indicate that there are some strategies that have been documented to be successful in reducing recidivism to the benefit of the individual, family, and community, further supporting investment in reentry as a moral choice.

B. Offender Reentry Policies and Practices

Reentry policies and programs are very broad. Reentry programs are not just administered upon release from prison. In fact, some can begin while offenders are in prison, to prepare them for adjustment to the outside world ("prerelease programming"). Also, postrelease reentry programs can be short term or long term. For example, there are sex offender reentry programs that require extended periods to accommodate long-term monitoring and services. This section summarizes the policies and practices under the broad umbrella of offender reentry.

Prerelease Programming

Many prisoners are provided an opportunity, particularly near the latter part of their prison term, to participate in programs to foster useful skills to prepare them for return to general society. It is possible that an offender lacks the necessary behavioral, emotional, or social skills to reintegrate successfully into his or her community. Further, independent housing, medical care, and employment introduce additional skills necessary to navigate these complex institutional and social structures. A prerelease program is meant to serve as a bridge toward a postrelease plan that might include some type of community **supervision** (for example, parole); treatment services, including substance abuse and mental health; and other supports such as temporary housing or employment services. These services may be made available to all prisoners entering a release stage, whether or not they will be on some type of postrelease supervision or parole. Some prisons offer "life skills" courses to help offenders close to their release date understand how to look for a job, find housing, create a budget, and so on. Recent changes to the health care law requiring all individuals to obtain health insurance introduces a new set of challenges for prelease planning in prison. For example, California's Safety Realignment Act of 2011 shifted many lower level offenders from state prison to county institutions, which requires coordinated planning to transition health care from correctional staff to a care provider in the community. It also requires correctional personnel to provide assistance for offenders in obtaining insurance or Medicaid prior to release. Although not formally part of "prelease programming," some states provide cash to prisoners upon release. However, these funds are often meager at best. In some states, prisoners may only get a few changes of clothes and a token amount of money for transportation on the day of their release to the community.

Parole and Release

Prisoners usually reenter society through three mechanisms: unconditional release, parole supervision, and mandatory supervision. Unconditional release is when prisoners reenter society without any supervision because they have served 100% of their sentence behind bars (Alarid, Cromwell, & del Carmen, 2008). About 20% of all prisoners reenter society this way (Alarid, Cromwell, & del Carmen, 2008). A very small number of inmates receive commutations, in which a president or governor issues an executive order to reduce the sentence. For example, in July 2015 President Obama issued an executive order commuting the sentences of 46 drug offenders who had received harsh punishment under federal sentencing guidelines (Liptak, 2015).

Most offenders (80%) who are released receive some type of supervision (Alarid, Cromwell, & del Carmen, 2008). In states that have a parole policy, offenders who are parole eligible have their cases reviewed by a governing body known as the parole board. This board is charged with the responsibility of assessing the probability that an offender will recidivate if he or she is released into the community. In some states a parole "hearing officer" may do the first investigation into the offender's suitability for parole and present a report to the parole board. The parole board also sets the conditions of parole that the offender must meet. The parole board makes its rulings based on information on the offender's criminal history, current crime, and record of performance while in the prison setting. The parole board must also take into consideration the probability of the offender recidivating or becoming a law-abiding citizen following release. In some sense, parole decisions are "predictions" about the potential for offender failure or success on the outside.

A modern justice innovation that has changed the "prediction" process is the validated risk assessment tool. These tools provide an empirically driven prediction (rather than one based on a more qualitative review of case files and the offender's response in the parole hearing) based on the given offender's risk and protective factors. The issue of risk and prediction is a significant moral one throughout the justice system and is discussed later.

Once the terms of parole are established and the offender is paroled, the offender is assigned to a parole agent for supervision. The parole agent (or parole officer) monitors the offender during his or her parole period to ensure the offender is meeting the conditions set by the parole board. The methods used for monitoring the offender could involve things such as drop-in visits to the offender's home and periodic scheduled meetings in the parole agent's office. When offenders do not meet the conditions set by the parole board, the parole agent has discretion to revoke the offender's parole, resulting in the offender being returned to serve the remainder of the sentence. Parole agents have to balance their responsibility to the community to prevent criminal activity with their responsibility to offenders to assist them in their reentry to society (APPA, 2015).

Some states have replaced discretionary parole with mandatory supervision, also known as "supervised release" or "postrelease supervision." Prisoners receive automatic supervision in the community at the expiration of their prison sentence. It is not decided by any governing body such as a parole board but is mandated by the legislature (Alarid et al., 2008). The number of prisoners being released to parole supervision has been shrinking due to the increase in determinate sentencing and mandatory release policies across the United States (Cole & Smith, 1996).

Not all offenders released to supervision require the same level of contact with parole agents or other supervision officers. For every sample of supervised offenders, there will be certain types of offenders who will have a greater likelihood of success (for example, nonviolent offenders, women, and those with few priors) with no or little supervision (Solomon et al., 2005). There will also be some offenders who require more frequent contact and surveillance to ensure their transition to the community. Many states have adopted *intensive supervision programs* for parole or post release supervision (in states that have mandatory supervision) to ensure that those offenders believed to be at higher risk for recidivism receive more contact with their supervising officer. The caseloads for officers assigned to intensive supervision are usually smaller to facilitate the more intensive strategies they may use (more frequent face-to-face meetings, more frequent urinalysis and drug testing, unannounced site visits to the offender's home or work place, and so on).

Other Types of Reentry Programs and Policies

Halfway Houses

A halfway house is a residence located in the community in which prisoners are placed, for the most part, to serve a period of time after being released from prison to prepare them for full reentry to the community. They have also been called "community corrections centers." Offenders who are placed in a halfway house are given much more freedom than while they were incarcerated. However, there are usually rules in *community corrections* settings such as curfews that ex-prisoners may have to abide by. Most halfway houses will offer job training and drug treatment services to help offenders with the reentry process. Some may require the offender to hold a job or go to school during the day but be back at the halfway house by a certain time each night.

Furlough

Inmates who are furloughed are released to the community for a specified time period (24 to 48 hours, for example) to accomplish certain things. This may include attending a funeral, spending time with a spouse (sometimes referred to as a conjugal visit), or looking for housing or employment when released (Bohm & Haley, 2008). Prison rules governing furlough usually reserve the opportunities for those who have demonstrated they are appropriate candidates to be released to the community. Providing a furlough to a prisoner is viewed as a reward for good behavior and as a method for helping the offender reintegrate back into the community once released.

However, furlough also requires a "prediction" of risk. Some inmates predicted to be low risk and eligible for furlough may still commit an offense. For example, during the 1988 presidential election, then vice president George H. W. Bush (the Republican Party candidate) heavily criticized Massachusetts governor Michael Dukakis (the Democratic Party candidate) for allowing a convicted murderer, Willie Horton, furlough from prison. Horton committed violent crimes against an elderly White couple while on his 10th furlough (Bohm & Haley, 2008). The charges made by Bush were criticized by many as playing on racism among Whites concerned with being victimized by Black males (Anderson & Enberg, 1995). While quite rare, this event, and others like it, highlights the issue of prediction and risk in nearly every area of reentry decision-making.

Work and Study Release

Another way that prisoners can leave the institution temporarily is for work or education. These release opportunities help inmates establish ties to work or educational establishments, preparing them for reentry into society (Bohm & Haley, 2008). Work release is more common and popular, since inmates generate income and also an employment history. In most work release programs, prisoners work a specified time period during the day and then return in the evening. Study release is less common, since inmates may have to pay for their own education, and study courses are sometimes offered within the prison itself. Again, inmates in study release are allowed to leave to attend classes and then return when the classes are over for the day. These temporary release opportunities also provide incentives for good behavior and provide a way for the prison authorities to test the "readiness" of a prisoner for eventual release (Bohm & Haley, 2008).

Therapeutic Communities

The rates of substance and alcohol abuse among offenders are very high compared to those who are not incarcerated. Prisons are challenged to provide treatment to substance-abusing offenders as well as prevent the introduction of drug-related contraband during the time of imprisonment. Reentry programs face even more challenges, given that offenders are now free in the community to engage in the same behaviors as they did prior to incarceration. There are many substance- and alcohol-treatment approaches used in reentry. One approach, known as *therapeutic communities*, is often used during pre- and postrelease to address the underlying abuse that led to crime and conviction (for example, addressing alcohol abuse among DWI offenders). Therapeutic communities are intensive service programs that provide substance-free clean living environment along with group therapy, and other health and education services, to address negative and improve lifestyle choices during transition into the community (NCBI, 1999).

C. Recent Innovations in Reentry

Although many reentry programs and policies have been in place for a long time, the growing importance of offender reentry has led to the development of innovative programming. Through the Second Chance Act, the federal government provides funding to states to support innovative programming to document and evaluate some of these new approaches. The Second Chance Act, established in 2008, provides funds for demonstration grants across a range of reentry topics that include reentry courts, mental health programming, co-occurring treatment, and capacity building for evidence-based programming such as employment and housing programs.

Reentry Courts

These courts were established to better coordinate offender's postrelease needs. Such courts often begin working with offenders prior to release from prison. The court establishes a structured appointment schedule with the ex-prisoners, and staff members at the court coordinate services such as job training, housing, drug abuse treatment, and transportation (Alarid et al., 2008). Reentry courts often use graduated incentives and sanctions to reward positive behavior and punish negative acts (Alarid et al., 2008).

Housing Programs For Ex-Prisoners

One challenge for ex-prisoners is finding suitable housing. During incarceration, particularly during longer terms, prisoners may lose connections to family and friends, thereby reducing the places they might be able to stay after getting out of prison. Chronic homelessness among ex-prisoners presents considerable hardship to the individual and an imposing barrier to successful reintegration into society.

Some programs have been developed that provide subsidized housing for ex-offenders, coupling that with support services and even job retraining or employment to assist them in making the reentry transition.

Mental Health Programming

Individuals in prison have higher rates of mental illness compared to those who are not system involved. Prisons and reentry programs have a moral and in many instances legal obligation to provide services that provide mental health treatment and support. Not providing comprehensive services puts the individual and community at risk for detrimental repercussions, since untreated and unmediated release prisoners are at heightened risk to recidivate in the community. Although rigorous evidence is still limited, programs that provide comprehensive continuum or care, or curricula-based programming that focuses on cognitive and mental well-being, have demonstrated significant reductions in recidivism among participants (Council of State Governments, 2015).

Interagency Comprehensive Supports Upon Release

The most critical period for reentry are the immediate post release period in which many ex-offenders are reintroduced to same criminogenic influences as prior to incarceration. The concern is escalated for violent and repeat offenders. Interagency comprehensive supports target these individuals and provide individualized supports and services to ensure successful integration over the days and weeks following release. The Boston Reentry Initiative is one such program; a quasi-experiment indicated that the program reduced recidivism by participants, compared to similar offenders not offered the programming (Braga, Piehl, & Hureau, 2009).

D. The Moral Choice in Practice

The sections above describe pre- and post release reentry policies and programming. The underpinnings of all reentry interventions are to establish a prediction of risk, provide supervision and surveillance to prevent recidivism, and protect individuals and the community. These underpinnings also, however, carry certain moral choices and goals that require consideration in practice.

Risk and Prediction

The justice system has many decision points. For example, police have wide discretion on whether to stop a vehicle or make an arrest. Prosecutors have wide discretion on whether to charge an individual with an offense. At the reentry stage, at least in states using discretionary parole, there is also some latitude among parole boards to determine to let offenders out of prison or keep them locked up.

The decision of whether to parole a prisoner or not brings to the forefront moral dilemmas for criminal justice actors such as parole board members. Parole boards have to determine whether the offender has been rehabilitated to the point that he or she no longer poses a threat to public safety. Since there is no completely foolproof, fail-safe method that will keep an offender from committing a new crime on the outside, parole boards have to weigh risk to the community with other aims they are trying to achieve. These other aims include providing a "release valve" for the overcrowding of the prison system, furthering the offender's rehabilitation, reuniting the offender with his or her family, and so on.

Political pressures may also influence this decision, as in cases in which the prisoner has committed a violent or notorious crime and paroling the person would incur citizen and media scrutiny. A classic example of this moral dilemma occurred in New Jersey. Thomas Trantino murdered two police officers in Lodi, New Jersey, in 1963. He received the death penalty, but when capital punishment was abolished in the 1970s, his sentence was commuted to life in prison. Trantino became a model prisoner and became eligible for parole in 1979. His parole, however, was continuously turned down because law enforcement and the public were outraged he was being considered. Trantino was finally released on parole in 2004.

The decision to parole an offender has been improved with the use of risk assessment instruments discussed earlier. Such instruments, using data collected from the offender's case file, produce scores that indicate level of risk of recidivism. None of these instruments are fail-safe: They all make errors in that some offenders predicted to do well in reintegration will commit a new crime (also known as the "false positive"). Conversely, some offenders predicted to be at high risk for recidivism who are denied parole may have done quite well on the outside (also known as the "false negative"). Advancements in risk assessment instruments have provided evidence of stability in the assessment process, limiting risk and helping decision makers arrive at a more accurate prediction. Successful approaches such as the risk-need-responsivity model, founded in Washington, use rigorous risk assessment to establish comprehensive needs that are then addressed through flexible and responsive programming. Research demonstrates that risk instruments such as these outperform "clinical judgment" alone; that is, the parole board making the decision without any empirically driven structure to guide it (Hoffman, 1996). However, using a risk instrument in conjunction with clinical judgement is recommended to produce the best possible prediction of community risk and offender rehabilitation.

Failing to use risk assessment or to use it properly endangers public safety by allowing prisoners at high risk for reoffending to be released before they should or not receive adequate supervision and treatment when released. But the flip side is harmful, as well. Prisoners who are very low risk for reoffending are subjected to unnecessary levels of supervision or treatment. This puts a drain on scarce resources, taking away funds from other public safety concerns.

Supervision and Surveillance

Closely related to the risk and prediction issue is the moral dilemma that supervision agents may face when working with ex-prisoners. Agents must balance community safety with the successful reintegration of the ex-prisoner. Agents are given power to recommend revocation of parole if in their judgment the ex-prisoner is violating the conditions of his or her parole. Such revocation returns the ex-prisoner back to prison to serve out the remainder of the sentence.

The goal of supervision is to monitor the offender to reduce recidivism risk and to help support the ex-prisoner in their reentry. However, with supervision comes greater surveillance of the offender's actions and whereabouts. In cases in which ex-prisoners have committed new serious offenses, there is little choice for the agent but to make an arrest or involve the police. But there are a host of things that a person may do while under scrutiny and parole supervision that are not criminal but do involve violations of parole conditions. Some of these may not be very serious. Should the agent recommend revocation, for example, if the ex-prisoner was not supposed to consume alcohol but had a beer at a local pub? Some have advocated for zero tolerance in monitoring supervised offenders, whether on probation or parole, so that when they violate conditions—no matter how seemingly trivial they are—they should be revoked (Grattet, Petersilia, & Lin, 2008).

A return to prison, however, puts any opportunity for the ex-prisoner to successfully reintegrate into society at risk. The agent may give the ex-prisoner a "break" and not recommend revocation or include it in any report. Because of this discretion on the part of supervision agents, some offenders may receive breaks and others may not. This can create moral problem such as unfairness, particularly if the group that does not get the break is of a certain racial or ethnic class.

Government Financial Support for The Moral Choice

Although the United States has long embraced offender reentry as a moral action, a question can be asked about how much the government supports this moral choice in practice. Offenders released from prison into the community are still faced with the same plethora of factors that led them to be incarcerated in the first place. For example, they face challenges such as substance abuse and mental health problems, unemployment or underemployment in menial labor, homelessness, lack of family support, and rejection by the community. All of these challenges and others are compounded by the individual being locked up in a prison system for a number of years. The institutionalization effect might include everything from being "hardened" by the prison experience to learning the "crime trade" from more experienced career criminals. Given these challenges and hurdles for the ex-prisoner, investing enough into reentry so that it could make a difference is another moral choice. It is one that is countered, of course, by many competing aims and priorities that government budgets must balance. We argue that there is a moral choice to support reentry efforts. However, complicating this is that it will require a significant investment to do it in a way that maximizes the released offender's potential and reduces the risk of harm to the public.

The federal government has enacted several initiatives in support of reentry during the past two presidential administrations (Bush and Obama). For example, in 2001 and 2004, the Bush administration allocated more than $400 million to support the reentry of criminal offenders, including funding for housing, job placement, mentoring services, and some faith-based initiatives (Wilkinson & Rhine, 2005). However, this funding, although substantial on its face, comes to about $50 per released offender (Wilkinson & Rhine, 2005). In another example described above, the Second Chance Act of 2008 was enacted by Congress and implemented by the U.S. Department of Justice to provide funding to state government entities to initiate programs and policies that would help reintegrate offenders back into society.

On the flip side, however, of the billions of dollars ($8.5 requested in 2015) allocated to the Federal Bureau of Prisons and Detention at the federal level, only about 7% of that budget was allocated to reentry programs to ensure the successful assimilation of offenders back to society after release (U.S. Department of Justice, 2015). Although there is no way to know what the "right amount" is, it would be hard to imagine that this investment in reentry would provide enough services to individual offenders to help them overcome the challenges discussed earlier.

Incarceration, Prison Terms, and Reentry

The explosion in the prison population in the United States may have influenced reentry aims in at least two ways. First, the rapid expansion of prison populations may be related to the decreased treatment and service provision to inmates in prison to help them work toward reintegration. For example, only 35% of inmates participated in education prior to prison release. This was down from 43% in 1991. Only 12% of inmates reported being involved in any prelease planning at all (Travis & Petersilia, 2001).

A second way that prison population expansion may have potentially impacted reentry is that state corrections authorities are under pressure to reduce those populations. Some of this pressure is financial, since state correctional budgets have increased significantly with the rise in prison populations. Some of the pressure is legal, since some correctional facilities are undergoing overcrowding, jeopardizing the health of offenders and correctional staff, and are under court order to reduce their prison populations.

In addition, offenders are being sent to prison for longer terms. The average sentence has increased in the United States due to mandatory determinate sentencing, including "truth in sentencing" laws that require some categories of offenders to spend at least 85% of their prison term incarcerated. However, this lengthening of the prison term means that offenders are spending a longer time institutionalized, with greater time away from their families and communities, which further undercuts reentry efforts (Travis & Petersilia, 2001). There are some communities, largely urban, that suffer from large rates of disconnected single-parent homes, which leads to a generational cycle of crime. Recent efforts through President Obama's My Brother's Keeper initiative are intended to address this intergenerational impact.

The prison experience presents several challenges for successful reentry. These challenges include prisonization and institutionalization (Gaines & Miller, 2007). Prisonization refers to the inmate adopting the subcultural norms of the prisoner subculture. The prison subculture emphasizes toughness, with admiration for violence and any kindness viewed as a weakness. Institutionalization involves the process by which prisoners become used to having every decision controlled by prison authorities (when to eat, when to sleep, and so on) in a strictly insulated environment.

Both prisonization and institutionalization are further exacerbated by the longer prison sentences being meted out on offenders. To successfully integrate into society, released prisoners must now change their mind-set in surviving the prison subculture to norms that law-abiding members of society hold. In addition, they must now make the move from a strictly controlled environment to one in which they have freedom to make their own day-to-day decisions.

Legal and Governmental Barriers to Successful Reentry

Sometimes the morally correct choice—in this case, offender reentry—can be undercut by other government priorities or aims. A classic example of this is the wide range of disenfranchisement—removal of voting privileges—that occurs following a felony conviction. Thus, although the United States has made a moral choice to support reentry efforts, it also pursues or allows a contradictory aim to provide a number of civil disabilities on ex-offenders, such as disenfranchisement. These policies present significant hurdles to any offender attempting to reintegrate back into society as a contributing member.

These barriers have been legislatively enacted to further restrict ex-prisoners. For example, a variety of laws has been enacted to further deprive ex-prisoners of their civil freedoms. In almost all states, felony offenders lose their right to vote (14 make this a permanent loss following a felony conviction). In some states, offenders cannot hold office or participate in jury duty.

There are many other penalties placed on an ex-offender as well, such as having to declare the felony record on every subsequent job application. In addition, certain jobs may not allow the hiring of an employee with a criminal record (for example, some states outlaw ex-prisoners from working in establishments that serve alcohol). Parole conditions may restrict areas where the ex-prisoner can live, sometimes keeping the offender in communities in which jobs are scarce and unemployment rates are high (Cole & Smith, 1996). Some unions may have eligibility criteria for membership that preclude ex-offenders, which further removes employment opportunities.

These additional "taxes" that ex-offenders pay are contrary to ideals about fairness. Such ideals would hold that once offenders have been incarcerated, they have paid their debt to society and punishment should end. These penalties ensure that the punishment continues to be paid—in most cases, until the offender's death.

These civil disabilities and additional punishments are complicated by labeling. Because ex-prisoners are now labeled as "criminals" or "felons," they are treated differently in the community (Farrington & Murray, 2012). They may come under more scrutiny from ordinary citizens, who may report their actions as suspicious to police or supervision authorities. Potential employers, even if they are allowed to hire ex-prisoners, may also shy away from engaging with the offender out of fear of being victimized or exposing other employees to criminal behavior.

The Duty to Evaluate

Although providing reentry opportunities to offenders is arguably a moral choice, there is a duty to evaluate such policies and programs to ensure that they work as designed, that they do not provide additional risk to the public, and that they do, in fact, assist prisoners in making a successful transition to the community. It is morally wrong to spend taxpayer money on failed programs and policies, particularly if there are more effective offender reentry strategies available. Even a cursory glance at the literature on reentry indicates that of the hundreds, if not thousands, of programs around the nation that would be defined as assisting offenders with reintegration into society, comparatively few evaluations meeting minimum quality standards are completed.

In most cases the will to conduct program evaluation is thwarted by a number of barriers. Programs are often underfunded, and state and county governmental agencies, or nonprofits running specific reentry programs, may not have the money to collect good quality data, let alone support a program evaluation. There is often fear of evaluation and what it might mean to the program if the evaluation reported negative findings. Would the program be terminated? Would those who supported its implementation suffer any fallout from that decision? Campbell (1969) argued that administrators should be rewarded for undertaking evaluation, particularly rigorous studies, of their programs and policies, but finding a progressive government culture in which this is practiced is a protracted and painful process.

There is also some debate over how one should judge the success of a reentry program. Although the main outcome of interest in recidivism, there is some argument to develop broader measures that would expand beyond "not getting arrested or revoked" to whether offenders remained sober, participated actively in treatment programs, and were more involved in family and community life (Gaines & Miller, 2007).

DISCUSSION QUESTIONS

1. As a parole agent, is your moral obligation to the offender, the community, or both?
2. If you controlled the federal funding for prisons and reentry, what would be your investment strategy to reduce recidivism?
3. How should social institutions address the detrimental community impact brought on by decades of mass incarceration?

REFERENCES

Alarid, L. F., Cromwell, P., & del Carmen, R. V. (2008). *Community-based corrections* (7th ed.). Belmont, CA: Wadsworth-Cengage.

American Probation and Parole Association. (2015). *Code of Ethics.* Retrieved from: https://www.appa-net.org/eweb/DynamicPage.aspx?Site=APPA_2&WebCode=IA_CodeEthics

Anderson, D. C., & Enberg, C. (1995) Crime and the politics of hysteria: How the Willie Horton story changed American justice. *Journal of Contemporary Criminal Justice,* 11(4), 298–300.

Bohm, R., & Haley, K. N. (2008). *Introduction to Criminal Justice* (5th ed.). Boston: McGraw-Hill.

Braga, A. A., Piehl, A. M., & Hureau, D. (2009). Controlling violent offenders released to the community: An evaluation of the Boston Reentry Initiative. *Journal of Research in Crime and Delinquency,* 46(4), 411–436.

Campbell, D. T. (1969). Reforms as experiments. *American Psychologist, 24,* 409–429.

Carson, A. E., & Golinelli, D. (2013). Prisoners in 2012: Trends in admissions and releases, 1991–2012. Bureau of Justice Statistics, National Prisoner Statistics Program, 1978–2012. Retrieved from http://www.bjs.gov/content/pub/pdf/p12tar9112.pdf

Center for Substance Abuse Treatment. Treatment of Adolescents with Substance Use Disorders. Rockville (MD): Substance Abuse and Mental Health Services Administration (US); 1999. (Treatment Improvement Protocol (TIP) Series, No. 32.) Chapter 5—Therapeutic Communities. Available from: http://www.ncbi.nlm.nih.gov/books/NBK64342/

Clear, T. (1994). *Harm in American penology: Offenders, victims, and their communities.* Albany, NY: SUNY–Albany Press.

Cole, G. F., & Smith, C. E. (1996). *Criminal justice in America.* Belmont, CA: Wadsworth.

Council of State Governments. (2015). *Justice center. Focus area: Mental health.* Retrieved from https://whatworks.csgjusticecenter.org/focus-area/mental-health

Department of Justice. (2011). *Attorney General Eric Holder Convenes Inaugural Cabinet-Level Reentry Council.* Retrieved from: http://www.justice.gov/opa/pr/attorney-general-eric-holder-convenes-inaugural-cabinet-level-reentry-council

Department of Justice (2015). *U.S. Department of Justice FY 2015 budget request.* Retrieved from http://www.justice.gov/sites/default/files/jmd/legacy/2013/09/07/prisons-detention.pdf

Farrington, D. P., & Murray, J. (Eds.). (2013). Labeling theory: Empirical tests. In *Advances in Criminological Literature* (Vol. 18). New Brunswick, NJ: Transaction.

Gaines, L. K., & Miller, R. L. (2007). *Criminal justice in action* (Instructor's ed.). Belmont, CA: Wadsworth.

Grattet, R., Petersilia, J., & Lin, J. (2008). *Parole violations and revocations in California*. Final report submitted to the US National Institute of Justice. Retrieved from https://www.ncjrs.gov/pdffiles1/nij/grants/224521.pdf

Hoffman, P. (1996). Twenty years of operational use of a risk prediction instrument: The United States Parole Commission's Salient Factor Score. *Journal of Criminal Justice, 22*, 477–494.

Kyckelhahn, T. (2012). *State Corrections Expenditures, FY1982-2010*. Washington, DC: Bureau of Justice Statistics.

Liptak, K. (2015). President Obama commutes sentences of 46 drug offenders. CNN. Retrieved from http://www.cnn.com/2015/07/13/politics/obama-commutes-sentences-drug-offenders

MacKenzie, D. L. (2008, October). *Reentry: Examining what works in corrections*. Paper presented at the 16th Annual International Community Corrections Association Research Conference, St. Louis, MO.

Schmitt, J., Warner, K., & Gupta, S. (2010). The high budgetary cost of incarceration. Center for Economic and Policy Research. Retrieved from http://www.cepr.net/documents/publications/incarceration-2010-06.pdf

Seiter, R. P., & Kadela, K. R. (2003). Prison reentry: What works, what does not, and what is promising. *Crime and Delinquency, 49*, 360–390.

Solomon, A., Kachnowski, V., & Bhati, A. (2005). *Does parole work? Analyzing the impact of postprison supervision on rearrest outcomes*. Washington D.C.: The Urban Institute.

Travis, J., & Petersilia, J. (2001). Reentry reconsidered: A new look at an old question. *Crime & Delinquency, 47*(4), 291–313.

Travis, J. (2005). *But they all come back: Facing the challenges of prisoner reentry*. Washington D.C.: The Urban Institute Press.

Visher, C. A., Winterfield, L., & Coggeshall, M. B. (2006). Systematic review of non-custodial employment programs: Impact on recidivism rates of ex-offenders. *Campbell Systematic Reviews, 1*. DOI: 10.4073/csr.2006.1

Wilkinson, R. A., & Rhine, E. E. (2005). The international association of reentry: Mission and future. *Journal of Correctional Education, 56*(2), 139–145.

Zara, G., & Farrington, D. P. (2015). *Criminal recidivism: Explanation, prediction and prevention*. Roxbury, MA: Routledge.

09

Are Social Control Efforts Shrinking Crime? Effects of Socializing Institutions

Robert Grantham

CHAPTER OUTLINE

KEY TERMS

- AGENTS OF SOCIAL CONTROL
- COLLECTIVE EFFICACY
- CULPABILITY OF GOVERNANCE NARRATIVE
- FORMAL SOCIAL CONTROL
- INFORMAL SOCIAL CONTROL
- INSTITUTIONAL ANOMIE THEORY
- REDLINING
- SOCIAL CONTRACTS

A. Introduction

Years ago—which now feels like an eternity, at a time that most college students today are probably not aware of—most Americans relied on the six o'clock evening news for their source of information. Ostensibly, ABC, NBC, and the CBS evening news stations (and their local affiliates) are where Americans everywhere heard about various issues of the day, including incidents of crime. Some people today, for example, may even recall the station where they first heard about the Kennedy or Martin Luther King Jr. assassinations, or about the Charles Manson killings, and whether they heard about the crimes from news anchors like Barbara Walters, Walter Cronkite, or Dan Rather. Traditional television of the past ultimately changed; and during the 1980s cable news networks emerged in the United States, making round-the-clock broadcasting of the news more possible. During this cable TV transformation, many analysts and researchers note that the media industry also began to consolidate, leading to fewer (but larger) new outlets.

Ironically, some critics argue that fewer news outlets makes it easier for TV stations to capitalize and benefit from overstating the realities of crime patterns in the United States. For example, in a study of how America profits from crime, Joel Dyer (2010) argues that as a consolidated news market emerged, "media corporations decided to dramatically increase their use of violent, crime-oriented content as a means of increasing ratings or pickup rates and thereby enhancing their profits." And in the process the strategy "created a by-product—an exaggerated apprehension of crime throughout the general population."[1] However, concerns about consolidated media outlets and their links to crime go beyond an advance of increased profitability. We are equally concerned about *any* shifts in the ability to actually control crime. Hence, if capacities to control crime are tied to unclear motivations (of any kind, including profits), can or should we consider arguments that allow us to rely on ethical dilemmas about how best to proceed in controlling or curtailing incidents of crime and delinquency? Moreover, is there a relationship between efforts of social control and patterns of crime? In this chapter, we explore this broad question by first examining what is meant by social control—its heritage and selected theoretical assumptions—in relation to dealing with crime. We discuss ways in which people are socialized, and the impact

governance—as an institutionalizing enterprise—on efforts of social control.

The chapter concludes by discussing the impact of governance; effectiveness of the criminal justice system as a vehicle for social control; and moral implications of social control efforts. As we proceed, consider this question: Should we ponder ethical questions, for example, when distorted information about racial groups[2] and ill-informed public opinion about crime[3] are used to validate the need for increased efforts of **formal social control**? We begin with a discussion of what we know about social control.

B. What Is Social Control?

Whenever students and individuals, in general, hear the words *social control*, they rarely think of theoretical and academic implication that the term invokes. Perhaps one thought about social control often imagined by some involves, for example, the manner in which crowds of rowdy fans are handled by law enforcement agents at sporting events. Think about when police were needed in 1995 after UCLA's men's basketball championship victory, amid reports of "raucous" victory celebrations, overturned vehicles, and beer

---

2 See Kang, 2005, in which he provides a literature review of issues surrounding implicit bias whereby Whites and others have an inward (at times subconscious) harsher and more punitive view of minority males, in general, relative to that of Whites.
3 See Roberts & Stalans, 2000, for complete discussion.

---

1 Dyer, 2010, p. 71.

bottles being thrown at police; or in 2002 when riot police were called in to deal with rioting University of Maryland students following the school's basketball championship victory. In the incidents described above—wherein **agents of social control** were needed (including resources for a deployment of police helicopters) to protect property and to ensure the safety of innocent bystanders—the perpetrators of illicit activities were characterized by the press as "ecstatic" and "overzealous" students.[4] Some may think of this as a sort of minimalist description by the media, stripping away criminal impressions about the students and maybe lessening a need for ongoing social control measures.

However, issues related to our understanding of social control endure a more critical distinction, since social scientists and criminologists rely on the conceptual heritage of the perspective, as well as theoretical arguments about the nuances and ideas of control, relative to crime and delinquency. Later in the chapter we consider aspects of social control within a context of crime trends, socializing institutions, efforts of government, and moral implications.

Social and Intellectual Heritage

Social control theory of delinquency and its appeal to conservative criminologists became one way to move beyond the viewpoints of late 1960s radical criminologists—who were more sympathetic with the ways in which conflict theorists viewed the social world.[5] Conflict theorists focus on how structural conditions—external to the individual—help predict patterns of crime, like economic policy provisions, availability of affordable housing, or joblessness. Conversely, conservative criminologists lean toward examining ways in which the weakness and negligence of individuals result in delinquent behavior. Broadly, one underlying theme for control theory arguments is the need to regulate human behavior. Assumptions embedded within these concerns lead control theorists to ask a different question than advocates of most other theories of crime. Instead of asking *why do people commit crimes*, control theory scholars agree that the concern should be: What is it about social interactions that actually discourage people from committing crimes, whereby they seek to obey the rules of society? Academicians commonly relate obedience to rules to a Hobbesian position, which was articulated by a 17th-century English philosopher.[6]

Thomas Hobbes believed that humans were instinctively evil beings who needed to be protected from themselves. By extension, society is at risk whenever disobedience to the social order and unchecked human endeavors are allowed to run rampant. Thus, Hobbes warned against the idea of a so-called war of all against all, related to hedonistic tendencies and selfish preoccupations. Recall the 1980 movie *Mad Max*, starring Mel Gibson? It portrays a "society perilously close to ruin, perhaps after

---

4   Moore & Maher, 1995; Allen, 2008.
5   Williams & McShane, 2013.
6   Williams & McShane, 2013; Chriss, 2013.

a nuclear war," in which motorcycle cops "struggle to control marauding biker gangs [who] terrorize the highways"[7] and disregard the rights of others and rule of law. Hobbes believed that to avoid such a calamity, individuals in communities ultimately enter into what he calls **social contracts**, which are sometimes informal (unwritten and/or unspoken) covenants whereby an agreement is understood by individuals among social groups to "forego the unbridled pursuits of gratification in exchange for the state's guarantee to step in and regulate everyone's pursuit of self-gratification."[8] From this argument, many social control theorists accept a Hobbesian perspective as an important epistemological assumption that dissuades people from becoming involved in criminality, or in other words, why people simply obey the law.[9]

Perhaps one way we might come close to considering the *social contract–social control* approach is by studying people who volunteer their time. Is it safe to assume that whenever people volunteer their time, this represents an act of virtue and/or a commitment to an unspoken covenant or social contract? In one study, researchers at the University of Minnesota explain that assumptions behind the development of social control theories help us to envision how voluntary service actually draws people slowly into accepting the virtues of a social contract. In other words, various coercive efforts of informal social control from family members, friends, or colleagues convince us to participate in benevolent acts. Specifically, their study of 1,000 adolescents tested the act of volunteering and its impact on arrest rates. They found, unsurprisingly, that the more youngsters who volunteered for different organizations in their areas, the fewer were arrested for various criminal offenses.[10] Can we consider this a viable example of existence of a social contract? It certainly pales in comparison to the calamity and chaos depicted in the movie *Mad Max*.

C. Theoretical Contributions

Whether social contracts exist (or not) could easily become the topic of intriguing discussions among students, while considering (for example) criminal acts and covenants between sports fans, their universities, and the community. It would surely be an interesting debate. However, specific theoretical arguments play a useful role in answering questions about crime and delinquency in society, relative to the need to ensure social control, which may or may not implicate social contracts. In any event, while giving credit to Hobbesian insights, criminologists and other scholars agree that the writings of 19th-century sociologist Emile Durkheim "form the basis on which social control theories are built."[11]

---

7   See discussion of Hobbesian principles and movies in Falzon, 2014, p. 187.
8   Chriss, 2013, p. 138.
9   Williams & McShane, 2013.
10   Uggen & Janikula, 1999.
11   Kubrin, Stucky, & Krohn, 2009, p. 168.

Durkheim believed that healthy and orderly societies are ones where people are adequately integrated with one another, combined with a proper balance of regulations in community settings. In other words, the more socially integrated the neighborhoods, the more effective they are in exerting **informal social control** to regulate behavior.[12]

Informal social control consists of nonphysical coercive measures used to regulate individual or group behavior, unlike formal social control techniques (*discussed later*) that are administered and sanctioned by the state through practices by police departments, court systems, corrections, and juvenile detention centers. However, there are important contributions made by informal social control arguments that deserve our attention here (see below), which admittedly is not an exhaustive account of the theory literature.

Social Control/Bond Theory

Many in the field of criminal justice and criminology consider Hirschi one of the most influential criminologists and scholars in the development of social control theory.[13] Consequently, much of what is examined today relative to informal social control owes a great deal of credit to Hirschi's (1969) work, in his book *Causes of Delinquency*. His work takes a more careful look than previous studies at why youth become involved in the commission of delinquent acts. Social bonds to community and society that are typically formed during the course of one's life, once weakened, contribute to youth involvement in delinquency, according to Hirschi. The assumption is that people, especially youth, feel constrained by informal relationships or bonds that they possess to others, which discourages them from involvement in delinquency.

Stop for a moment to consider your adherence to rules; whether it involves residential life programs at school, team sports, church group organizations, or family outings. Since these are often loosely organized events, we characterize them as both social and informal. Hirschi believes that such activities tie us together in ways that avoid delinquency, while describing four broad elements of informal social bonds[14]: (a) *attachment*, characterized by the emotional closeness that we feel to our families; (b) *belief*, the ideas that orient us toward goals of a common value system that essentially convinces us that we should obey rules in society; (c) *commitment*, the cognitive dimension of social bonds that some criminologists equate with a commonsense orientation where we make rational calculations regarding commitments to conformity; and (d) *involvement*, which represents the time we spend in conventional activities (like grocery shopping, birthday parties, or doing yard work) whereby a behavioral disposition

12 See Durkheim, 1951, for discussion on social integration/regulation relative to his study of suicide rates.
13 Kubrin et al., 2009.
14 See Cullen and Agnew, 2011; Kubrin et al., 2009; or Chriss, 2013, for full discussion of elements of social bonds.

can be observed. Today studies in the literature continue to link the four elements of social bonds (or lack thereof) to various types of delinquency. However, some crime scholars note methodological and demographic shortcomings regarding the model, which perhaps led Hirschi to re-conceptualize an additional understanding of social control.

General Theory of Crime and Social Capital

As Hirschi stirred things up for the world of crime and deviance—after having established himself as a prominent voice in the study of crime and delinquency—many criminologists and social scientists believe that he slightly abandoned the initial views of his social bond thesis in favor of a conceptually different view of control. The new approach embraces the theme, perhaps, of a 2012 report by the U.S. Department of Health and Human Services that equates parents using drugs in front of their children as tantamount to child abuse.[15] Such unfortunate occurrences are often linked to bad behavior and delinquency.

Approximately 2 decades before the 2012 U.S. report on parenting discussed above was released, in 1990 Travis Hirschi and criminologist Michael Gottfredson coauthored the book *A General Theory of Crime* (1999). The focus of the book switches from the more sociological experiences of youth implicated in the social bond thesis and more toward self-control, the wayward habits of their parents, and poor decisions made by their parents as they were reared.[16] Overall, the *general theory of crime* posits that a lack of self-control—that forms with young kids as a result of complicated practices of parenting—is the source of criminal and illicit behavior. Specifically, youth internalize a sense of low self-control, leading to involvement in illicit activities such as drug abuse, skipping school, unwanted pregnancies, joy-riding, and so on. This thesis of low internal social control departs from the more sociological implications of Hirshi's social bond thesis. However, there exists mixed empirical support in the literature for Gottfredson and Hirschi's internal self-control argument.[17]

Social capital thesis arguments—which consider advantages gained through personal interactions with prominent others and/or links to established processes—move away from focusing on the internal control of delinquents. The approach considers lack of access to social and economic benefits—compared to more fortunate people—that is believed to accrue through belonging to various social associations and community networks. For example, youth who live in troubled urban communities often lack the social capital gained from access to voluntary organizations (for example, parent–teacher associations, Little League Baseball teams, and after-school programs), which researchers believe help youngsters avoid becoming involved in delinquent behavior. One study in 2012 of high schools

---

15   Child Welfare Information Gateway, 2012.
16   Cullen & Agnew, 2012.
17   Cullen & Pratt, 2000; Tittle, Ward, & Grasmick, 2003.

in the state of Maryland observed that dynamics of social capital—derived from student involvement in interscholastic sports programs, compared to noninvolvement—increased the chances that school officials would have positive resolutions to delinquent disturbances among students, which occur every now and then during after-school activities.[18] Said differently, officials who work at schools where students lack access to (or fail to volunteer for) interscholastic sports programs probably have a more difficult time dealing with unexpected disturbances that become defined as delinquent behavior, according to social capital thesis arguments. On the other hand, social capital thesis arguments, delinquency, and whether one volunteers or becomes civically involved in social networks may a bit of an oversimplified analysis.

Although Harvard political scientist Robert Putnam concedes that a reduction in delinquent behavior is often linked to the willingness of individuals—across all communities—to get involved in social activities (for example, voter participation, church attendance, school programs), he points out that new trends are emerging that show higher rates of participation in *individualistic* self-help groups.[19] "Through self-disclosure, members share their stories, stresses, feelings, issues, and recoveries. They learn that they are not alone; they are not the only ones facing the problem."[20] They seek to address problems related to alcoholism, gambling, dietary issues, smoking, or other personal vices. For our purposes, however, whether the increased interest in self-help groups over traditional civic engagement activities has an impact on social control efforts of communities that lead to less delinquency require further investigation in the social control literature.

Social Disorganization Theory

Social capital thesis arguments are somewhat related to those expressed by theorists from the Chicago school of thought[21] who turned their attention in the mid-1900s toward ecological aspects of the city, while studying urban problems, social control and delinquency. Social scientists who study ecological conditions focus on growth patterns related, for example, to spatial realities, populations, technology, and density. Specifically, urban sociologists from the Chicago school considered urban spatial dynamics, while conceptualizing cities as being organized in ways that help researchers study crime. For example, cities were said to be arranged in five concentric zones, with the center of the city (zone 1) designated as the central business district, while the area immediately surrounding the central business

---

18   Langbein & Bess, 2012.
19   See Chriss, 2013, for full discussion of Robert Putnam's positon on social capital.
20   See Ahmadi, n.d. for broader current discussion.
21   The University of Chicago established the first department of sociology in 1892. One argument of the school, which became the core of the Chicago school of thought, is that human behavior is developed and changed by the social physical environment of the person, rather than by genetic structure. See Williams and McShane, 2013, for full discussion.

district (zone 2) was referred to as the zone of transition. The last three zones were of less interest, relative to crime and delinquency: (zone 3) the working class zone, (zone 4) the residential zone, and (zone 5) the commuter zone.

In the mid-1940s, sociologists Clifford Shaw and Henry McKay were most interested in the zone in transition, since it is conceptualized as the area that consists of high crime and where new immigrants, less well-off residents, and minority populations move in and out of. They argued that communities within this zone are socially disorganized, allowing researchers to predict patterns of crime. Socially disorganized areas are characterized by a breakdown of social institutions such as families, schools, churches, and others, which makes it difficult for community members to exert effective informal social control over delinquency. Said differently, disorganized communities lack a sense of **collective efficacy**—described broadly as a sort of relational interdependence between residents, which is found to have an inverse (or reverse) relationship on crime and delinquency.[22] In other words, studies in the social disorganization literature help us understand that as collective efficacy increases, communities experience lower crime rates. These benefits are explained by an increased capacity of residents to coordinate social control activities that discourage poor behavior.

Criminologists and sociologists believe that until about the early 1980s, social disorganization theory arguments lost the interest of researchers; but insist that the perspective was revitalized by scholars who turned more of their attention to structural dynamics (that is, poverty, economic inequality, and transiency) that shape residential interactions. The different structural approach arguments challenged cultural of poverty and violence theses that had emerged in the literature regarding the poor and racial minorities.[23] For example, one widely accepted study of urban areas found that measures of racial inequality help researcher predict levels of violence, thereby challenging the notion that inadequate social control efforts and social breakdown *alone* explain delinquency.[24] In a 2005 paper, criminologists Ruth Peterson and Lauren Krivo insist that the new emphasis on structure in the literature during the early 1980s set off "a flurry" of other studies that added to what we know today about social control and predictors of delinquency. Essentially, these studies put less emphasis on describing informal social control and more on structural determinants of informal social control that explain crime.

The most recent arguments added to the social disorganization literature propose that researchers go even further by examining wider macro forces (related to deindustrialization, outmigration of more affluent residents from cities, housing discrimination, and certain government decisions) that may help shape the structural relationship to disorganization and delinquency from a social control perspective.[25]

---

22 See Sampson, Raudenbush, & Earls, 1997, for a discussion of collective efficacy.
23 See Groves & Sampson, 1987, for a complete discussion of cultural arguments.
24 Blau and & Blau, 1982.
25 See Sampson & Wilson, 1995, for a discussion.

D. Socializing Institutions

Now that we have some background information about theories of social control, we are positioned to later consider the issue as social control relates to crime in society. Recall, however, that social bond theory helps us understand why people obey the law; general theory of crime explains how inadequate parenting is the culprit for one's inability to control internal delinquent impulses; whereas social disorganization theory explains consequences of poor social control in communities, while also considering conditions in society that help us predict weakened capacity to avoid delinquency. In this section, we discuss socializing institutions as a way to further clarify some specifics and give us an additional layer of understanding of how individuals and groups fit within aspects of social control relative to crime.

Sociologists have long understood the process of socialization and how people come to be aware of certain things. One assumption of becoming socialized is that we learn and are conditioned by interaction between genetics and environments, which is a broad understanding of socialization.[26] However, scholars often analyze to what degree heredity versus the environment influences the process of socialization, while evaluating studies of primates and of humans reared from birth, totally isolated from civilization. We feel the need to note that the debate does exist, without getting into any of the details. Here, we are decidedly more interested in simply accepting the assumption that a socialization process occurs: at the individual developmental level and more importantly (for this chapter) in ways that shape our overall perception of the world, which we argue should force us to think more critically and ethically about efforts of social control. At the individual level of awareness, Sociologist Richard Schaefer (2010) writes that our understanding of who we are and what is meaningful to us emanates from our social and self-identity. As we evolve throughout the course of our lives, our identities, he writes, are often molded by two different processes—when we rehearse and prepare for future social relationships (anticipatory socialization) and when we discard former behavior patterns in order to accept new ones (resocialization).

At an interactive and more external level, we become socialized institutionally through what Schaefer (2010) calls agents of socialization, or the group or social context whereby socialization takes place. For example, the family, schools, church, the media, and the government all act as agents of social control and are said to operate institutionally in our lives. Thus, by many accounts, here is where we are often conditioned to accept, reject, or question things going on around us in the social world. Considering agents of socialization within a context of crime and social control may help us better discuss and/or interrogate ethical and policy-related matters in society. Below, we briefly discuss examples of two socializing institutions, the family and the media.

---

26   See Schaefer, 2010, for a full discussion of socialization.

The Family

When we think about dynamics of family, we often consider how children learn and are socialized to be courteous, be responsible, and follow the rules, while parents and other family members model the best practices of being a citizen, student, worker, friend, and romantic partner, to name a few. However, the idea that the family plays the biggest role in socializing children[27] raises concerns about whether families today are uniquely positioned to produce the most desirable outcome while assuming this role. Consider shifting family dynamics, before *even* contemplating positive socialization of children, social control, and crime. A recent article in the *Washington Post* asks whether the "picture-perfect" family actually exist today. The paper points out that as the country witnessed the Obamas, Bidens, and McCains in 2008 showcase their families as the perfect embodiment of the institution of family, divorce had become the norm, with more than half of marriages in the United States ending in divorce. This is further complicated by the fact that "the traditional family unit has been replaced by a wide variety of living arrangements," and that only "58 percent of children live with two married, biological parents."[28]

These trends raise different challenges for poor families, where indigent women are less likely to get married than non-poor women; and for Black families, where studies of the so-called marriage market indicate that at age 25 there were "three unmarried Black women for every Black man who had adequate earnings."[29] However, despite these dynamics, some evidence suggests that Black single mothers have made positive adjustments, while all is not lost for minority and poor families. For example, some evidence suggests that many single Black mothers are coping with the absence of Black fathers, relative to effective socialization techniques that they have adopted for their children.[30]

The Media

As an agent of socialization, the media plays a role—almost without us realizing it—in what we think about society. It signals who the heroes and villains are, discourages us from becoming involved in illicit acts, and reminds us of proper social norms in society.[31] However, complaints about media are rampant. For example, one of the most consistent criticisms of the media as a socializing institution involves a debate surrounding whether children imitate violent behavior from movies and television and whether certain images depicted on the screen comport with the values of decency in American Society. For example, the National Rifle Association and its proponents, like Second Amendment scholars Joyce Lee Malcolm, resist the idea that guns in society or on television lead to more violence.

---

27   Schafer, 2010.
28   Cherlin, 2010, p. 247.
29   Coontz & Folbre, 2010, p. 189.
30   Macke & Morgan, 1978; Burt & Simmons, 2015.
31   See Schaefer, 2010, for a discussion of the media.

In *Guns and Violence*, Malcolm compares violence in the United States to violence in England and argues that reductions in crime in the United States point to the right to bear arms in defense of oneself, whereas the rise in violence in England (comparatively) is related to gun laws that actually prevent British citizens from similar individual protections.[32] Thus, it stands to reason from Malcolm's perspective that television programming depicting guns bears little to no responsibility for violence among children. Conversely, one study published in 2008 by the *American Behavioral Scientists* states:

> *Fifty years of research on the effect of TV violence on children leads to the inescapable conclusion that viewing media violence is related to increases in aggressive attitudes, values, and behaviors. The changes in aggression are both short term and long term, and these changes may be mediated by neurological changes in the young viewer. The effects of media violence are both real and strong and are confirmed by the careful reviews of research evidence by various scientific and professional organizations. (Murray, 2008, p. 1212)*

The issue of guns and violence will likely continue to be debated within the context of whether violence on TV programming inappropriately socializes children. The issue will likely spur continued provocative discussions among many in society, including college students.

However, the issue of decency of program and image depictions on television is also controversial, for different reasons slightly different than of gun violence. The claims often implicate transgression against accepted values and norms. For example, in 2004 singers Janet Jackson and Justin Timberlake were performing during the halftime show of Super Bowl XXXVIII when (unexpectedly) Jackson's wardrobe supposedly "malfunctioned," exposing her breast for about 9/16th of a second. Following the incident, assisted by groups like the Parents Television Council, several complaints were filed with the Federal Communications Commission (FCC), claiming that the exposure of Jackson's breast amounted to the type of indecent exposure that is both inappropriate for children and also threatens the national morality. As a result, the FCC considered issuing stiff fines for the incident. The FCC ultimately fined the CBS network (not Jackson or Timberlake) $550,000 for the mishap, which was ultimately struck down by the courts. Later, however, the matter led Congress to adopt the Broadcast Decency Enforcement Act (2005), which would give the FCC more authority to levy fines against future violations of decency.

Essentially, the discussion above positions the media (through television programming) as a socializing institution (for example, affirming conventional social norms), which provides us with some social

---

32   Malcolm, 2002.

context regarding social responses to other events, even those related to crime. We will return later to the topic of the media relative to social control, crime and ethics.

E. Impact of Government Policy on Efforts of Social Control

Our discussions thus far allow us to think about theories of informal social control that suggest why people obey the law and void delinquent behavior, as we conserved how people are socialized. In addition to what we have learned about efforts of informal social control and socializing institutions, formal social control efforts implicate specifically the role that governance plays in dealing with crime. This understanding leads us to include a discussion of criminal justice practices, as scholars argue that flawed policies enshroud our awareness of how best to defeat crime. We begin, however, by situating this discussion within a necessary and broader context.

Culpability of Governance

Concerns for families, groups, and others in our social world are intertwined unavoidably with dynamics of governance that include implementation of formal social control methods at various levels of government (federal, state, or local). One assumption is that governments are responsible or culpable for outcomes of its institutions that are connected with unexpected or lopsided social outcomes. Similarly, in *Urban Society: A Shame of Governance*, the editors insist that **culpability of governance narratives** question, for example, whether an *imbalance of governance* obscures a society's ability to eradicate the seeds of crime and criminogenic conditions—as researchers consider decisions tied to prisons, drug policies, policing, and the criminal justice system.[33]

Broadly speaking, imbalances of governance are situations or arrangements that "cause cumulative increases in the relative power of stronger parties and vicious spirals of relative power loss for weaker ones"[34] that often render some groups into a persistent vulnerable position. More specifically, some researchers examine the criminal justice system and argue, for example, that an imbalance in governance is characterized by dominant voices from various policy communities[35] who advance a tough-on-crime rhetoric, which some believe is linked to longer sentences of incarceration for nonviolent offenders who often lack resources to adequately defend their cases.[36] We argue that governance plays some role in the development of such conditions. For our purposes, governance refers

---

33 Grantham & Chorbajian, 2010.
34 Galanis, 2011, p. 327.
35 Policy communities, for example, include police associations, bar associations, judicial organizations, and correctional associations. See Fairchild, 1981.
36 Barkow, 2005.

to decision making efforts at federal, state, or local levels of government that impact interdependent cross-sections of society. We will first discuss larger social context of governance, via describing macro structural thesis and crime and neoliberalism influences on macro socializing institutions, before discussing formal social control and ethics.

Macro Structural Arguments and Crime

Earlier in our discussion we noted that structural conditions like poverty, unemployment, and racial inequality help researchers predict crime in inner cities, but that social disorganization scholars also believe that wider macro structural forces (for example, housing, deindustrialization, or various political decisions) are tied to policies, which shape structural conditions mentioned above. In other words, if poverty helps predict crime in socially disorganized areas, what macro structural forces (tied to policies) help to predict inner-city poverty? Some scholars even write that "deliberate policies disrupt the social institutional order (of cities) in ways that threaten the social organization of communities."[37] From this argument crime scholars believe that "structurally induced social disorganization"[38] helps researchers predict urban crime, which ostensibly suggests a culpability of governance. If we accept this assumption, does it suggest that actions or inactions of governance weaken social institutions of communities? Consider discriminatory housing for a moment.

In *Capital and Communities in Black and White*, Gregory Squires (1994) argues that discriminatory practices of lending through a technique redlining of minority communities make it difficult for inner-city residents to obtain loans and purchase property. Redlining is when banks and other financial institutions identify areas that ultimately make it more difficult for residents in the area to get loans, insurance, and other services. Squires argues that during the 1980s and 1990s, federal regulators failed to enforce provisions in the law, which signaled a lax environment for banks and other financial institutions regarding lending practice, as complaints of redlining ensued. Today residents of minority communities continue to file complaints of being redlined. However, in 2015 New York attorney general Eric T. Schneiderman filed charges against various New York banks (for example, Evans Bank and Five Star Bank) for **redlining** practices that denied mortgages and credit to African Americans, regardless of their credit worthiness. In one case, *Five Star Bank* of New York was penalized and agreed, as part of the settlement, to open two new Rochester-area branch offices located in neighborhoods with a minority population of at least 30%.[39] Ultimately, many believe that actions of this nature economically deprive families of needed resources and show how, in many ways, minorities and the poor often pay more for goods and services, since they settle for higher prices and higher interest rates. One notable

---

37   Peterson and Krivo, 2005, p. 335
38   Peterson and Krivo, 2005, p. 335
39   Schneiderman, 2015.

study in the social disorganization literature ties examples of how urban residents are economically deprived and actually links types of deprivation to patterns of crime.[40]

Neoliberal Logic of Governance and Crime

In *A Brief History of Neoliberalism* (2007), David Harvey argues that social policy in the United States since about the mid-1970s has adopted the logics of commercial and business entities. For example, one study details how construction of public housing in U.S. cities over the past 40 years has been undermined by corporate pressures to reduce the supply of affordable housing units in favor of private development—as public officials and economic developers laud the financial rewards for doing so.[41] Steven Messner and Richard Rosenfeld argue in *Crime and the American Dream* (1997) that relations between public officials and private parties described above demonstrate that American social institutions are routinely dominated by economic institutions (for example, banks, insurance companies, mortgage firms), which harm society in measurable ways. For example, in an earlier study they found that homicide rates are higher in countries that are dominated by economic institutions.[42] They describe this situation as a form on institutional anomie or normlessness.

F. Formal Social Control and Ethical Considerations

Formal social control involve official efforts by the state, which entail courts, the police, juvenile detention centers, prisons, and legal actions designed to maintain order. Fortunately, we now have some useful tools that help us consider efforts of formal social control relative to social institutions, crime, and ethics, all within a context of governance. One major surrounding issue of formal social control in the United States is that justice is often meted out within what some researchers refer to as a flawed criminal justice system. This critique comes amid some important questions about the effectiveness of imprisonment and whether high incarceration rates in the United States explain changes in crime rates, for example. A complex part of this inquiry confronts the disparate impact of the criminal justice system on racial groups and whether differences in outcomes and/or practices raise overall ethical dilemmas for society.

---

40   See Bursik & Grasmick, 1993, for a discussion on social disorganization and economic deprivation.
41   See Harvey, 2007, for a discussion of neoliberalism; Hackworth, 2007, for a discussion of public housing; and Messner & Rosenfeld, 2013, for a discussion of institutional anomie.
42   Messner & Rosenfeld, 1997.

Crime Rates in the United States

Former secretary of state and First Lady of the United States Hillary Rodham Clinton gave a speech in April 2015 at Columbia University in New York, leading up to her campaign to become the Democratic nominee for the 2016 U.S. presidential election. During the speech, she decried the imprisonment system in the United States, saying that it is "time to end the era of mass incarceration" and that "we need to have a true national debate about how to reduce our prison population while keeping our communities safe."[43]

Keeping our communities safe? Could it be that no one told the former secretary of state that crime rates in the United States have been falling since about the 1990s? That's true. Overall crime rates in the United States—according to Uniform Crime Reports—have been in decline. Between 1990 and 2013 the United States experienced a 50% decline in violent crime and a 46% decline in property crime over the same period.[44] Perhaps the former secretary of state got a bit ahead of herself in implicit calls for prison reform. Maybe imprisonment is actually working to drive down crime. However, researchers at the Brennan Center for Justice at the New York University Law School conducted an extensive study of declining U.S. crime rates and did not reach that conclusion.[45] The study found that decreased crime rates are almost irrelevant to increasing numbers of people that are incarcerated in U.S. prisons. Overall, most crime experts agree that rising incarceration rates do not explain declining crime rates that began during the mid-1990s.[46] Alternatively, the report concluded that certain social, economic, and environmental factors played a role in the crime drop. Specifically, "the aging population, changes in income, decreased alcohol consumption, consumer confidence and inflation contributed to crime reduction."[47]

Criminal Justice

While acknowledging positive law enforcement efforts that are widely acknowledged and understood by many crime scholars, research on criminal justice systems in the United States during the past 2 decades has been intense, leading to endless analyses that suggest that the system is a flawed

---

43   Bump, Phillip, 2015
44   UCR Data Online, n.d.
45   Roder, Eisen, & Bowling, 2015.
46   Belbot, 2012.
47   Roeder et al., 2015, p. 4.

enterprise[48] that is characterized by ahistorical color-blind approaches to law and order, prone to brush aside legacies of racism in the United States,[49] that has resulted in higher incarceration rates of Black males disproportionate to their representation in society; that has resulted in the administration of the death penalty such that it executes murderers of affluent and White victims at higher rates than those of Black or poor victims; that has meted out a so-called war on drugs that ensnared nonviolent offenders whereby between 2001 and 2013 (at the federal level alone), more than half of prisoners serving sentences of more than 1 year in federal facilities were convicted of drug offenses;[50] and finally, that embraces controversial legal codes (for example, stop and frisk, three strikes, and stand your ground), despite how application of the statutes are thought to impact the poor and minority groups disproportionately. Below are three brief descriptions of codes listed above, as an example of items recently in the news.

> **Stop and frisk**, *"a brief, non-intrusive, police stop of a suspect: The Fourth Amendment requires that the police have a reasonable suspicion that a crime has been, is being, or is about to be committed before stopping a suspect."* *In 1967 the U.S. Supreme Court upheld that if the police reasonably believe that a person is armed and dangerous, 'they may conduct a frisk and a quick pat-down of the person's outer clothing.'"*[51]

> **Three strikes,** *"any law that requires, upon conviction of a third felony, that the offender serve either a life sentence or a sentence that is significantly longer in duration than would otherwise be mandated". Such laws "emerged in the early 1990s amidst public outrage over repeat violent offending that had drawn media attention."*[52]

> **Stand your ground**, *simply means that, "if you reasonably believe that you face imminent death, serious bodily injury, rape, kidnapping, or (in most states) robbery, you can use deadly force against the assailant, even if you have a per- fectly safe avenue of retreat." In non-stand-your-ground states, when someone faces such threats outside the home (and, in some states, their business), only deadly force against the assailant is allowed if a perfectly safe avenue of retreat*

---

48   Reddington & Bonham, 2012.
49   Michelle Alexander (2012) makes this argument in her book *The New Jim Crow*.
50   Carson, E.A, 2014.
51   Cornell University Law School, n.d.
52   Hanser & Gomila, 2012, p. 101.

is not available.[53] *In 2005 Florida was the first state to enact the law. Since then 24 other states have adopted versions of the law.*

G. Social Control: Flawed Policy and Ethics

As we consider issues of social control, specifically formal social control mechanisms that impact groups differently, it forces us to consider policy implications relative to issues surrounding criminal justice. Crime scholar Gene Bonham Jr. (Reddington & Bonham, 2012) gives us a useful guideline for having this discussion. Policies related to criminal justice, he argues, are flawed whenever they do not produce the intended effect or whenever they produce unintended consequences. Social science researchers and journalists provide evidence in wide support of the flawed policy thesis, on the basis of unintended consequences and other reasons. For example, one study reviews the literature on three-strikes legislation (discussed above) and finds that racial disparity exists, as the policy is implemented.[54] In the state of California alone, the study points out that African Americans make up 6.5% of the state population, 30% of the prison population in the state, 36% of second-strike offenders, and 45% of third-strike offenders. Latinos are 32% of the state, 36% of the prison population, and 32.6% of all second and third strikers; whereas Caucasians offenders make of 47% of the state, but only 29% of prison population, 26% of second strikers, and 25.4% of third strikers. While the literature consists of evidence regarding inconsistent policy outcomes, our objective is to help provide an opportunity to link this information with social control and institutional dynamics that implicate governance and raise ethical questions.

Bonham argues that current criminal justice policy practices such as 3-Strikes laws and others are shaped by political actors, whereby lower rungs of society are manipulated into accepting proposals to fight crime; middle class citizens of society are (at times) consulted with by elites but ultimately placated by politicians; while upper class citizens enjoy the most control over policy formation. Such inconsistent messaging, he insists, has lead researchers and others to scrutinize decisions made within the criminal justice system influenced by (a) extralegal factors—like race, ethnicity, and socio-economic status—rather that legal ones; (b) a historical emphasis of punishment in the U.S. system; (c) selective prosecution of weak and less powerful individuals; (d) ambitions of politicians who are willing to misapply of evidence from research for their own ideological purposes; and finally (e) unhealthy alliances between the media, and government officials within dominant policy communities. This final point raises ethical concerns, which lead us to the next point of this discussion.

---

53   Volokh, 2014.
54   Hanser & Gomilla, 2012.

Ethical Considerations

Consider Tamir Rice, a 12-year-old African American male, playing with a toy gun in a park in Cleveland, Ohio in 2014. According to news reports, a police officer—within 2 seconds of exiting the police car—shot and killed the 12-year-old. Consider Walter Scott, a 50-year-old African American fleeing from the police in Charleston, South Carolina, in 2015, after being pulled over for a nonfunctioning break light. A videotape of the event shows a police officer shooting Scott in the back several times, killing him. Consider Freddie Gray, a 25-year-old African American male, who was falsely arrested and detained by the police in Baltimore, Maryland, in April 2015. While in custody he reportedly suffered an injury to his spinal cord and died; six police officers have been charged with manslaughter. Lastly, consider Antonio Zambrano-Montes, a 36-year-old unarmed Mexican man who was fleeing from the police in the state of Washington to avoid being served with a warrant. Seventeen gunshots were fired at him as he turned toward the police officers, killing Zambrano-Montes.

Ethically based arguments (relative to events described above, for example) often energize critical discussions—regarding policy, racial bias, and crime—in nuanced ways that are bound to implicate governance. Therefore, implicating government action in a discussion of criminal justice and ethics is necessary, as "for the past two centuries, institutions of criminal justice have been predominately agencies of or accountable to government."[55] Additionally, how matters of crime are dealt with in the United States has also been influenced by a confluence of media actors, the private sector, and arms of government in ways that challenge institutional practices, social norms, as well our own resolve about ethical dilemmas. However, few ethically based arguments in the literature allow us to integrate concerns of interest discussed earlier in this chapter.

Scholars describe ethics as a branch of philosophy concerned with the study of questions of right and wrong and how we ought to live. Ethical arguments fall into three categories: those that insist that we ponder individual levels of conduct; those that consider grouped-relations with others; and the most underdeveloped part of the traditional ethics literature involve those that allow us to integrate multiple levels of concern that raise moral questions about actual systems of governance. Each of these categories overlap within specific studies of ethics that focus on language, logical structures, rational for interpreting ethical terms, standard ways of behaving, and solving practical moral problems

---

55   Kleinig, 2008, p. 1.

that arise.[56] Ethical arguments that focus on individual levels of conduct, for example, debate issues relative to notions of morality as it differs from person to person, or whether one is or *should be* willing to defend powerless individuals in society, or abuses of power—as a violation of the role authorization[57] granted to someone in an official capacity as an agent of government. Ethical argument that debate our grouped-relations to others consider, for example, a need to understand different cultures based on the perspective of the different culture, or tolerate and accept existing differences between diverse ethical perspectives.

Finally, ethical arguments that allow us to integrate multiple levels of concern in society that implicate systems of governance are perhaps the most under represented. For example, they consider issues relative to legislation, various statutes, and governmental regulations and whether the issues conflict with other ethical standards.[58] Ultimately, integrating multiple levels of concern in society compels us to make moral and ethical judgements about decisions or inactions of governance that are linked to problematic social outcomes. Relative to issues of crime, Cynthia Banks (2013) argues that resolving ethical dilemmas in criminal justice require citizens to think critically about broad social policy and to avoid assuming a posture of helplessness. Herein lies a potential problem: that is, whether individual citizens imagine a set of norms or ethics about systems of governance that link social policy and elements of criminal justice.

H. Revisiting an Earlier Discussion

Recall **institutional anomie theory** (IAT) arguments provide a framework that allow us to interrogate the normative order of governance, relative to crime, social policy, and the uncritical nature of the American citizenry. Essentially, we believe that IAT is normative perspective (or ethic) that allows us to integrate multiple levels of concern of crime, which forms a basis to judge systems of governance. IAT is critical of neoliberal forms of governance that adopt strong commercial characteristics. Thus, the argument is that whenever economic institutions dominate and encroach upon the norms of social institutions (family, schools, churches, aspects of governance), anomic conditions emerge that disarm social institutions of their regulatory capacity, which help researchers predict crime. Thus, IAT challenges us to decipher judgments about a moral or normative disposition regarding links between economic dynamics and social order. Moreover, what social mechanisms are in place that possibly affects an individual's critical thinking about such relations, which raise ethical concerns elsewhere? IAT arguments suggest that the public's preoccupation with materialism and individualism confounds

---

56   See Banks, 2013, for a full discussion of studies of ethics.
57   See Hanser & Gomilla, 2012, for a full discussion.
58   Banks, 2013.

the critical thinking skills concerning such matters of importance, while tolerating potentially unethical conditions linked to crime and governance.

Therefore, as researchers insist that neoliberal policies—that shape criminal justice programs in the United States—promote individualistic punitive conceptions of and responses to crime[59]; might we better understand public appetite and/or silence about formal social control processes and legal remedies (imprisonment, three-strike laws, stand your ground, stop and frisk) that disproportionately impact Black and Latino males? Couple this trend with one review of the literature on implicit bias published in *Harvard Law Review*, which found that during simulated target practice games, participants in the study were consistently more likely to shoot an unarmed Black male versus an armed White male. This may provide us with insights into recent shooting tragedies in the United States that involve the police and unarmed Black males or the punitive disposition toward Black males that result in history of police violence in Black communities. In any event, *Harvard Law Review* links implicit bias studies to relaxed rules adopted by the FCC—that granted more flexibility to local TV news stations, leading to increased over-coverage of Black males involved in criminal acts.[60] This is but one example of governance (FCC) that may have gone astray that remind us of a need to develop increased ethical arguments that integrate governance and crime. As a corollary, just as appeals by parents to the FCC (discussed earlier) regarding the indecency of exposing children to Janet Jackson's breast during the Super bowl were made; who among us are prepared to appeal to the FCC on the basis of ethics and indecency that usage of the public airwaves that create moral panics and expose young children to caricatures of Black and Latino men (as social malefactors) is equally as indecent?

Finally, an overall ethical question to consider: When lopsided social outcomes persist in society, relative to marginalized disorganized communities and claims of disparate treatment by the criminal justice system, does this encourage us to interrogate aspects of a governmental order whose actions or inactions threaten the outlook (repeatedly) for too many of its citizens, while also simultaneously undermining the nation's capacity to assess sincere progress toward crime reduction?

DISCUSSION QUESTIONS

1. Discuss the focus of the different informal social control perspectives.
2. How do formal social control dynamics implicate a culpability of governance?
3. Discuss the media as a socializing institution as well as an example of failed governance.
4. Discuss the relationship between crime rates and mass incarceration.

---

59   See Harvey (2007); and Bell (2011).
60   Kang, 2005.

REFERENCES

Ahmadi, K. S. (n.d.) "What is a self-help group?" PsychCentral. Web. 3 November 2015.

Alexander, M. (2012). *The new Jim Crow: Mass incarceration in the age of colorblindness*. New York: New Press.

Allen, S. "Overzealous fans create riot trend." *Daily Bruin*. 8 January 2008. Web. 3 November 2015.

Banks, C. L. (2013). *Criminal justice ethics: Theory and Practice*. Thousand Oaks, CA: Sage.

Barkow, R. E. (2005). Panel four: The institutional concerns inherent in sentencing regimes. *Columbia Law Review, 105*(4), 1276–1314.

Bell, E. (2011). *Criminal justice and neoliberalism*. New York: Palgrave Macmillan.

Blau, J. R., & Blau, P. M. (1982). The cost of inequality: Metropolitan structure and violent crime. *American Sociological Review, 47*, 114–129.

Bump, Phillip. "Hillary Clinton hopes to undo the mass incarceration system Bill Clinton helped build". *The Washington Post*. 28 April. 2015. Web. 3 November 2015.

Bursik, R. J., & Grassick, H. G. (1993). Economic deprivation and neighborhood crime rates, 1960–1980. *Law and Society Review, 27*(2), 263–283.

Burt, C. H., & Simons, R. L. (2015). Interpersonal racial discrimination, ethnic-racial socialization, and offending: Risk and resilience among African American females. *Justice Quarterly, 32*(3), 532–570.

Carson, E.A. "Prisoners in 2013". *Bureau of Justice Statistics*. 16 September 2014. Web. 3 November 2013.

Cherlin, A. J. (2010). The picture-perfect American family? These days, it doesn't exist. In B. J. Risman (Ed.), *Families as they really are* (pp. 246–250). New York: Norton.

Child Welfare Information Gateway. (2012). 'Parental drug use as child abuse." Web. 3 November 2015.

Chriss, J. J. (2013). *Social control: An introduction*. Malden, MA: Polity Press.

Coontz, S., & Folbre, N. (2010). Briefing paper: Marriage, poverty, and public policy. In B. J. Risman (Ed.), *Families as they really are* (pp. 185–193). New York: Norton.

Cornell University Law School. (n.d.). Legal Information Institute. "Stop and frisk." 3 November 2015.

Cullen, F.T., & Agnew, R. (2011). *Criminological Theory: Past to Present*. New York, NY: Oxford University Press.

Durkheim, E. (1951). *Suicide*. Glencoe, IL: Free Press.

Dyer, J. (2010). Profiting from prisons. In R. Grantham & L. Chorbajian (Eds.), *Urban society: The shame of governance* (pp. 69–74). Cornwall-on-Hudson, NY: Sloan.

Fairchild, E. S. (1981). Interest groups in the criminal justice process. *Journal of Criminal Justice, 9*, 181–194.

Falzon, C. (2014). *Philosophy goes to the movies: An introduction to philosophy*. New York: Routledge.

Galanis, M. (2011). Vicious spirals in corporate governance: Mandatory rules for systemic (re)balancing? *Oxford Journal of Legal Studies, 31*(2), 327–363.

Gottfredson, M., & Hirschi, T. (1999). *A general theory of crime*. Stanford, CA: Stanford University Press.

Grantham, R. & Chorbajian, L. (Eds.). (2010). *Urban Society: The shame of governance*. Cornwall-on-the-Hudson, NY: Sloan.

Groves, W. B. & Sampson, R. J. (1987). Traditional contributions to radical criminology. *Journal of Research in Crime Delinquency, 24*(3), 181–214.

Hackworth, J. (2007). *The neoliberal city*. Ithaca, NY: Cornell University Press.

Hanser, R. D., & Gomila, M. N. (2012). The consequences of three strikes laws. In F. Reddington & G. Bonham Jr. (Eds), *Flawed criminal justice policies* (pp. 101–120). Durham, NC: Carolina Academic Press.

Harvey, D. (2007). *A Brief History of Neoliberalism*. New York: Oxford University Press.

Hirschi, T. (1969). *Causes of delinquency*. Berkeley: University of California Press.

Kang, J. (2005). Trojan horses of race. *Harvard Law Review, 118*(5), 1489–1593.

Kleinig, J. (2008). *Ethics and criminal justice*. Cambridge, MA: Cambridge University Press.

Kubrin, C. E., Stucky, T. D., & Krohn, M. D. (2009). *Researching theories of crime and deviance*. New York: Oxford University Press.

Langbein, L., & Bess, R. (2012). Sports in school: Source of amity or antipathy? *Social Science Quarterly, 83*(2), 436–454.

Macke, A. S., & Morgan, W. R. (1978). Maternal employment, race, and work orientation of high school girls. *Social Forces,* 57(1), 187–204.

Malcolm, J. (2002). *Guns and violence: The English experience*. Cambridge, MA: Harvard College.

Messner, S., & Rosenfeld, R. (1997). Political restraints of the market and levels of criminal homicide: A cross-national application of institutional anomie theory. *Social Forces, 75*, 1393–1416.

Messner, S., & Rosenfeld, R. (2013). *Crime and the American dream*. Belmont, CA: Wadsworth.

Moore, M., & Maher, A. "Wild Westwood: Police have to restrain raucous victory celebration by UCLA fans". *Los Angeles Times*. 4 April 1995. Web. 3 November 2015.

Murray, J. (2008). Media violence: The effects are both real and strong. *American Behavioral Scientist, 51*(8), 1212–1230.

Peterson, R.D. & Krivo, L. (2005). Macrostructural Analyses of Race, Ethnicity, and Violent Crime: Recent Lessons and New Directions for Research. *Annual Review of Sociology* 31, 331–356.

Pratt, T. C., & Cullen, F. T. (2000). The empirical status of Gottfredson and Hirschi's general theory of crime: A meta-analysis. *Criminology, 38*(3), 931–964.

Reddington, F. P., & Bonham, G., Jr. (Eds.). (2012). *Flawed criminal justice policies*. Durham, NC: Carolina Academic Press.

Roberts, J. V., & Stalans, L. J. (2000). *Public opinion, crime, and criminal justice*. Boulder, CO: Westview.

Roeder, O., Eisen, L. B., & Bowling, J. (2015). What caused the crime decline? Report, Brennan Center for Justice, New York University School of Law, New York. Retrieved from https://www.brennancenter.org/sites/default/files/publications/What_Caused_The_Crime_Decline.pdf

Sampson, R. J., Raudenbush, S. W., & Earls, F. (1997). Neighborhoods and violent crime: A multi-level study of collective efficacy. *Science, 277*(5328), 918–924.

Sampson, R. J., & Wilson, W. J. (1995). Toward a theory of race, crime, and urban inequality. In J. Hagan & R. D. Peterson (Eds.), *Crime and inequality* (pp. 37–54). Stanford, CA: Stanford University Press.

Schaefer, R. T. (2010). *Sociology*. New York: McGraw-Hill.

Schneiderman, E. T. (2015). A. G. Schneiderman secures agreement with Five Star Bank to end racially discriminatory mortgage lending practices in Rochester [Press release]. Retrieved from http://www.ag.ny.gov/press-release/ag-schneiderman-secures-agreement-five-star-bank-end-racially-discriminatory-mortgage

Squires, G. D. (1994). *Capital and communities in Black and White: The intersections of race, class, and uneven development*. New York: SUNY Albany Press.

Tittle, C., Ward, D. A., & Grasmick, H. (2003). Self-control and crime/deviance: Cognitive vs. behavioral measures. *Journal of Quantitative Criminology, 19*, 333–365.

UCR Data Online. (n.d.). Uniform Crime Reporting Statistics. Retrieved from http://www.ucrdatatool.gov/index.cfm

Uggen, C., & Janikula, J. (1999). Volunteerism and arrest in the transition to adulthood. *Social Forces, 78*(1), 331–363.

Volokh, E. (2014, June 27). What 'stand your ground' laws actually mean. *Washington Post*. Retrieved from https://www.washingtonpost.com/news/volokh-conspiracy/wp/2014/06/27/what-stand-your-ground-laws-actually-mean

Williams, F. P., & McShane, M. D. (2013). *Criminological theory*. Upper Saddle River, NJ: Prentice Hall.

10

The Future of Criminal Justice

Carolyn Petrosino

KEY TERMS

- CYBERCRIME
- DECARCERATION
- MINORITY COMMUNITIES
- POLICE–SOLDIERS
- RISK ASSESSMENT
- SENTENCING OPTIONS
- SOCIAL MEDIA
- SPECIALIZED COURTS

A. Introduction

The criminal justice system in the United States has changed in dramatic fashion over the past 300 years. Its earliest steps were based on limited notions of crime and the criminal. The criminal was perceived as one overpowered by evil supernatural forces and personal sin. Therefore, the goal of the early justice system, as it existed then, was to require repentance of the offender and his or her rebuke of evil. The criminal justice system was steeped in the religious notions and the superstitions which were common beliefs at the time. It lacked any objective criteria in which to guide justice practices and policies. Today's criminal justice system has received the benefit of decades of research on crime and criminal behavior. Still, despite the advancements made in theory and practice, somethings have been very slow to change. What is as common today as it was in the past is that the justice system deals far more often with members of the underclass, the poor and the powerless, than with those from higher socioeconomic classes. This is a reality despite the fact that deviance (the violation of rules and norms) occurs across all socioeconomic classes. Moreover, crimes are committed by those from upper classes (that is, white collar, corporate crimes, and so on); however, the justice system responds to these categories of crime differently from conventional crimes.

The purpose of this chapter is to consider emerging trends and new perplexing issues occurring in society that are yet to be effectively engaged by the criminal justice system. We also examine the pressures brought by these developments on future policies and practices in the criminal justice system in the United States. Finally, this chapter concludes by suggesting that the criminal justice system should embrace a moral framework in guiding policy development so that a fairer and more just system evolves.

B. Crime and Criminal Law

Computer Hacking

A challenge for lawmakers today and tomorrow is enacting laws that will effectively address the complexities of computer-based crime. The public is beginning to learn of how impactful computer-based crime, also referred to as **cybercrime**, is on society. So many modern conveniences are run by computers. It is not unusual to find even in kitchens of today many computerized appliances.

This writer had to recently "reboot" my microwave when it was acting peculiar. Samsung now sells a Wi-Fi-enabled LCD refrigerator equipped with a grocery manager app that tracks the expiration date of perishable foods and assists in generating a supermarket shopping list for the consumer. Comparable technology is found in washers, dryers, and dishwashers. Apple recently launched the Apple Watch (also called a "smartwatch"), which is a personal computer worn on the wrist. It has several functions that include heart monitoring and banking functions through Apple Pay.

On a much larger scale, we know that gas stations, water treatment plants, and electrical power systems are run on a power grid—each of these depend upon computer systems. Along with society's growing dependency on computer technology is the increasing vulnerability to hacker attacks. One of the earlier well-publicized occurrences of computer hacking involved identity theft via large scale data breaches of retail stores. In 2013 Target's customer database was breached. More than 70 million records containing the names, mailing and e-mail addresses, and credit card information of Target customers was stolen. It is estimated that the thieves acquired $53.7 million as a result of their crimes.[1] As of the date of this writing, no charges have been brought against anyone for this massive crime. Does society have the means to police and investigate this type of crime? Does society have laws that would appropriately punish this type of crime? According to the U.S. Department of Justice

---

1 Krebs on Security , 2014.

(DOJ), "Cybercrime is one of the greatest threats facing our country, and has enormous implications for our national security, economic prosperity, and public safety."[2]

Federal prosecutors have seen some success in bringing indictments in some computer hacking cases. But the fact is there are insufficient numbers of trained investigators who are experienced enough to fully comprehend these complex crimes and are able to obtain the requisite evidence needed to gain a conviction. But the DOJ is forming Computer Hacking/Intellectual Property Units, which specialize in these types of crimes. As federal prosecutors gain more expertise in computer-based crime, it is expected that more effective policies will be developed to respond to these crimes. Financial theft and identity theft are serious crimes sustained by victims, but the next two computer-based crimes to be discussed threaten to physically injure those victimized.

Two recent developments with the potential to cause serious injury or death challenge the criminal law: the hacking of cars and the equipping of drones with firearms. What was previously the stuff of Hollywood stunts and trickery is now a very real possibility in ordinary life. That is the notion that a car's computer system can be hacked and thereby controlled while on the highway by someone other than the driver. This frightening idea is far more dangerous than the first red flag that appeared several years ago: the ability of thieves to steal a car without breaking into it by smashing windows. Car thieves began using an electronic hacking device that enabled them to intercept signals from key fobs and open car doors as easily as the owner and then steal the car—inconspicuously.

Now hackers are closer to having the ability to take over a car while it is being driven and create terror and worse. *Wired* magazine and other news outlets recently published the story (and a video) showing the hijacking of a Jeep. With a *Wired* staffer driving, a Jeep automobile was taken over, via the Internet, by two security researchers. The researchers, Miller and Valasek, were able to take over the car's steering, transmission, and brake system. They wanted to warn the auto industry that Chrysler's Uconnect dashboard computer system was vulnerable to cyberattack.[3] Chrysler responded by recalling more than 1 million of their vehicles with the Uconnect computer system. Some would argue that it is just a matter of time before hacking events with tragic results occur. The question is, are there any laws currently existing that would address the hacking of automobiles? No, not as yet. But it is reported that Senators Ed Markey and Richard Blumenthal are proposing legislation that would require the auto industry to meet new standards to be developed by the National Highway Traffic Safety Administration[4] that would prevent auto hacking. Still, legislators must prepare for the possibility of hackers breaching new industry standards and doing harm.

Drone Technology and Firearms

---

2   U.S. Department of Justice, n.d.
3   Greenberg, 2015a.
4   Greenberg, 2015b.

The public has become familiar with drone technology through the Obama administration's efforts in the war on terrorism. The media has frequently reported on successful drone attacks waged by the United States on al-Qaeda and now ISIL or ISIS leaders. Drones are unmanned aircraft that are used for either surveillance purposes or for firing weapons on hostile targets. Although there is some controversy surrounding the use of drones in war (for example, innocent persons are sometimes killed or nonmilitary sites are destroyed by a drone attack), there should be far more concern with this recent domestic development. There are now some individuals who have outfitted their privately owned drones with firearms.

A recent news story showed 18-year-old Austin Haughwout controlling what he called the "Flying Gun"—"a homemade multirotor drone hovering off the ground and firing a semiautomatic handgun"[5] on private property. As frightening as this prospect appears, law enforcement officials have stated that they are unsure whether this act violated any law.

The month of July 2015 alone witnessed more than 30 mass shootings.[6] Now there is the possibility of a motivated malcontent to program a drone to shoot and kill multiple persons. Haughwout was not arrested for his flying gun exploit, but the Federal Aviation Administration (FAA) is currently investigating this matter. Currently there are no FAA standards regarding the use of civilian drones. But there are those who contend that ordinary citizens who may pursue utilizing a drone to fire a weapon may be protected by the Second Amendment.[7] Clearly, this is another emerging issue that the criminal law must quickly address.

Terrorist Groups and the Internet

The last example of an issue that may need further legislative action is the use of **social media** by terrorist organizations and extremist groups to recruit and radicalize others. On June 17, 2015, Dylann Roof, a 21 year old white male, entered Charleston, South Carolina's Emanuel African Methodist Episcopal Church, where he was welcomed by the African American parishioners to join them for midweek Bible study. After sitting among the church members for about an hour, he stood and began shooting them with a Glock 41 handgun. He murdered nine of them. His motivation was hatred of Black Americans.

How did a 21-year-old with a minimal criminal record transform into an unscrupulous killer? Thus far, the investigation of the Charleston shootings reveals that Roof spent a sizable amount of time on the Internet at websites that spewed the language of White supremacy, racism, anti-ethnic sentiments, and anti-Semitism. Today, included in the many uses and benefits of the Internet is its use to promote

---

5   Phys.org, 2015.
6   Mass Shooting Tracker, n.d.
7   Kobler, 2013.

murder and other acts of violence. Websites that are dedicated to ugly vitriol and revisionist perspectives of world and U.S. history are well represented. Individuals who tap into these sites and chatrooms will be exposed to articles, message music and other forms of expression that advocate the violent overthrow of government and the brutalization of identified "enemies." Can the intent to radicalize others and inspire them to become foot soldiers for the cause be criminalized? Should this be an area to be *further* regulated by law?

The FBI recently reported during a Senate Intelligence Committee hearing that "more than 200 Americans"[8] have tried to join up with ISIS (Islamic State in Iraq and Syria). ISIS is not alone in discovering the effectiveness of social media outlets to influence and recruit those who are vulnerable to these tactics. It is reported that approximately 90% of terrorist activity on the Internet takes place through social media venues.[9] Domestic hate groups such as the Ku Klux Klan, Aryan Nations, and neo-Nazi groups also use the Internet and social media tools for their purposes, as mentioned previously. Bakas describes the variety of reasons why such groups rely on this form of mass communication:

- To share 'best practices';
- Coordinate attacks;
- Expand the reach of their propaganda to a global audience;
- Recruit new members;
- Communicate with international supporters and ethnic diasporas;
- Solicit donations, and;
- Foster public awareness and sympathy for their causes.[10]

The fact that terrorist groups use social media and the Internet in effective ways is a thorny issue for the justice system. On the one hand, the Department of Homeland Security and the law enforcement community in general would prefer to *prevent* the radicalization of others who plan and sometimes carry out horrendous attacks on citizens. On the other hand, it is through these outlets that intelligence might be gathered. Nevertheless, the ability to gain useful intelligence is not an easy one. The Internet is largely unregulated and it is accessible to millions perhaps billions of individuals. Law enforcements' intelligence gathering from publicly available social media websites is referred to as Social Media Intelligence.[11] Monitoring social media can yield critical information and can help thwart the violence planned by these individuals.

---

8   Hattam, 2015.
9   Bakas, n.d.
10   Ibid.
11   Ibid.

Groups like ISIS seek to influence youth to join their cause which is why social media (widely popular among millennials) is a preferred strategy. There have been several news reports that young girls targeted for recruitment had successfully traveled overseas to join up with ISIS fighters to become their wives. Some who are recruited are *minors*. Perhaps minors can be better protected by criminalizing efforts to recruit or proselytize or indoctrinate minors to join a criminal organization. The use of social media to intentionally target youth, even minors is an exposed area that must be more carefully considered by the criminal justice system now and in the future.

C. Policing

The years 2014–2015 will be remembered as one of the most disturbing, turbulent, and tension-filled time periods between police, the African American community, and others who are committed to the ideal of equal treatment before the law. Following the deaths of two African American men at the hand of police, two communities—Ferguson, Missouri, and Baltimore, Maryland—became unhinged. What unfolded was counterproductive interplay between some community members who had had enough of feeling angry, frustrated, and targeted for police abuse and some police who felt that their legitimacy was not recognized or respected by Black Americans and other citizens. The larger question for criminal justice is what can be learned from Ferguson and Baltimore that can make the policing of **minority communities** far more productive.

On August 9, 2014, Michael Brown, an African American teenager, was shot and killed by White police officer Darren Wilson in Ferguson. Wilson's defense is that he felt that his life was threatened by the actions of Brown and that lethal force was justified. The prosecutor saw things Wilson's way and chose not to bring charges against him. What occurred afterward received worldwide attention. Although many residents were incensed by the prosecutor's decision, some reacted by committing acts of arson and looting of neighborhood businesses, throwing rocks or even shooting at police. Police responded in full riot gear and used tear gas, rubber bullets, and other tools to try and disperse and dissuade the growing crowds from destructive actions. Eventually county law enforcement and even the National Guard were brought into Ferguson.

One of the most controversial news photos from the Ferguson conflict shows police officers outfitted like soldiers in a war zone. Questions arose as to the wisdom of equipping police with tanks, other armored vehicles, assault weapons, night vision gear, and the like in a community that already sees itself as unfairly set upon by police. The symbolism of police–soldiers in Black communities is akin to American soldiers fighting enemies of the United States in Afghanistan and Iraq. Is that an appropriate stance to take? A second question asks, are local, county or even state police trained well enough to use these tools of warfare appropriately in American communities? Local police are able to obtain this sophisticated military equipment through the availability of federal grants. The 1033 program (created by the National Defense Authorization Act of Fiscal Year 1997) allows the secretary of defense "to transfer, without charge, excess U.S. Department of Defense … supplies and equipment to state and local law enforcement agencies."[12] By way of the 1033 program, police departments have acquired "435 armored vehicles, 533 planes, over 93,000 machine guns, and over 400 mine-resistant armored trucks—over $4 billion dollars' worth of equipment."[13] The potential for accidental or intentional use of *lethal force* grows exponentially with the use of this equipment. Remembering that the armed forces can never be used against the American people, unless under extraordinary circumstances of civil unrest—we now have police departments that use the same equipment as the military, with the purpose of use against the American public. Is this ethical? The criminal justice system must look more carefully at the appropriateness of this development and the rules of engagement and policies that may be in place to govern the use of this equipment.

Lastly, as a result of the DOJ's investigation of the Michael Brown incident, a disturbing practice was uncovered. The primary objective of the Ferguson police and the municipal court was to develop and maintain an additional revenue source. This was done by penalizing poor and Black residents of Ferguson with never-ending fees and fines. This perspective caused the local justice system to see Ferguson residents first as potential offenders and second as sources of revenue. According to the DOJ report, "the court primarily uses its judicial authority as the means to compel the payment of fines and fees that advance the City's financial interests."[14] This practice was particularly devastating to financially struggling residents. The DOJ report describes the following:

> *We spoke, for example, with an African-American woman who has a still-pending case stemming from 2007, when, on a single occasion, she parked her car illegally. She received two citations and a $151 fine, plus fees. The woman, who experienced financial difficulties and periods of homelessness over several years, was charged with seven Failure to Appear offenses for missing court dates or fine payments on her parking tickets between 2007 and 2010. For each Failure to Appear, the court issued an arrest warrant and imposed new fines and fees. … As of December 2014, over seven years later, despite initially owing a $151 fine and having already paid $550, she still owed $541.[15]*

---

12 JUSTNET, n.d.
13 Bouie, 2014.
14 U.S. Department of Justice Civil Rights Division. 2015, p. 6.
15 Ibid. p. 7.

With such policies in place, it is clear that those who least can afford it are drained of the few dollars they have over extended periods of time. Such policies (which some would say are tantamount to a new form of slavery) subordinate public safety and community service objectives to exploiting citizens for the sake of financing the local justice system. Should not the future of criminal justice include the eradication of such practices?

Few outside of the city of Baltimore would recognize the name Freddie Gray. On April 12, 2015, Gray was arrested by Baltimore police for possession of a switchblade-like knife. He was placed in a police van to be transported, but when he was removed he was unable to walk, talk, or breathe. Several days later, Gray was dead. The medical examiner determined that his death resulted from a devastating spinal cord injury caused by a high-energy impact. Protestors, who were mostly high school age and younger, took to the streets following the death of Gray. Many thought the response to these young people was slow and ineffective. Protest devolved into riots involving looting, arson of businesses and automobiles, as well as attacks on police. It is important to note the difference between peaceful protest and rioting. The public witnessed both during the Baltimore conflict (as it did in Ferguson), and the media covered it all for several days and nights. Clergy, civic groups, and community activists worked diligently, along with public officials, to encourage residents to observe the evening curfew. The Maryland National Guard was deployed to help bring order. Eventually the destructive actions of some diminished resulting in constructive planned community actions and peaceful demonstrations. Gray's death was ruled a homicide, and six Baltimore police officers were charged with assault and involuntary manslaughter.

But what are the lessons that can be learned from Ferguson and Baltimore that can be useful to all concerned going forward? What changes should occur in policing? Perhaps the following:

1. Diverse police departments are an asset. The Ferguson police department was almost entirely composed of Caucasian officers; only 4 out of 53 officers were African American[16] at the time of the Brown incident. The community of Ferguson, however, is predominately African American. The absence of a diverse police department enabled a police culture that devalued the poor as well as African American residents.

2. The militarization of local law enforcement may compound the us versus them mentality for both law enforcement and the citizenry. The Pentagon transferred surplus military equipment worth close to half a billion dollars to local law enforcement agencies. Should law enforcement ever respond to American communities like an occupying force? There can only be detrimental effects, particularly in racial minority communities, when police utilize this type of military-grade equipment. Citizens respond angrily and police react with more

---

16   Buchanan et al., n.d.

force, creating an unnecessary escalation of tension and violence. During the Ferguson conflict, an obviously tense police officer was captured on camera shouting at protesters, "Bring it, all you fucking animals! Bring it!"[17]

3. <u>The financial exploitation of the African American community by Ferguson police further delegitimizes police authority.</u> The DOJ's Civil Rights Division investigated the practice by police and the municipal court of fining community residents as a means of generating revenue. The data maintained by the Ferguson police revealed a race effect in this practice that penalized Black citizens more than any other group and that the disparity was the result of "discriminatory intent." This practice exacerbated the distrust of the African American community toward the Ferguson police department.

4. <u>A diverse police department alone does not guarantee the development of good police–community relations.</u> In the Freddie Gray tragedy, half of the officers who were implicated in his death were racial minorities. Thus, being a Black, Hispanic, or Asian police officer does not preclude the possibility of abuse of minority residents. Police leadership must create and maintain a work ethos that respects citizens and seeks to serve them, regardless of whether they are law abiders or law violators.

5. <u>Police–community relations must be ongoing and not begin at the time of a crisis.</u>

Rioting is never justified. But as was often quoted during the Baltimore conflict, "Riot is the language of the unheard," stated by Martin Luther King Jr. during the civil rights movement. Clearly the relationship between the Black community and the Baltimore police department was anemic at best. The callous treatment of Freddie Gray and the outrage of the community is evidence of long-standing poor police–community relations. Emphasizing the commitment to building and maintaining good police–community relations is paramount now and in the future.

Many incidents have occurred in the world of policing from which improvements can be made for the future. The social costs of missteps can be enormous, including the loss of life and impact the very integrity of law enforcement as an institution. The same came be said for corrections. The next section discusses what we've learned in corrections that can markedly improve this component of the criminal justice system.

---

17   Voorhees, 2014.

D. Corrections

The explosion in correctional populations that has occurred over the past 30 years has many levels of costs and implications:

- We have incarcerated 2.2 million persons—a dubious distinction.
- The expenditures required to build, fill, manage, and maintain correctional facilities has become cost prohibitive.
- Other and more prosocial human services are now underfunded in many states as a result of the increasing cost of incarcerating offenders.
- Support of reentry programs have not kept pace with the incarceration rate.

More could clearly be added to this list, such as the impact on the children of incarcerated parents and the racial disparities and racial discriminatory practices which causes negative generational effects. The future of corrections perhaps will see a departure from these counterproductive policies.

Research has provided reliable evidence on these and related problems which could positively impact future corrections policies. What is clear from the evidence is that the correctional population explosion was caused mostly by crime policies and not by increases in crime. Blumstein and Beck found that "only 12% of the increase in incarceration rates was attributable to increase in crime."[18] Thus, 88% of the expansion was caused by changes in penal law and in sentencing policies. Principal were the new drug laws that required longer mandatory sentences. Even for nondrug offenses, use of truth-in-sentencing models and Three-strikes laws in addition to decrease use of discretionary parole release all caused more individuals to languish in prison for longer periods of time. The ability to reverse overreliance on prisons can be accomplished by revising current crime policy.

Doris MacKenzie authored an extensive report[19] that examined the state of corrections in the 21st century. Although the report was published in 2001, most if not all of her observations are still valid 14 years later. The future of corrections must involve the use of sanctions other than incarceration. There are a variety of **sentencing options** available to the courts, which include (a) a more strategic use of fines and community service, (b) increased use of restorative justice models, (c) smarter and more frequent use of intermediate sanctions, and (d) the use of more options in managing offenders who are supervised in the community through probation or parole. Even though MacKenzie as well as other researchers have observed a greater presence of **risk assessment** measures throughout corrections, this reality does not preclude consideration of other sanctions that are short of incarceration.

---

18   as cited in MacKenzie, 2001, p. 14.
19   Ibid.

A wide variety of community-based corrections programs that address the needs of targeted offender populations can be found across the United States. When such programs demonstrate an acceptable amount of success, they should be further funded by the state. Greater utilization of other sentencing options, with a conscious effort toward **decarceration**, should see correctional costs come down and movement toward a more community-justice oriented outcome.

In addition to making greater use of sanctions outside of incarceration is the further use of **specialized courts**. The primary objective of such courts is to focus on the treatment needs of specific offenders along with requiring accountability, responsibility with supervision to avoid the pattern of failure and more criminality. There are specialized courts to deal with the problems of drug offenders, youth, returning war veterans, reentry, and perpetrators of domestic violence, for example. The very existence of specialized courts indicates that interest in rehabilitation and treatment for the offender is a viable goal worthy of investment by the justice system. A concentrated focus on specific offender problems makes more sense than mindless incarceration. Another potential area that will impact future criminal justice processes and procedures is the incorporation of technology.

It is likely that the role of technology will certainly expand in the future of criminal justice. There are many areas where the use of sophisticated technologies could only improve the justice system. As a researcher interested in pursuing correctional data, we commonly find antiquated file systems in classification and other key information systems. Just as the medical profession made a concerted effort several years ago to computerize patient records so that important information is instantly available to authorized parties—criminal justice agencies should do similarly. Information such as the offender's criminal history, outstanding warrants, restraining orders, motor vehicle records, institutional and/or community program participation, adjustment to supervision, and other pertinent information can be computerized and made available to court, correctional, and law enforcement agencies—at a moment's notice. The standardization of offender records—across states will become increasingly important in the future due to the transient nature of all people, including offenders.

Another key role for technology is in the monitoring of offenders in the community. The importance of risk assessment will not decrease particularly if decarceration becomes a serious crime policy. Therefore risk assessment will loom in importance. The United Kingdom, particularly London, is known for the prevalence of cameras and closed-circuit television. Cameras will likely continue to increase in use in the United States. Also, as drone use becomes more routine in police work; we will likely see it in other venues in the criminal justice system. Perhaps probation and parole officers, both with responsibility for supervising offenders, would use drone technology to make sure their charges are at work or in other approved places. Drone technology could supplement electronic monitoring, and even surveil the comings and goings of registered sex offenders.

The following saying has been credited to several individuals, but most often to Mahatma Gandhi: 'It is often said that 'a nation's greatness is measured by how it treats its weakest members.' Gandhi's quote should perhaps frame the direction of the future of criminal justice in the United States. How do we treat the offender? Should it indicate the moral character of American society? Can it be said that offenders represent the "weakest" members of society? The critical criminologist would say that the criminal justice system is structured in a way to exploit those who are the most vulnerable—the poor, the young, the uneducated, and racial and ethnic minorities. The Bureau of Justice Statistics provides a profile of those who are incarcerated in state and federal prisons:

- The majority of inmates are age 39 or younger; White prisoners are on average older than Black and Hispanic prisoners.
- As of December 31, 2013, 37% of male prisoners were Black; Blacks are 13% of the population so this reflects an overrepresentation in prisons.
- As of December 31, 2013, 32% of male prisoners were White; Whites are 78% of the population reflecting an underrepresentation in prisons.
- For males ages 18 to 19: The imprisonment rate of Black males (1,092 inmates per 100,000 Black males) is more than 9 times greater than that of White males (115 inmates per 100,000 White males).[20]
- 68% of state prison inmates do not possess a high school diploma.

After reviewing these data, we may be able to say confidently that prisoners tend to come from groups that lack education, financial resources, and political capital. This would arguably make them comport to Gandhi's description of "weaker" members of society. The next question to ask is, does the criminal justice system, in general, handle offenders in ways deemed "civilized"? Probably not.

First, it has been acknowledged that the United States has created mass incarceration (of the weak) at a rate that surpasses most other nations around the globe. Second, this condition has been artificially created as a result of intentional policies to punish (the weak) offenders for longer periods of time. Third, there are several policies and regulations that act as effective obstacles to the reintegration of (the weak) the offender back into society. What are some of these barriers? The Legal Action Center[21] provides the following list:

- Most states allow employers to deny jobs to people who were arrested but never convicted of a crime.
- Most states allow employers to deny jobs to anyone with a criminal record, regardless of how long ago or the individual's work history and personal circumstances.

---

20   Carson & Bureau of Justice Statistics, 2014.
21   Legal Action Center, 2004.

- Most states ban some or all people with drug felony convictions from being eligible for federally funded public assistance and food stamps.
- Most states make criminal history information accessible to the general public through the Internet, making it extremely easy for employers and others to discriminate against people on the basis of old or minor convictions, for example, to deny employment or housing.
- Many public housing authorities deny eligibility for federally assisted housing based on an arrest that never led to a conviction.
- All but two states restrict the right to vote in some way for people with criminal convictions.

How do these policies and regulations aid those who have committed crime but wish to make a go of prosocial behavior and try to lead a productive law-abiding life? They don't. These regulations are not in support of the ex-offender; they merely further marginalize him or her, which increases the likelihood of continued criminality. This structure bogs down poor Black and Brown communities with a cycle of social disruption and removal of young men of color (and women) from homes and neighborhoods, increasing the level of dependence on public assistance; residents are less desirable as potential employees, and fewer people from these communities are eligible to vote and influence the very policies that have created these structural hindrances. How moral is this?

Ethics offers several frameworks that could enable the determination of crime policy, law, and regulations that fit *moral* principles. The result may bring a fairer and more just criminal justice system that does not target and further exploit the weakest segments of our society. The final sections of this chapter discuss the merits of this perspective for the future of criminal justice.

E. Policy Analysis in Criminal Justice. Needed: A Moral Outlook

Not unlike the nature of public policy analysis in other areas such as public health, education, and health care delivery systems, analysis methods in crime and justice are similar. The conventional analysis approach to public policy and program initiatives typically includes implementation, outcome, and/or impact. While the examination of these substantive areas are extremely informative and assist in determining effectiveness, they do not provide insight into the basic rightness or wrongness (morality) of the policy at issue. As an additional aspect of analysis, moral assessment requires the application of ethical theories and principles. These theoretical principles serve as standards that may be used to evaluate crime policy.

Conventional approaches to policy analysis usually suffer from the following limitations: (a) a narrow focus, (b) an overemphasis on the perfunctory aspects of a program, (c) the absence of long-term effects measurement, and (d) the nonexistence of moral considerations. The consequences of these limitations can be impactful when other factors that may be pertinent to the issue of effectiveness are not sufficiently considered. Crime policy is often symbolic and reflective of assumptions and social values that have real moral implications for the criminal justice system and society at large.

Unfortunately, it is apparent that stakeholders possess little interest on whether a policy is morally right until a highly publicized negative event occurs and is brought to the public's attention (that is, Ferguson fines as tax revenue policy). Without the effort to examine the moral aptitude of a policy, its advocates may presume that it is ethically sound. But is this assumption sufficient? Do the conventional approaches allow us to ascertain the moral worth of a policy? The application of moral theory may assist in providing additional insights into the social impact and potential consequences of a given policy. This may benefit future criminal justice policy.

F. Moral Theory as an Assessment Tool

The determination of the moral worth of new initiatives could be helpful to policy-makers and funding agencies. Research universities, private research centers and state and local government agencies are all competing for shrinking research dollars in order to fund programs. Programs that are also able to demonstrate a moral center may benefit in this competition. It should be desirable to stakeholders to support policies and programs that are morally beneficial to society. This may be a commonsense conclusion; however, there are popular programs that are proven to be ineffective and even iatrogenic, that is, counterproductive and even immoral (Finckenauer, 1982; 1999; Petrosino, Turpin-Petrosino, & Buehler, 2003). The prevention of unintended consequences or other negative developments may be avoided through the moral evaluation of policy. This must be embraced in future criminal justice initiatives. For crime policy, this could be an invaluable approach to analysis. After all, crime control policies are loaded with ethical concerns. As discussed earlier, we currently see morally questionable developments: increasingly militarized weaponry and tactics by police departments, the use of private prisons to manage the convicted, the use of supermax prisons for incorrigible inmates, and so on. Such practices raise important concerns beyond that of fiscal responsibility or other administrative criteria. Criminal justice policies should undergo moral assessment which causes consideration for the ethics of policy and the subsequent implications for crime control, the criminal justice system and society in general.

G. Conclusion—A More Moral Criminal Justice System in the Future

The application of the major ethical systems inherent to criminal justice, such as utilitarianism, ethical formalism, peacekeeping or Rawlsian ethics, may shed additional light on the moral value of a crime policy. Although there are many ethical theories, these four are perhaps most relevant to the evaluation of crime policies. Utilitarian theory provides justification for the primary aims of punishment. Ethical formalism focuses on the intrinsic worth of human beings and the importance of equality—providing similar treatment to similar cases. Peacekeeping reminds us of the connectedness of all human beings. Finally, the ethical system of John Rawls's justice as fairness concerns itself with the primacy of the social contract, impartiality, and the equal distribution of goods and services in society. This theory considers the broader social and political context of crime policy.

The moral assessment of crime policy requires an in-depth analysis. The following elements are necessarily included: (a) familiarity with the etiology of the social problem addressed by the policy; (b) awareness of the effects of the problem and what groups are impacted directly and indirectly; (c) an examination of the immediate outcomes and what they mean for the groups mostly or peripherally impacted; (d) speculation on the long-term effects of the program on the group or community impacted, or even the criminal justice system itself; and (e) speculation on any future moral concerns that may development.

What are the potential benefits of applying moral theory as a part of policy analysis? First, a more ideologically coherent justice system. The American criminal justice system primarily reflects utilitarian ethics. Analyzing crime policies in accordance with utilitarianism theory will permit us to see if programs and policies are in concert with the moral values reflected in this system or not. This means ethical theory may act as a central organizing focus for considering developments. Second, a greater ability to discern ethical issues that are embedded in policy initiatives in general. Not unlike the perspective advocated by Callahan and Davis regarding the use of ethics as an analytical tool, it provides an additional dimension to the process of policy analysis (Kleinig & Smith, 1996). Third, examining policy within an ethics context facilitates a deeper understanding of the theoretical underpinnings of the policy. Discerning implicit theory aids program assessment in general. Fourth, a greater sensibility regarding the impact of policy on the human family. How policy impacts human relationships and how these relationships impact society is considered in the application of ethical systems. Essentially, applying moral theory to policy assessment permits a new critical perspective on the benefits and consequences of policy, which provides an additional tool for policy makers, practitioners and academics. Utilizing a moral lens in the examination of criminal justice policies could have prevented some aspects of Ferguson, and perhaps all of Baltimore's chaos, particularly the death of Freddie Gray. Emerging social problems such as the increasing dangers of computer hacking or the ability of ordinary citizens to weaponized drones, and other future developments will require the enactment of crime policies that must be vetted for its moral and ethical implications. It is the mandate of the criminal justice system to not only protect public safety, but to have the foresight to administer effective crime policies that are just and that are based on sound moral principles. Such crime policies would reflect the high ideals in which the standard of justice was forged.

1. This chapter discussed new potential crimes that have serious consequences on those who are victimized by these acts. In what ways can the criminal justice system become more proactive in anticipating harmful acts that will likely become proscribed by law?

2. How can consideration of moral principles become more a part of the process in the conceptualization and development of crime policy in the future?

REFERENCES

Bakas, J. A. (n.d.). "#Terrorist:" The use of social media by extremist groups. Retrieved from https://www.academia.edu/9015149/_Terrorist_The_Use_of_Social_Media_By_Extremist_Groups

Bouie, J. (2014, August 13). The militarization of the police: It's dangerous and wrong to treat Ferguson, Missouri, as a war zone. *Slate*. Retrieved from http://www.slate.com/articles/news_and_politics/politics/2014/08/police_in_ferguson_military_weapons_threaten_protesters.html

Buchanan, L., Fessenden, F., Lai, K. K. R., Park, H., Parlapiano, A., Tse, A., ... Yourish, K. (n.d.). What happened in Ferguson? [interactive map]. *New York Times*. Retrieved from http://www.nytimes.com/interactive/2014/08/13/us/ferguson-missouri-town-under-siege-after-police-shooting.html?_r=1#tension

Carson, E. A., & Bureau of Justice Statistics. (2014). Prisoners in 2013. Retrieved from http://www.bjs.gov/content/pub/pdf/p13.pdf

Finckenauer, J. O. (1982). *Scared straight! and the panacea phenomenon*. Englewood Cliffs, NJ: Prentice Hall.

Finckenauer, J. O. (1999). *Scared straight—The panacea phenomenon revisited*. Prospect Heights, IL: Waveland Press.

Greenberg, A. (2015a, July 24). After Jeep hack, Chrysler recalls 1.4M vehicles for bug fix. *Wired*. Retrieved from http://www.wired.com/2015/07/jeep-hack-chrysler-recalls-1-4m-vehicles-bug-fix

Greenberg, A. (2015b, July 21). Senate bill seeks standards for cars' defenses from hackers. *Wired*. Retrieved from http://www.wired.com/2015/07/senate-bill-seeks-standards-cars-defenses-hackers

Hattam, J. (2015, July 8). FBI: More than 200 Americans have tried to fight for ISIS. *The Hill*. Retrieved from http://thehill.com/policy/national-security/247256-more-than-200-americans-tried-to-fight-for-isis-fbi-says

JUSTNET. (n.d.). The 1033 Program. Retrieved from https://www.justnet.org/other/1033_program.html

Kleinig, J., & Smith, M. L. (1996). The development of criminal justice ethics education. In J. Kleinig & M. L. Smith (Eds.), *Teaching criminal justice ethics: Strategic issues* (pp. vii–xix).

Kobler, J. (2013, May 21). The next gun debate? Armed drones could be protected by the Second Amendment. *US News and World Report*. Retrieved from http://www.usnews.com/news/articles/2013/05/21/the-next-gun-debate-armed-drones-could-be-protected-by-the-second-amendment

Krebs on Security. (2014). The Target breach by the numbers. Retrieved from http://krebsonsecurity.com/2014/05/the-target-breach-by-the-numbers

Legal Action Center. (2004). After prison: Roadblocks to reentry. A report on state legal barriers facing people with criminal records. Retrieved from http://www.lac.org/roadblocks-to-reentry/upload/lacreport/LAC_PrintReport.pdf

MacKenzie, D. L. (2001). *Sentencing and corrections in the 21st century: Setting the stage for the future*. Report. Retrieved from https://www.ncjrs.gov/pdffiles1/nij/189106-2.pdf

Mass Shooting Tracker. (n.d.). Retrieved from http://www.shootingtracker.com

Petrosino, A., Turpin-Petrosino, C., & Buehler, J. (2003). "Scared straight" and other juvenile awareness programs for preventing juvenile delinquency (Updated C2 Review). In *The Campbell Collaborative reviews of intervention and policy evaluations* (C2-RIPE). Philadelphia: Campbell Collaboration.

Phys.org. (2015, July 24). Police arrest US teen who built gun-firing drone. Retrieved from http://phys.org/news/2015-07-police-teen-built-gun-firing-drone.html

US Department of Justice. (n.d.). Cyber crime. Retrieved from http://www.justice.gov/usao/priority-areas/cyber-crime

US Department of Justice Civil Rights Division. (2015). Investigation of the Ferguson Police Department. Retrieved from http://www.justice.gov/sites/default/files/opa/press-releases/attachments/2015/03/04/ferguson_police_department_report.pdf

Voorhees, J. (2014, November 25). Everything that's going wrong in Ferguson. *Slate*. Retrieved from http://www.slate.com/articles/news_and_politics/politics/2014/08/ferguson_police_timeline_a_comprehensive_chronological_accounting_of_the.html

About the Authors

(in alphabetical order)

Trevor Fronius

Trevor A. Fronius, MS, is a senior research associate at the WestEd Justice & Prevention Research Center. His expertise includes conducting rigorous experimental and quasi-experimental field studies, national-level complex secondary data analysis, and systematic reviews in justice and public health. His current research explores areas related to urban youth violence, socioenvironmental factors of crime, public policy, and determinants to juvenile crime and delinquency.

Robert Grantham

Currently serving as an assistant professor in the Criminal Justice Department at Bridgewater State University in southeastern Massachusetts, Grantham completed his doctoral degree in sociology at Purdue University in West Lafayette, Indiana. His research focuses on aspects of governance that help explain urban crime and other problematic conditions in large cities. He coedited *Urban Society: The Shame of Governance*, which was published in 2011.

Sarah Guckenburg

Sarah Guckenburg, MPH, is a senior research associate at the WestEd Justice & Prevention Research Center. She serves as a codirector and researcher on projects focusing on school climate, bullying, youth violence, restorative practices in schools, teen pregnancy, and school safety. She currently codirects a community-based randomized controlled trial of a Latino/a teen pregnancy prevention program and a study of restorative justice practices in schools. She is also part of the evaluation team for the South Carolina Safe and Supportive School initiative addressing school climate and serves on the team evaluating the Safe and Successful Youth Initiative, a statewide urban violence prevention strategy in Massachusetts.

John Hobson

After decades of law enforcement experience, Jack Hobson retired from police work, where he specialized in proactive juvenile justice initiatives and delinquency prevention. He received his EdD from Nova Southeastern University in 2001. His doctoral work focused on violence and bullying prevention at the elementary and middle school level. As a juvenile officer, he directed the regional school district's D.A.R.E. (Drug Abuse Resistance Education) and SRO (school resource officer) programs. He was instrumental in establishing Alternative High School Program Excel: Learning for Life. Other initiatives included a youth program that linked police officers with high-risk youth in academic and recreational settings. As a member of the adjunct faculty of the criminal justice department at Bridgewater State University, his academic and teaching interests focus on the social–psychological hurdles experienced through adolescence. To that end, he published his first book, *Drifters: Stories from the Dark Side of Delinquency*, in 2013.

Feyisara Olotu

Feyisara Olotu is the president, partner, and cofounder of Olotu & Olotu, P.C., a boutique law firm started in 2009. Her area of practice includes criminal, immigration, and personal injury law, among many other types of law. She is a member of the Volunteer Lawyers Project and the Black Alumni Network at Boston College Law School. Olotu has served as an adjunct professor at Bridgewater State University since 2010. She earned her BA in sociology at Boston College in 2006. She went on to earn her JD at Boston College Law School in 2009. She has been admitted to the Massachusetts Bar since 2009.

Mia R. Ortiz

Mia R. Ortiz is an assistant professor in the Criminal Justice Department at Bridgewater State University. Ortiz received her PhD from the Graduate Center of the City University of New York. Her research interests include quality of life offending, pretrial release, specialized courts, and juvenile delinquency.

Anthony Petrosino

Anthony Petrosino, PhD, is director of the WestEd Justice & Prevention Research Center, project director and senior research associate in the Learning Innovations program at WestEd. He is also a senior research fellow at George Mason University's Center for Evidence-Based Crime Policy. Petrosino has more than 25 years of experience collaborating on research and evaluation projects, with many of them focused on justice, prevention, and safety topics. In addition, he has authored and coauthored more than 100 articles, book chapters, and technical reports.

Carolyn Petrosino

Carolyn Petrosino, PhD is professor of criminal justice at Bridgewater State University in Bridgewater, Massachusetts. She has nearly 18 years of experience as a correctional social worker, correctional unit supervisor, and parole hearing officer in the New Jersey correctional and parole systems. She earned her doctorate at the Rutgers School of Criminal Justice in Newark, New Jersey. Her current research interests include the political nature of hate crime, its effects on victims and communities, and its national and global persistence. Her focus also includes special correctional populations, the impacts of correctional policy on poor and minority communities, and reentry and control policies governing offenders in the community. Petrosino is coauthor of *American Corrections: The Brief* (3rd edition) for Cengage. Her most recent book, *Understanding Hate Crime: Acts, Motives, Offenders, Victims and Justice*, was published in 2015 for Routledge.

Francis Williams

Francis Williams, PhD, has been a practitioner, researcher, scholar, public speaker, and educator on issues of law enforcement, police and community relations, race and crime, crime policy, and more recently, online education for more than 38 years. Williams spent more than 27 years as a practitioner in the field of criminal justice, which included working with juveniles in the streets and in schools, security administration for more than 10 years, plus years in service as a probation officer initially working with juveniles, and ended by specializing in the supervision of sexual offenders. He received his PhD in law and public policy from Northeastern University in Boston, Massachusetts in 2007. Williams is a published author who, in addition to a book on school prevention program models in 2008, has published other articles or book chapters that focus on police minority community relations, race and crime, and sex offenders. His varied research interests include law enforcement, strategic policy formation, police and minority community relations, and race and crime and has more recently delved into the Scholarship of Teaching and Learning. Since 2008, Williams has been an associate professor of criminal justice at Plymouth State University in Plymouth, New Hampshire.

Wendy L. Wright

Wendy L. Wright is an assistant professor of criminal justice. She completed her PhD in the Department of Political Science at Rutgers University in New Brunswick, New Jersey, in 2013. Her research focuses on political theory in the interpretation and critique of law and policy. She is currently working on the manuscript of her first book, *The Failure of Punishment*, which examines the relationship between the justifications for punishment and the practice of punishment in the American context with a special focus on race and critical theory.